Praise for Peter Weddle's Books & Guides

A Multitude of Hope:
A Novel About Rediscovering the American Dream

"… engaging and thoughtful."

—Joyce Lain Kennedy, Syndicated Career Columnist

"… a provocative take on the job search … holds a lot of weight."

—Rathin Sinha, CEO America's Job Exchange

"… one of the bravest books I've read in a long time. Its depiction of today's unforgiving, anxiety-inducing world of work is accurate and honest."

—Christine Ramsey, President Boxwood Technology

"As a long-time consultant working with individuals exploring career opportunities, I highly recommend this book. … by bringing the Horatio Alger story up-to-date, *A Multitude of Hope* lives up to its name."

—Joan Learn, Regional Manager The Ayers Group

"I am an author of a research guide for older Americans as well as founder of RetiredBrains.com, a website that includes information on finding employment and *A Multitude of Hope* is one of the best reads for Boomers who are seeking a job or interested in getting the inside story on what some very smart people have done and are doing with their lives."

—Art Koff, CEO RetiredBrains.com

WEDDLE's Guide to Employment Sites on the Internet

"Restaurant patrons looking for quality dining have Zagat to guide their cuisine needs. For the recruitment industry, the name is Weddle … Peter Weddle that is."

—American Staffing Association

"I've known Peter Weddle for years. He is an immensely likeable guy. He is also extremely knowledgeable. Highly recommended!"

—Richard Nelson Bolles, *What Color is Your Parachute?*

Work Strong

"A wealth of updated and useful information."

"WEDDLE's is a very useful tool that recruiters and HR professionals will find helpful."

"When in doubt, consider WEDDLE's ... an industry standard."

"If you're looking for an objective guide to employment Web-sites, ExecuNet recommends WEDDLE's Guide.
—ExecuNet Center for Executive Careers

Work Strong: Your Personal Career Fitness System

"Peter Weddle's Career Fitness System empowers you to take your job search to the next level and achieve lasting career success."

—Diana Miller, CEO Community Job Club

"There are few people in the world who are as passionate about our careers and our own unique talents as Peter Weddle. Work Strong changes the paradigms of career management books and is sure to give you a new perspective on how to Work Strong in your own career."

—Aaron Matos, CEO Jobing

"This book is a guide to finding yourself and to charting a new course for a 21st Century career. A must read!"

—Kevin Wheeler, CEO Global Learning Resources, Inc.

"A lifetime of career happiness in a single book!"

—Dan Honig, COO DiversityJobs.com

In today's world, it's not enough to work hard. You also have to work strong and perform at your peak. That's the power and promise of this book."

—John Bell, CEO Boxwood Technology

Generalship: HR Leadership in a Time of War

"... a wake-up call for those of us in HR. We need to take on the accountability for effecting change. ... This book provides a great strategy for doing just that."

—Regina DeTore, VP/HR Sepracor, Inc.

"... a must-read book for human resource professionals, especially those who seek to be true leaders in their corporation."

—Jerome N. Carter, SVP/HR International Paper

"Human Resources is now facing extra-ordinary challenges. This demanding time requires the kind of bold, thoughtful and thorough leadership suggested by this book."

—Guy Patton, EVP/HR Fidelity Investments

"Don't miss this book. It's Machiavelli's *The Prince* and Covey's *7 Habits of Highly Effective People* all rolled into one for the HR profession."

—Donna Introcaso, VP/HR iVillage

"This book is a must-read on HR leadership, not only for HR practitioners, but for every CEO and Company Director, as well.

—Robert S. Nadel, President Nadel Consulting

Recognizing Richard Rabbit: A Fable About Being True to Yourself

"A magical way to explore the essence of you."

—Jennifer Floren, CEO Experience

"… a very intriguing and unique book."

—Patrick Erwin, *The Work Buzz CareerBuilder.com*

"… if you're thinking about making changes in your personal life or want a pep talk about being true to yourself, check out this book."

—Celeste Blackburn, Managing Editor, *Resources for Humans*

"The story inspires useful reflection and a practical rethinking of your own personal effectiveness in work and life."

—Jonathan Goodman, *Review on Social Median*

Career Fitness: How to Find, Win & Keep the Job You Want in the 1990s

"This book is phenomenal! It'll help you run the race of your life at work each day."

—Harvey McKay, *Swim With the Sharks Without Being Eaten Alive*

"… street-smart wisdom, coupled with practical career workout tools … sure to be useful to people at any point in their career."

—Madelyn Jennings, SVP/HR Gannett Company, Inc.

Also By Peter Weddle

A Multitude of Hope: A Novel About Rediscovering the American Dream

The Success Matrix: Wisdom from the Web on How to Get Hired & Not Be Fired

Job Nation: The 100 Best Employment Sites on the Web

The Career Activist Republic

Work Strong: Your Personal Career Fitness System

Recognizing Richard Rabbit: A Fable About Being True to Yourself

Generalship: HR Leadership in a Time of War

Career Fitness: How to Find, Win & Keep the Job You Want in the 1990s

Postcards from Space: Being the Best in Online Recruitment & HR Management

WEDDLE's Guide to Employment Sites on the Internet (biannually: 1999-present)

WEDDLE's Guide to Association Web Sites

WEDDLE'S Guide to Staffing Firms & Employment Agencies

'Tis of Thee: A Son's Search for the Meaning of Patriotism

The Career Fitness Workbook

How to Find, Win & Hold Onto the Job of Your Dreams

Peter Weddle

Work Strong

Published by WEDDLE's LLC, celebrating over a decade of publishing for America's workers, employers, and recruiters. WEDDLE's books are distributed by Independent Publishers Group, 814 North Franklin Street, Chicago, IL 60610, PH: 312-337-0747, www.ipgbook.com.

ISBN: 978-1-92873473-4

WEDDLE's
www.weddles.com

WORK STRONG

This Book Has Been Especially Designed for Two Kinds of People

Job Seekers

Career Activists

Those who want to enhance their credentials in the job market so they will have their pick of employment opportunities that will increase the paycheck and the satisfaction they bring home from their work.

Those who want to advance themselves in their profession, craft or trade so they can increase their success on-the-job and their access to ever more interesting and rewarding opportunities in the workplace.

About the Author

Peter Weddle has been described by *The Washington Post* as "a man filled with ingenious ideas." Over a span of more than two dozen books, he has offered his readers both unique insights into the modern world of work and powerful techniques for achieving job search and career success.

Peter has been a columnist for *The Wall Street Journal* and *National Business Employment Weekly* and contributed articles and guest columns to *Huffington Post*, *Money*, MSNBC.com, CNN.com, Yahoo! Finance, CBS MoneyWatch and numerous other publications.

Previously, he was the CEO of Hay Systems, Inc., University Research Corporation and Job Bank USA. He was also appointed to a Federal Science Board and received the Commander's Award for Public Service from the U.S. Department of the Army.

An Airborne Ranger, Peter was graduated from the United States Military Academy at West Point. He holds advanced degrees from Middlebury College and Harvard University. He lives in Stamford, CT with his wife and two long-haired dachshunds.

What You'll Find in This Workbook

The Secrets to Job Search and Career Success... All in One Book!

A description of the new world of work in the United States and how it has changed the definition of:

What it means to be a "qualified candidate" when you're looking for a job; and

What it means to be a "qualified performer" when you're working on-the-job.

The **4 Career Fitness principles** that will power you to job search and career success in the new world of work.

The **7 Career Fitness practices**—activities that will take up a fraction of your day while positioning you as the candidate employers have to hire and the worker employers refuse to lose.

Specially tailored versions of the **7 Career Fitness practices** for:

- First-time job seekers; and

- Those reentering the workplace after an extended absence or long period of unemployment.

The best ways to:

Discover your unique talent—what you love to do and do best;

Set rewarding career goals—"career victories" that are meaningful to you;

Build the resume you deserve—a record that every employer will respect; and

Find your Dream Team—the right employer and coworkers for you.

And much, much more!

Table of Contents

Chapter One 15

The Economic Singularity

Why Career Fitness Can't Wait

Chapter Two 19

How to Become a World Class Career Athlete

Chapter Three 25

Your Career Fitness Checkup

Chapter Four 37

Career Fitness

A System for Working Strong in the 21st Century

Chapter Five 55

Step #1: Understanding

Learning the Principles of a Healthy Career

Chapter Six 75

Step #2: Preparation

The Career De-Stress Test

Chapter Seven... **105**

Step #3: Warm Up

Your Career Fitness Plan

Chapter Eight **121**

Step #4: The Career Fitness Work-in

How to Build a Healthy Career Every Day

Chapter Nine.. **253**

Step #5: Cool Down

Maintain a Career Record

Appendix 1 .... **281**

Rookies and Comeback Pros

How to Enter & Reenter the World of Work

Appendix 2 .... **287**

Which Employers Should You Work For?

How to Pick Your Own Dream Team

Appendix 3 .... **295**

A Summary of Sources

My Career Fitness Notes

_____

_____

_____

_____

_____

_____

_____

_____

_____

_____

_____

_____

_____

_____

_____

_____

_____

_____

Career Fitness

Step #1: Understanding

Step #2: Preparation

Step #3: Warm Up

Step #4: The Career Fitness Work-in

Step #5: Cool Down

Chapter One

The Economic Singularity
Why Career Fitness Can't Wait

"You have no control over what the other guy does. You only have control over what you do."

A.J. Kitt, Champion skier

In 1993, the science fiction writer and academician Vernor Vinge introduced the concept of a "technological singularity." In essence, the term designated that point in time when machines would become smarter than humans. Vinge wasn't predicting the rise of Terminators, but rather the advent of machines that could work harder, safer, with greater precision and higher quality than people.

Today, however, the U.S. is facing a very different challenge. It is best described as the "economic singularity." What does it denote? The economic singularity is the point in time when the workers in other countries become smarter than the workers in the United States.

While Vinge prophesized that we would not reach the technological singularity until 2045, however, we have already passed the economic singularity. American employers are no longer competing with rivals that have cheaper labor. They are—at this very moment—competing against those that have smarter labor.

The employees of companies outside the U.S. now have more education and higher skills than do many employees inside the U.S.. As a consequence, those companies are now achieving higher productivity, greater product and service innovation, better customer service and stronger financial results than ever before.

What's that presage for working men and women in the United States?

It signals two disruptive changes:

- **First, the definition of "qualified" has now changed.** Without any announcement or explanation, employers have set a higher standard for a job seeker to be considered a "qualified applicant" and for an employee to be seen as a "qualified performer."

  What is this new standard? Employers are no longer satisfied with people who can do a job. They want those who will excel at it. Competence is simply insufficient in the face of the higher level of competition in the global marketplace. What employers need are people who deliver superior work. Every day and from the first day of their employment.

- **Second, every worker must step up their game.** Regardless of their profession, craft or trade, their educational degrees and certifications, their level of experience and seniority, they must perform at their peak and do so every day.

  How is that accomplished? Working harder is clearly important, but it is insufficient for victory in the face of smarter competition. While some may not be pulling their share of the load in today's workplace, most Americans are already putting in long hours and great effort on-the-job. So, what's also required? **Working strong**—being the best a person can be every moment they're on-the-job.

Practicing Career Fitness isn't, therefore, a nice but noncritical habit to develop. It isn't a well meaning resolution that you can put aside without consequences. And, it isn't something that you can dabble in as your schedule or mood allows.

> **American employers are no longer competing with rivals that have cheaper labor. They are—at this very moment—competing against those that have smarter labor.**

Career Fitness is the only way to be competitive in today's winner-takes-all global marketplace. It prepares you not to hang on and survive, but to step up and prosper. It enables and empowers you to be the champion you were meant to be … and the champion you must be if you expect to enjoy success at work.

That's why more and more Americans are already transforming themselves into career athletes. Whether they realize it or not, they are establishing themselves as the captain of their career and beginning to manage their employment according to the principles and practices of Career Fitness.

Where's the proof?

Consider these facts.

- The 2001 recession was a deep economic downturn that produced a lengthy "jobless" recovery. In 2003, two years after it began, there were still 16 million Americans out of work.

  That same year, however, the U.S. Department of Education reported that there were 92 million Americans enrolled in some form of adult education. In other words, even if all 16 million unemployed persons had gone back to school, there were also 76 million Americans who were heading off to work each day and then hustling off to an academic course or training program at night or on their weekends. They were engaged in "pumping up their career cardiovascular system."

- The 2008 recession was the most severe economic calamity in the U.S. since the Great Depression. In 2010, two years after it began, there were still 13 million Americans out of work.

That same year, however, the U.S. Department of Labor reported that, between February and April, more Americans resigned from their jobs than were laid off. Two million people left their positions voluntarily, while 1.7 million got a pink slip. A group equal in size to the city of Houston was taking charge of their careers and setting their sights on new employment opportunities that would better position them to advance their careers by "working with winners."

Why are these workers taking such extraordinary steps?

As just noted, for some it's a defensive strategy. They are engaging in activities that will protect them from the potential pitfalls and demanding tests of the post-singularity workplace.

For others, however, it is very much an offensive strategy. The new world of work may be hard to understand and impose new and different demands, but it is also filled with more opportunity and greater prospects for success than ever before.

The 21st Century workplace offers each and every person—regardless of their field of work, age or gender—a chance to reaffirm the American Dream. It gives them the genuine opportunity to reach for the best of what's inside them and bring it to work each day.

Those who accept that challenge—those who resolve to practice Career Fitness and aspire to excellence—will join them on the victory stand. Let that be you.

Chapter Two

How to Become a World Class Career Athlete

"The principle is competing against yourself. It's about self-improvement, about being better then you were the day before."

Steve Young, Former professional football player

It's the same in neighborhoods just about everywhere. Almost every day, you'll see people running and walking, bicycling and inline skating, playing tennis and exercising to stay in shape. Whatever the weather, they'll be out there—solitary figures and chattering groups—trying to keep themselves physically fit.

Maybe you're one of them. It is, after all, the lifestyle of our modern American culture. No matter how hectic things become, no matter what the demands we face at home and work, most of us realize that life is best enjoyed when we stay healthy. Good health enables us to live a good life.

Physical health doesn't happen by serendipity, however. Those of us who are out there staying active understand that. We know that being fit is not our natural human state. We accept that it is not a right, a guarantee, a promise or even a reasonable long term expectation.

Our bodies age and are constantly exposed to a host of potential dangers. Illnesses, commuting, business trips, office environments, even the weather can degrade and harm our physical well-being. It's up to us, therefore, to preserve and protect it.

We are individually responsible for achieving and maintaining our good health, and we have to work at it every single day. Consciously or unconsciously, most of us recognize that obligation, and a growing number of us are committed to meeting it. To measuring up. We have made maintaining our physical fitness a central feature of the way we live our lives.

Transforming Yourself Into a Career Athlete

This book begins with a very simple premise: taking care of your career in the challenging 21st Century world of work is a lot like taking care of your health. In order to find a new or better job and achieve lasting career success, you must re-imagine yourself as a "career athlete." You must see yourself as a new breed of worker-champion.

Your model is not that of the athletes engaged in professional sports, but rather, the athletes who are most like you. Worker-champions are the workplace version of Olympians, at least Olympians as they were originally envisioned. They may be amateurs, but they are dedicated professionals in their sport.

These athletes have a number of special attributes:

- **They are independent.** They decide where and when they will exercise their physical abilities and under what conditions. It might be running in a local marathon or playing in a tennis tournament, but they determine the content and duration of their activity.

- **They are passionate about their sport.** They love the doing of it and are energized and fulfilled by that activity. It strengthens and conditions them, exhilarates and rewards them, and leaves them with a pervasive sense of physical and psychological well-being. Indeed, athletic endeavor can actually create a pleasurable physiological response—what is sometimes called a "runner's high"—that replenishes the spirit as well as the body.

- **Their goal is to be the best they can be in their chosen sport.** An athlete continuously strives to excel and then extend the limits of their performance. There is no end to their effort because they believe there is no limit to what they can achieve.

- **They can be anyone.** Athletics are a democratic activity. All of us have a body, so all of us have the inherent ability to engage in and enjoy physical activity. Sure, some of us will perform better than others, but all of us can be athletes, and all of us can reach for and attain the peaks of our own personal excellence.

> **In order to find a new or better job and achieve lasting career success, you must re-imagine yourself as a "career athlete."**

Working men and women are also athletes; they are "career athletes." Whether they are looking for a new job or for more success in the job they have, their attributes are identical to those who are engaged in sports:

- **They are independent.** Career athletes decide where and when they will work and under what conditions. It might be for one employer rather than another or as an independent contractor, but they determine the content and duration of their activity.

Work Strong

- **They are passionate about their field of work.** They love the doing of it and are energized and fulfilled by it. It strengthens and conditions their self-expression, exhilarates and rewards their personal growth, and leaves them with a pervasive sense of mental and emotional well-being. Indeed, a career athlete's work can actually create a pleasurable physiological response—what is sometimes called "flow"—that replenishes the spirit as well as the body.

- **Their goal is to be the best they can be in their profession, craft or trade.** A career athlete continuously strives to excel and then extend the limits of their performance. There is no end to their effort because they believe there is no limit to what they can achieve.

- **They can be anyone.** Career development is a democratic activity. All of us have a mind, so all of us have the inherent ability to engage in and enjoy the work we do with it. Sure, some of us will perform better than others, but all of us can be career athletes, and all of us can reach for and attain the peaks of our own personal excellence.

You can't become a successful career athlete, however, by simply stating your intention to do so. You also can't rely on serendipity or depend on fate or good fortune, and you cannot look to others—your employer, your boss, your mentor, your teacher or your parents—to make it happen. You won't transform yourself into a career athlete by wishful thinking or by being loyal and dependable and showing up for work every day.

There is only one sure way to establish yourself as a genuine career athlete, and that's to practice Career Fitness.

The Power and Promise of Career Fitness

Career Fitness is based on two lessons all of us have learned about our physical health. From our earliest days as a child, we are taught that:

- Each of us is individually responsible for the well-being of our own bodies;

    and

- We must work at strengthening and protecting our physical well-being every single day.

These responsibilities are nontransferable and nonnegotiable. When we ignore them, we harm ourselves; and when we accept them, we better all of our life.

In the 21st Century workplace, the same facts of life apply to our careers, as well:

- Each of us is individually responsible for the well-being of our own career;

    and

- We must work at strengthening and protecting the health of our career every single day.

These responsibilities are also nontransferable and nonnegotiable. When we ignore them, we harm our standard of living; and when we accept them, we better the one-third of our life we spend at work.

Career Fitness enables you to become a career athlete and overcome the challenges and capture the opportunities in the modern American workplace. It gives you a new vision for your work and the fortitude and self-confidence with which to redesign the nature of your employment. It transforms the reality of your workday experience. It alters the possibility in your life from simple survival to prosperity and fulfillment.

Career Fitness will restore you—it will reinforce your confidence in the American Dream—but it will not recreate the past. It will not bring back the gold watch or a workplace built on old fashioned and obsolete career ladders. Instead, Career Fitness enables you to re-set the conditions of your reality.

It empowers you to achieve your full potential at work and to reach for the extraordinary occupational goals that you are naturally capable of achieving. It liberates you to build a successful career on the talent with which you have been endowed. Ultimately, Career Fitness gives you the vision and the tools to transform your work into a personal and potent pursuit of Happiness.

Indeed, Career Fitness is based on a simple, yet powerful vision that runs counter to the prevailing view of work in the modern American workplace. This alternative vision, ironically, takes you back to your roots, enabling and, hopefully, inspiring you to believe that:

- Happiness can and, indeed, should be achieved on-the-job;

- the pursuit of that Happiness is the definition of a healthy career;

  and

- there are specific career self-management activities which, if implemented correctly, will give you the occupational stamina and strength necessary to execute your pursuit successfully.

Understand and accept those three statements—begin with the foundation they provide—and the practice of Career Fitness will have its full and best effect. It will dramatically improve the sense of purpose as well as the rewards you earn from your work.

The Five Empowering Steps in Career Fitness

As you will shortly learn, Career Fitness is a system for **career self-management**. It encompasses both a philosophy of working and a regimen of activities to implement that philosophy in your career. Their purpose is to reposition the work you do so that it plays a more meaningful and rewarding role in your life.

Said another way, the Career Fitness system will empower you to develop the strength, reach and endurance of your career. And, in the challenging world of work of the 21st Century, a fit career is the only way you can find, win and hold onto the job of your dreams.

That may sound like a big commitment, but the Career Fitness system actually involves just five steps:

STEP 1: You learn the unique guiding principles of Career Fitness, so you understand the purpose and power of the various activities you will perform to build up your ability to compete in today's job market and excel on-the-job.

STEP 2: You use a series of worksheets to discover your special talent—the intersection of what you love to do and do best—so you know the kind of work that will maximize both your success and your happiness.

STEP 3: You use a series of worksheets to set three key goals: a near term goal to enhance your performance in your current job, a mid-term goal to advance your career toward new challenges and opportunities, and a developmental goal to acquire the necessary qualifications for success in both.

STEP 4: You will learn the seven career building activities of the Career Fitness regimen—a one-of-a-kind program for peak performance in a job search and on-the-job—and then use a series of integrated worksheets to apply those activities to your own career.

STEP 5: You will learn how to monitor your progress in practicing Career Fitness so you recognize your career victories—on a resume employers will respect and in a private record you will value—and to take appropriate actions when you fall short of your goals.

Those five steps are fully described in this Career Fitness Workbook. Everything you need to find, win and hold onto the job of your dreams is right here at your fingertips. It's your playbook for success in today's challenging world of work.

Equally as important, the Career Fitness system is an equal opportunity career building program. It will benefit you whether:

- you're in transition or fully employed;

- you're happy in your job or turned off by it;

- you're a mid-career professional or just starting out in the world of work;

- you're a senior manager or executive or a new member of the workforce;

- you wear a white collar, blue collar or no collar at all;

    or

- you have thirty years of experience or thirty minutes.

Whatever your specific situation, the Career Fitness system will enable and empower you to increase the paycheck and the satisfaction you bring home from work.

Chapter Three

Your Career Fitness Checkup
How Healthy is Your Career?

"Doctors and scientists said that breaking the four-minute mile was impossible, that one would die in the attempt. Thus, when I got up from the track after collapsing at the finish line, I figured I was dead."

Roger Bannister, after he became the first person to run a sub four-minute mile in 1952

How healthy is your career? Are you building solid occupational strengths? Are you developing the level of competence and endurance you'll need to find your first job or a new job or long term success in your field of work? Or, is your career showing symptoms of being out of shape? Are you professionally flabby? Do you seem to be slowing down and unable to reach for new opportunities or better ones?

As is often the case with their physical fitness, many people don't know the answers to these basic questions about their occupational health. They assume that all is okay because they've seen no warning signs of trouble. They conclude that the day ahead will be just like the day before because they aren't suffering from career cardiac arrest, or what most of us call unemployment.

But careers can be sick long before the pink slip arrives. There can be all kinds of hidden illnesses gnawing away inside a person's career, weeks, months, even years before the symptoms visually manifest themselves in the workplace. As with many physical diseases, you often can't see these afflictions early on, but they are very real, and they are definitely career-threatening.

So, what should you do? How can you protect yourself from these career illnesses? How can you build and maintain a healthy career?

The solution is deceptively simple. It involves taking just two actions:

- First, you have to pay attention to your career.

You have to keep an eye on it, because there are little signs which you can see, signs that can alert you to possible career problems ahead.

- Second, you have to take preventive actions in your career.

You have to Work Strong, because if you adopt healthy career habits—if you commit yourself to a regimen of career enhancing activities—you can probably prevent most problems from ever occurring.

We're all busy, of course, so it's easy to overlook the signs and put prevention on the "to do" list that we never get around to doing. That course, however, has never been more hazardous to the health of your career.

> **There can be all kinds of hidden illnesses gnawing away inside a person's career, weeks, months, even years before the symptoms visually manifest themselves in the workplace.**

The massive restructuring that is sweeping through the 21st Century world of work—jobs that are moving offshore or being outsourced to third party vendors, the introduction of ever more advanced technologies on the manufacturing floor and in the office cubicle, company mergers and the acquisition of one company by another, the rise of global markets and global competition in U.S. markets—all of that turmoil makes it impossible to assume that yesterday's (or even today's) healthy career will inevitably continue unaffected and unperturbed into the future.

There is only one way to protect yourself in this environment: you must constantly monitor the fitness of your career. The more insight you have, the better you will be able to prepare for and protect yourself from the turbulence brought on by these shifts and, no less important, to take advantage of the opportunities they also present. To put it another way, knowing and managing your career status is the key to surviving and prospering in the modern American workplace.

Such self-awareness, however, does not come easily. It requires both personal courage and an effective method of assessment. Only you can provide the former; the following Career Fitness Checkup provides the latter.

Each question in this self-assessment is keyed to a specific principle or activity for building a healthy occupational experience. If you muster the will power to answer all of them forthrightly, therefore, they will enable you to determine both how prepared you are for a successful job search and continued career advancement and which areas require your attention.

The scoring key for the evaluation is detailed in a later section of this chapter entitled, "How Well Did You Do?". Your score will enable you to gauge the current state of your career's health. It assigns a numerical value to your own critical review of key variables in your work and employment.

You can then calibrate that score with the "Standards for Career Fitness" that follow the key. This final step places your assessment at a specific point along the continuum of career health—from a career that is in great shape to one that is dangerously out of shape. It helps you pinpoint the exact status of your career and what you must do to care for it.

In all likelihood, you'll find that there are some areas where your career is in pretty good shape and others where remediation is appropriate. To help you strengthen those areas of vulnerability, the scoring key identifies the specific Career Fitness principle or activity addressed by each question and where it is discussed later in the book. You can use these references to find and explore the specific areas of Career Fitness that will be most helpful to you.

For most, however, the best way to use the Career Fitness system is to start at the beginning and move sequentially through all five of its constituent steps. The principles and practices of the system have been carefully integrated to provide a uniquely comprehensive and effective job search and career building program. So, using the entire program ensures that you receive all of the benefits it can provide.

> **... knowing and managing your career status is the key to surviving and prospering in the modern American workplace.**

Your Career Fitness Evaluation

1. Have you completed your education in the profession, craft or trade in which you work?

[ ] Yes   [ ] No

2. When was the last time you sat down and evaluated the course of your career and the satisfaction you derive from your work?

[ ] Within the last 90 days

[ ] Within the last six months

[ ] Within the last year

[ ] More than a year ago

[ ] Never have

3. Do you set aside time to use your skills in a community support, social service, environmental or similar endeavor?

[ ] Yes   [ ] No

4. How often would you describe yourself as happy at work?

[ ] Almost always

[ ] Occasionally

[ ] Rarely

[ ] Never

[ ] I don't think it's possible to be happy at work

5. Do you use both traditional and online networking to connect with and get to know others in your field?

[ ] Yes   [ ] No

6. Who oversees the course of your career and ensures that you get the training you need and the opportunities you deserve? (Choose only one)

[ ] Your boss

[ ] Your parents

[ ] Your employer's Human Resource Department

[ ] Your mentor

[ ] You

7. Are you currently enrolled in a training or academic program to add to the knowledge, skills, and abilities you can use in your work?

[ ] Yes   [ ] No

8. With whom will you compete to win your next job? (Choose only one)

[ ] Your coworkers

[ ] Individuals outside the organization

[ ] Your boss

[ ] Yourself

9. Do you evaluate the employers that hire in your field and seek employment opportunities with those that are the clear leaders?

[ ] Yes   [ ] No

10. Have you identified your career objective and committed yourself to accomplishing it?

[ ] Yes   [ ] No

11. How much vacation time have you used in the last two years?

[ ] All of the days allotted to you by your employer

[ ] Approximately half of the days allotted to you

[ ] You take little or no vacation time

[ ] You take the time, but stay in touch with the office

[ ] More than your allotted time

12. Do you keep an up-to-date, written record of your work performance, when you're employed as well as when you're not?

[ ] Yes   [ ] No

13. When do you do your best work? (Choose only one)

[ ] When you're earning a large paycheck

[ ] When you like your boss

[ ] When you can work whenever and wherever you want

[ ] When you're recognized for the contributions you make

[ ] When you're exercising your natural talent and abilities

14. Have you identified the next job you'd like to have or the next level of work you'd like to perform?

[ ] Yes   [ ] No

15. When you're employed, do you look for information that will help you monitor the current status and future prospects of your employer?

[ ] Yes   [ ] No

How Well Did You Do?

Tally your Career Fitness score using the key below. For each question in the evaluation, the answer that will best advance the health of your career is worth 5 points; answers that will contribute to, but sub-optimize the vitality of your career yield between 4 and 1 points, depending on their potential impact; and answers that will actually detract from or hurt your career's health are worth 0 points.

After you've tallied your score, evaluate it with the Standards for Career Fitness presented at the end of this chapter. The results will tell you what kind of shape your career is in and how you should use the Career Fitness philosophy and regimen to strengthen your performance on-the-job and your potential for advancement in the workplace.

1. Have you completed your education in the profession, craft or trade in which you work?

Yes	Value = 0	Your Score
No	Value = 5	_____

(If you answered "Yes," see Chapter Five, Career Fitness Principle #4.)

2. When was the last time you sat down and evaluated the course of your career and the satisfaction you derive from your work?

Within the last 90 days	Value = 5	Your Score
Within the last six months	Value = 4	
Within the last year	Value = 3	
More than a year ago	Value = 1	
Never have	Value = 0	_____

(If you scored less than 5, see Chapter Seven, Evaluating Your Performance.)

3. Do you set aside time to use your skills in a community support, social service, environmental or similar endeavor?

Yes	Value = 5	Your Score
No	Value = 0	_____

(If you answered "No," see Chapter Eight, Exercise VI.)

4. How often would you describe yourself as happy at work?

Almost always	Value = 5	Your Score
Occasionally	Value = 3	
Rarely	Value = 2	
Never	Value = 0	
I don't think it's possible to be happy at work	Value = 0	_____

(If you scored less than 5, see Chapter Four, The Career Fitness Philosophy.)

5. Do you use traditional and online networking to connect with and get to know others in your field?

Yes	Value = 5	Your Score
No	Value = 0	_____

(If you answered "No," see Chapter Eight, Exercise II.)

6. Who oversees the course of your career and ensures that you get the training you need and the opportunities you deserve?

Your boss	Value = 0	Your Score
Your parents	Value = 0	
Your employer's HR Dept.	Value = 0	
Your mentor	Value = 0	
You	Value = 5	_____

(If you scored less than 5, see Chapter Five, Career Fitness Principle #1.)

7. Are you currently enrolled in a training or academic program to add to the knowledge, skills, and abilities you can use in your work?

Yes	Value = 5	Your Score
No	Value = 0	_____

(If you answered "No," see Chapter Eight, Exercise I.)

8. With whom will you compete to win your next job?

Your coworkers	Value = 0	Your Score
Individuals outside the organization	Value = 0	
Your boss	Value = 0	
Yourself	Value = 5	_____

(If you scored less than 5, see Chapter Four, A System for Working Strong.)

9. Do you evaluate the employers that hire in your field and seek employment opportunities with those that are the clear leaders?

Yes	Value = 5	Your Score
No	Value = 0	_____

(If you answered "No," see Chapter Eight, Exercise V.)

10. Have you identified your career objective and committed yourself to accomplishing it?

Yes	Value = 5	Your Score
No	Value = 0	_____

(If you answered "No," see Chapter Six, The Purpose of Your Work.)

11. How much vacation time have you used in the last two years?

All of the days allotted to you by your employer	Value = 5	Your Score
Approximately half of the days allotted to you	Value = 3	
You took little or no vacation time	Value = 0	
You take the time, but stay in touch with the office	Value = 0	
More than your allotted time	Value = 3	_____

(If you scored less than 5, see Chapter Eight, Exercise VII.)

12. Do you keep an up-to-date, written record of your work performance, when you're employed as well as when you're not?

Yes	Value = 5	Your Score
No	Value = 0	

(If you answered "No," see Chapter Nine.)

13. When do you do your best work?

When you're earning a large paycheck	Value = 0	Your Score
When you like your boss	Value = 1	
When you can work whenever and wherever you want	Value = 2	
When you're recognized for the contribution you make	Value = 3	
When you're exercising your natural talent and abilities	Value = 5	_____

(If you scored less than 5, see Chapter Five, Career Fitness Principle #3.)

14. Have you identified the next job you'd like to have or the next level of work you'd like to perform?

Yes	Value = 5	Your Score
No	Value = 0	_____

(If you answered "No," see Chapter Seven, Setting Goals.)

15. When you're employed, do you look for information that will help you monitor the current status and future prospects of your employer?

Yes	Value = 5	Your Score
No	Value = 0	_____

(If you answered "No," see Chapter Eight, Exercise IV.)

Your Total Score   _____

(Add up your scores for questions 1 - 15.)

The Standards for Career Fitness

The State of Your Career's Health

YOUR SCORE **YOUR RECOMMENDED USE OF CAREER FITNESS**

 Your career is in great shape!

Congratulations, you have already developed very healthy career habits and are likely to achieve sustained success in your job search and/or at work as long as you stay true to those practices. Use the Career Fitness system to:

- Gain an appreciation for what you have accomplished with your career;

  and

- Embark on activities that will strengthen your good habits so you reinforce and sustain the vigor of your career for the long term.

 Your career is in moderately good health.

You have developed a number of genuine career strengths, but they are weakened by one or more areas of vulnerability that could undermine your job search and/or your ability to perform at your peak on-the-job. Use the Career Fitness system to:

- Learn the full scope of healthy career behavior;

  and

- Embark immediately on those activities that will remediate the vulnerabilities in your career and then undertake the full range of activities that will sustain its vitality for the long term.

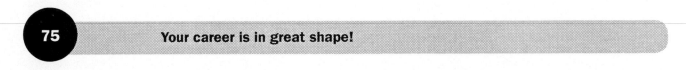 **Your career is suffering and needs your attention right away.**

You must quickly focus on the health of your career as its general weakness makes you especially susceptible to the harmful effects of today's fast-paced changes and challenges in the job market and the workplace. Use the Career Fitness system to:

- Acquire an understanding of and commitment to the principles of a healthy career;

- Learn the full scope of healthy career behavior;

  and

- Embark on the full regimen of activities required to stabilize your career in the near term and then sustain its vitality for the long term.

If you aren't already experiencing career cardiac arrest, you likely will be soon. To put it another way, your ability to acquire and hold on to gainful employment is in grave danger unless you devote your full and immediate attention to resuscitating your career. Use the Career Fitness system to:

- Focus your work on the relentless pursuit of the best you can be;

- Acquire an understanding of and commitment to the principles of a healthy career;

- Learn the full scope of healthy career behavior;

   and

- Embark on the full regimen of activities required to stabilize your career in the near term and then sustain its vitality for the long term.

The Career Fitness Evaluation will give you a good idea of just how healthy your career is and just how ready you are to deal with the demanding challenges of the 21st Century job market and workplace. Clearly, it doesn't test every aspect of your occupational anatomy, but it probes enough of the critical dimensions to provide an accurate profile of your "career expectancy"—the likely length and vigor of your work experience.

Equally as important, this self-assessment will also point you toward a regimen—a daily, weekly, monthly and quarterly schedule—of common sense and practical activities that you can undertake from the first day of your career to the last. If you will accept the responsibility for practicing the exercises in that regimen and if you do so diligently, you will position yourself for success:

- in the job market, if you're in transition;

   or

- on-the-job, if you're currently employed.

That's the power and the promise of Career Fitness.

Chapter Four

Career Fitness
A System for Working Strong
in the 21st Century

"I enjoy what I do, whether or not I've won a few tournaments in the last few months. When you push yourself so hard and you reach such a level to reach that next step, sometimes you might have to go backwards to get forward."

Annika Sorenstam, Former professional golfer

What is Career Fitness? How do you achieve it? And, why bother? What is it going to do for you?

First, let's explore what Career Fitness is <u>not</u>. There is a simple, but very important reason for this approach: Career Fitness is unlike anything you've ever been taught in the past about how to find a job and achieve a successful and rewarding career.

Career Fitness is not about your ability to attain a certain position in a company's hierarchy. It's not a way to work yourself up to be a store manager or the director of your department or the supervisor of your work group. Although such an outcome is definitely possible with Career Fitness, that's not its purpose.

In the old world of work circa the 20th Century, these positions were important because they would usually tell you whether or not your career was healthy and moving you toward success. Work was organized vertically as a competition with others to move up a career ladder of clearly defined positions within an organization.

You could determine a position's relative importance on the ladder by the pay it offered and the number of subordinates it supervised. It was a highly structured one-way pathway for advancement that was almost always managed by your employer.

Today, that well defined career pathway is gone. Increased global competition, rapid technological advances, shifting consumer preferences and changing market dynamics are continuously creating, eliminating and rearranging positions. As a consequence, the career ladder has largely been abandoned.

While upward mobility is clearly still possible, there's less certainty about how to achieve it. The stepwise progress provided by the career ladder has been replaced by a new and seemingly less certain pathway.

In the 21st Century workplace, you must manage your own career and you must do so on what is best described as a "career jungle gym." Rudimentary as that metaphor may seem, it provides an accurate image of how careers will unfold in today's constantly shifting world of work.

As you may recall from your childhood days, there are two truisms about jungle gyms:

- *First, they are liberating.* Unlike just about everything else in a child's life, there is no specified direction, no parent, teacher or rule to tell you which way to go. You get to choose the course you will take, the way you will move across the maze of pipes to get to wherever you want to go.

  It's a challenge, sure—no one is pointing the way for you so you have to figure it out on your own—but, it's also empowering and exciting. You have permission both to define the objective you seek and to choose the path you will take across the bars to pursue that goal.

- *Second, on a jungle gym, moving forward doesn't necessarily mean moving up.* In fact, moving directly up is often all but impossible, at least for any sustained stretch across the rungs. Instead, the jungle gym forces you to find your way forward by moving in many different directions—sometimes up, sometimes sideways and, sometimes, even backwards or down. The pursuit of your goal is not deterred by these course corrections, however, if you keep your eye on your objective, if you remember your goal and keep working toward it.

In the 21st Century workplace, you must manage your own career and you must do so on what is best described as a "career jungle gym."

So, what's this brand new career metaphor mean for you? Simply this: if you're worried about what seems like a lack of security, a sense of uncertainty, or a loss of control in your career, you can put that anxiety aside. The new world of work is no more threatening to your employment success than was the workplace of the past. In fact, if you were good on the school yard jungle gym—and who wasn't, it's an equal opportunity experience—then, you're going to be great in the new world of work in the 21st Century!

Managing your career has now become a new and interesting challenge precisely because there is no longer a fixed path for you to follow, either within a single company or even within the American workplace. The journey—the pursuit of your career objective—has happily evolved into a personal experience that is unique to you. From now on, your career is going to be just like swinging across that crazy contraption of twists and turns and angles and bends to find your way forward to wherever it is you want to go.

The experience may be a bit disconcerting or discomforting, at least at first. It is, after all, unlike anything that you've done or even been able to do at work in the past. It will also be demanding because it requires clear vision and genuine skills to do well. That initial unease, however, will quickly disappear because more than anything else, this new career experience is filled with the potential for self-exploration and discovery. For the first time ever in the world of work:

- you get to plot the direction your career will take;

  and

- you are the one who makes it happen.

The Old Definition of Success

Historically, employers have defined career success for their employees, and their definition was expressed with the career ladder. It was the measuring stick of advancement. Rising up the corporate ladder meant that you had made progress in your career. You were successful—at least as far as your employer was concerned—and more often than not, that produced substantive organizational rewards. Your compensation went up, your office or cubicle got larger, and your status in the corporate pecking order was enhanced.

Despite those advantages, however, many in the workforce were left with a vague sense of unease. All too often, ascending an organizational ladder was unable to generate the self-satisfaction we rightly associate with success. Advancement as defined by our employer's structure didn't automatically yield an equal measure of personal progress. In fact, the sprint up the organization chart to fame and fortune frequently left us worn out with careers that failed to enrich our sense of well-being or our pride of accomplishment.

Reaching the next higher rung in the corporate hierarchy simply failed to provide either lasting happiness or the fulfillment we seek in our work. Instead, many, maybe even most of us felt used up and worn out. Worse, we often came out of the experience disappointed in ourselves as we thought about the choices we had to make and the actions we had to take to "get ahead."

The results of a 2007 survey by the human resource consulting firm DDI reveal the residue of this structural malaise. The career ladder may be gone, but the time we spent on it continues to haunt us to this day. According to the poll's respondents, getting promoted is now the single, most stressful experience in their lives. The psychological and emotional trauma of moving up in the corporate hierarchy has become more difficult to deal with than even the anxiety of a divorce or the despair of a death in the family.

Although most employers didn't encourage it, the unintended consequence of the career ladder was competition. Advancement became a contest in which a single person got to win, and everyone else had to lose. Indeed, those who didn't make it to the next higher rung were left to feel inadequate and unsuccessful. Everything from their job titles to office furniture, from assigned parking spaces to designated seating around its conference tables reinforced the diminished stature of those left behind. It's no surprise, therefore, that most of us ended up feeling acutely dissatisfied, even painfully unhappy with the state of our careers.

Employment became something to be endured. It was the ultimate no-win experience. Why? Because there were lots of people climbing the ladder at the same time, and only one person could occupy the job represented by a specific rung on the ladder at any one point in time. If you define success as moving up the ladder—as was the case in many organizations—everyone else not on that rung was, by definition, a failure. No matter how high you climbed there was always someone ahead of you, and their position higher on the ladder robbed you of any satisfaction or happiness on-the-job.

Of course, this situation was laden with irony. It made even the "winners" feel like losers. Their first rush of excitement, their pride and feeling of accomplishment, didn't last very long. The structural recognition by their employer—that coveted promotion they had achieved—just didn't seem to deliver the deep and enduring self-respect they had anticipated. Grabbing the next rung up on the ladder made for greater institutional rewards, but all too often, it didn't make their work any more meaningful or their accomplishments any more satisfying to them.

So, what did they and the rest of us do? We got back in the race. We began the chase for the next higher rung on the ladder, and then, the one after that and the one after that. Our careers became a junkie's journey, only the high we chased was the pleasure of victory dosed out by our employers. We craved their confirmation of our worth represented by the next higher rung, and we would do whatever we had to do to get it.

As with habit-forming drugs, however, the pleasure of each step up grew less and less intense and its duration more and more fleeting. Even as we rose up through the hierarchy, we sank lower and lower in our own self-esteem. We were being forced to see our personal success as a victory over others, not as a victory of our own, and that malformed prism deflected us from the pride and sense of accomplishment we seek in our work. And deserve from it.

A System for Self-Fulfillment

Career Fitness provides a very different view of your career. Think of it as an alternative prism, one that enables you to see your work with a much more wholesome and self-affirming purpose.

Career Fitness, in essence, is a system for centering your job search and career on the workplace activity which will bring you true and lasting self-fulfillment. It provides the means with which you can actually work at your pursuit of Happiness. It is a guidebook to exercising your inalienable rights as a citizen-worker in the United States of America.

Career Fitness is a system because it encompasses two distinct, but integrated components. They are:

- A philosophy that defines the purpose of your work;

    and

- A regimen of activities for implementing that philosophy in your career.

The regimen is the "what" of Career Fitness—the steps you will take to achieve a healthy 21st Century career; the philosophy is the "why" of Career Fitness—the underlying rationale and principles that justify and shape those actions.

The Career Fitness Philosophy

The only way out of the self-limiting environment that was the unintended consequence of the career ladder is to redefine success on your own terms. It is to realize that a healthy career is not measured by what employers can give you—wealth or status or power—but rather, by what you can give yourself—personal satisfaction, self-respect and fulfillment. The purpose of your work, therefore, is to be your personal best at an endeavor that has meaning and importance for you.

To be your personal best is to draw on the special talent and capability with which you were born. It is to give expression to the self-defined and self-created excellence that resides within you and each and all of us. It is to enjoy your Natural, your unique occupational talent—the workplace activity at which you excel and in which you feel the most challenged, purposeful, happy and complete. This endeavor is your calling, and it is the only work that isn't onerous, dissatisfying and, ultimately, harmful to the health of your career.

> **The purpose of your work is to be your personal best at an endeavor that has meaning and importance for you.**

Many of us never get to work at our Natural. In fact, we don't even know what it is. That's why there has been so much focus, in recent years, on helping us to achieve "work-life balance."

The term implies that work is a negative activity that has no intrinsic value other than a paycheck. Our jobs cannot lift us up, but can only drag us down, so we must find a way to counteract them. We must balance our experience in the workplace with activities that occur someplace else and do have enduring value. And sadly, survey after survey confirms that balance is exactly what a growing number of Americans are struggling to achieve in their lives.

Why is this so? Why are so many American workers determined to spend less of their waking day at work?

- For some, of course, it is a reaction to increased pressures and demands at work. Americans have always been a hardworking people, but the global marketplace has forced workers to do even more. They seek balance in their careers, therefore, so they can still have a life and enjoy their relationships with family and friends.

- For others, however, the push for balance is caused by what's missing from their work. They are investing a third or more of their lives in their career, and that endeavor lacks any sense of purpose or meaning for them. They seek balance in their careers, therefore, so their employment experience is both appropriately engaging and consistently satisfying.

For the first group, work-life balance is a benefit that employers provide. It is controlled by them and necessarily subject to fluctuations in their fortunes. This kind of balance is important to have, to be sure, but in the 21st Century workplace, it is often hard to come by.

The pressures of competition leave little room in employer budgets for the kinds of activities and resources that would provide a credible counterweight to workplace requirements. As a consequence, when employers want to provide a balance, they often can't, and when they can provide it, employees often feel as if they already have it.

For the second group, in contrast, work-life balance is self-created. It is controlled by the individual and is largely unaffected by the fortunes of any employer. The individual seeks and accepts only those jobs where they can be their personal best. They transform their work from a negative to a positive experience by structuring their employment so that it has enduring value for them. They do that by focusing their career on the development and expression of their Natural.

What is a Natural?

Some people are lucky. They just know—they somehow figure out—often at an early age, what their Natural is. They recognize that they were meant to work at communicating complex ideas so everyone could understand or at disaggregating large and difficult problems into more manageable tasks or at showing compassion to those who are sick or in need. They positively identify their special talent—the intersection of what they love to do and what they do best—and they devote themselves to working at it all of their lives.

For most of us, however the essence of our Natural is a mystery, a conundrum, an unknown. That's why a 2005 survey found that six-out-of-ten American workers have no deep and enduring commitment to their work. They have never taken the time, made the effort, or given themselves permission to discover what gives it meaning. Our Natural is the self only we can know, and yet, it's the secret that far too many of us keep from ourselves.

As shown in the figure below, our work experience can fall anywhere along a three-stage continuum.

- In simple employment, you are indifferent to what you do. You take jobs because you have to earn a living. You need to pay bills and put food on the table for yourself and your family. The work, therefore, is less important than the paycheck that you earn. And, your investment in that work is limited to attaining the minimum qualifications necessary to perform the job well enough to get by.

- Mastery, on the other hand, involves taking jobs where the work is inherently interesting to you or involves activities in which you are able to develop an expertise over time. You still want and need that paycheck, but now you earn an additional form of compensation from your work. You take home the feeling of pride that comes from doing your work competently. You are motivated, therefore, to achieve a level of capability that will enable you to continue your effective performance on-the-job.

**Figure 1:
Your Life's Work**

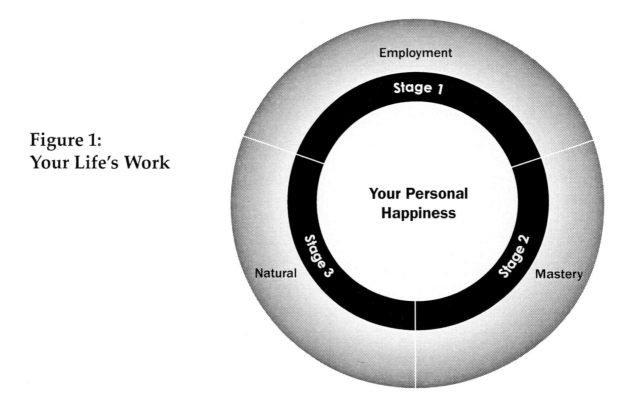

Most American workers toil in careers stuck somewhere between these two stages, between employment and mastery. They hold themselves back or allow themselves to be held back from the ultimate or third stage in the continuum. As a consequence, they never listen to their calling, and they never discover or learn how to work with their Natural.

Your Natural involves work that is magnetically engaging and deeply meaningful to you. Unlike any other endeavor, the substance of it—the composition of its tasks, the character of its responsibilities and the role of its results—touches you on both an emotional and intellectual level.

When you are employed at your Natural, you are uniquely challenged and fulfilled. You are driven, therefore, to be the best you can be in your work and that peak performance produces a double reward. You earn a monetary <u>and</u> a spiritual paycheck. You are paid an income and an extraordinary outcome—the profound happiness that arises when you are employed at what you most like to do and have the natural talent to do well.

But, how do you achieve that end? How do you pinpoint your Natural so you can devote your career to developing and expressing it? How do you determine exactly what it is that will make your work intrinsically interesting and meaningful to you?

There are three factors you must consider:

- **You have to accept that determining your Natural is hard work.**

Identifying your Natural is the entry level job that all of us must take. It is also an endeavor that requires your very best effort. Yet sadly, many of us put it off until it's too late or never even bother. We procrastinate right up to the very last minute—the second semester of our senior year in college or, worse, the point at which we've spent 30 or more years in an unsatisfying and boring career field—and then we get around to it.

If figuring out your Natural were that inconsequential, however, no one would be unhappy with their employment. We would all be heading out the door each morning and actually looking forward to our work. Regardless of its day-to-day difficulties and irritations, we would be powerfully stimulated by what we're doing and absolutely convinced that it is the very best way we could possibly spend our time on-the-job.

The reality, of course, is something else altogether. Countless surveys have revealed an enormous level of unhappiness among American workers.

One poll, for example, found that almost nine-out-of-ten people (88 percent) daydream about quitting their job "to become a success at something totally different." In other words, no matter how much money they were making, no matter how high up the old corporate ladder they had climbed, no matter how many country club memberships and exotic vacations and invitations to limited access events they had accumulated, they had yet to achieve anything that felt like genuine success at work.

Miserable as a lack of happiness can be, most of us have an even more unpleasant experience in the workplace. All too often, we either hate our jobs and careers or we are totally uninterested in them.

Work is a four-letter word that defines the obligations, the misplaced dreams, the insecurities that hold us back and keep us down. It is, with precious rare exceptions, the least engaging, least exciting, least fulfilling part of our lives. Indeed, according to the Conference Board, at least half of all American workers go off to work each day holding their noses or their heads in their hands. The experience is so unappealing that it actually undermines their physical and mental health.

And, the very magnitude of that distress underscores the scope of the challenge involved in finding our Natural. So many of us aren't working at what we most like to do and do best because, consciously or unconsciously, we realize just how difficult it is to figure that out. The examination is intrusive, introspective and requires far more honesty and candor than we're used to or comfortable with.

Discovering your Natural can only be accomplished if you push aside your surface assumptions and probe into the core of who you truly are. You have to silence the noisy interactions of your external existence and search for the quiet voice calling within you.

In the normal course of events, that's far more personal than most of us want to get with ourselves. It's simpler and much less demanding to put up with stultifying jobs and careers. So, we shy away from the hard work of self-exploration and set out on the path of least resistance, even though such a course almost always leads to meaningless work and a mediocre paycheck.

- **You must accept that knowing your Natural is not an off-on switch, but instead, a process of self-discovery.**

Discovering your Natural doesn't happen and then you're done, but instead, begins and continues on. The origin of the process is the recognition of your Natural—what it is—but from that point, with that self-knowledge, you embark on a life-long quest to develop and express that talent to its fullest dimensions.

At times along the way, your passage will provide moments of great happiness and fulfillment as you achieve goals that enable you to experience more of the best you can be. Working with your Natural is the one sure way to reach for the career champion within you, and that stretch to your best self is the only way to survive and prosper in the demanding world of work in the 21st Century.

The self-discovery process and the pursuit of Happiness is unlikely to be a straight line, however. That's not the way life unfolds, nor is it the way a career progresses, even when it's correctly centered on your Natural.

The experience will almost certainly have detours and dead-ends and may, from time-to-time, bring frustration and even some disappointment. It can take you to kinds of work that are absolutely wrong for you and to work that you think and feel is right, only to learn otherwise as your career unfolds.

You might, for example, love playing tennis and devote an extraordinary amount of time and effort to honing your skills in the sport, only to find out that you simply do not have the physical talent to make it your life's work. Similarly, you might enjoy the subject of anthropology during your school days, but discover upon graduation that what was exciting to read about in the classroom is unpleasant or uninteresting in the workplace.

These are setbacks, to be sure, but they do not change the fundamental promise of the American workplace. The journey is open to all. Some may start with disadvantages, and others may be mistreated—situations that we can and must fix—but all of us have the opportunity to embark on the search for the champion within us.

The quest may ultimately take us to a management position in professional sports or to a research job in the advertising field. Whatever the outcome, however, the fact remains: there is the capacity for superior work within each and all of us. We are born with it and hold it within us forever.

Every single person has the inherent ability to discover and live with the unique talent that is their special gift. And, imperfect as it may be, the United States of America—better than any other place on earth—encourages us to do just that. It alone guarantees a birthright to the pursuit of Happiness.

Starting out, like heading west on a wagon train into the frontier of America, takes personal courage and resolve. It is a commitment to yourself, a determination to stay true to what is an integral part of who you are as an individual being.

In day-to-day terms, it means you do not seek employment in those fields and jobs that pay the most or are the most convenient or others think are best for you. Instead, you center your work on that to which you feel naturally and perfectly connected.

Of course, you still aspire to the best possible quality of life for yourself and your family. The foundation of that quality, however, depends not on money or commuting distance, but on the inner pioneering you can do, during your career-long trek through the workplace.

- **The map to your Natural is etched within you.**

Your Natural is as integral a part of you as your personality. There is no global positioning system to help you pinpoint it, however. Instead, you must find this special talent the old fashioned way—by using two cardinal directions. As with longitude and latitude, each of these directions is incomplete without the other, so it's important that you use both and do so by integrating them into a single, unique point of reference.

What are these cardinal directions? In essence, your Natural is the intersection of:

o   An occupation or field of work in which you have sufficient inherent talent to acquire the expertise necessary to sustain a standard of living that is acceptable to you and your family.

o   An occupation or field of work that so engages and challenges you that the doing of it enables you to feel fully expressed as a talented person and thus happy during and at the conclusion of your employment experience.

As basic as these guidelines may seem, they are often misunderstood. And, when they are, unfortunately, they direct your journey into a course that is wrong for you and harmful to the health of your career. They lead you away from your Natural and thereby prevent you from realizing the growth and fulfillment you seek in your work.

Why do such misinterpretations occur? They are caused by the incorrect assumptions many of us make about the modern American workplace. Specifically:

o   *Knowing the ropes doesn't mean you know who you are.* Having expertise, in and of itself, does not mean that you are working with your Natural. Many of us get into a career field, are employed there long enough to gain significant knowledge and skill, and perceive the satisfaction that comes from the exercise of that competency as proof that we are working at our Natural.

Such satisfaction, however, does not necessarily mean you are fulfilled. And happy. It does not automatically signal that the work you are doing enables you to develop and express your special talent and thereby feel fully challenged and rewarded.

To put it another way, "know how" does not equate to "know you." On the other hand, if you first get to "know you" and then develop "know how," you are on your way to a meaningful and satisfying career. You are building competency in what is an integral and natural part of who you are rather than in a set of tasks defined and directed by your employers. In essence, you work at becoming good at you, not at being good at some job.

o *Being a satisfied consumer doesn't mean you are happy.* Career choices—whether they are made at the beginning of your career or at some point along the way—are often colored, even decided by the standard of living one field or another will afford. Increasingly, the only "acceptable" standard, at least in today's American culture, is one that enables us to possess every product and service urged on us by our consumer-based economy.

When you give in to that addiction to acquisition, however, you demote your Natural to the status of a hobby—the one activity you most enjoy doing, but can only get around to after your work is done.

There can be but one primary priority in a career, and consumerism demands that it be cash compensation. Personal growth and accomplishment—the building blocks of fulfillment and happiness—become less important than your ability to buy whatever you want.

Admittedly, there are many career fields that do not pay enough for you to own the latest model car or a continuously updated wardrobe or a home in an upscale neighborhood. You can, however, work in these fields if you redefine "acceptable" to mean the standard of living that will support your family <u>and</u> your spirit.

You can pursue these careers if you recalibrate your quality of life to a level that is achievable by everyone, but only with two kinds of compensation: the financial capacity to provide adequate food, clothing and housing for yourself and those in your care and the psychic capacity to provide a non-cash-based and non-consumable reward—happiness. If you conceive of "wealth" as the attainment of both of those paychecks, you will be the most successful people you ever know ... regardless of the brand of sunglasses or jeans or sneakers that you wear.

o *Choosing the best career field (for you) doesn't mean your work is more important than that of your peers.* We all know that some careers and jobs are perceived to be more worthwhile than others. That's why well-meaning parents, spouses and friends urge us in one direction and away from another. In their view, there's no redeeming value in doing work that lacks prestige or is onerous or dirty.

They believe there is a hierarchy of work, and only those with no other choice will take on an occupation that is generally considered to be undesirable.

Such social evaluations, however, have absolutely nothing to do with what makes you happy. The way you feel about work is personal, profound and should, therefore, be unaffected by social norms and popular values.

That truism has been illustrated time-and-again by Mike Rowe, the host of the Discovery Channel show Dirty Jobs. He's tried occupations ranging from treating sewage to harvesting taro and cleaning bird guano from ocean buoys.

He describes those who are actually employed at such work this way: *"These people take great pride in what they do. Everyone I've met who has a dirty job knows that if you removed them from the chain, then the whole thing falls in on itself. You'll see a lot of optimism and cheerfulness. These are happy people."*

Dirty jobs are no better or worse than working in an office cubicle for ten hours a day, or bussing tables in a restaurant or caring for incontinent patients in a hospice. In fact, work is inherently neutral. Outsiders may (and probably will) have their view, but only those on the inside—those who are actually employed in an occupation—know what it's really like.

Only they are in a position to judge its value. Their assessment, of course, won't ignore market value—what employers are willing to pay for such work—but it will give precedence to personal value—what the work does for them. And, the measure of that value depends primarily on their personal experience, on the sense of purpose and the feeling of self-worth they derive from doing the work.

o   *Working at your passion is not always what you first dream it to be*. While many of us would like to be a professional athlete or a movie star or a best-selling author, our physical attributes or intellectual capacity may not be sufficient for us to do so. In fact, that's probably the case for many, if not most of us. So, the conventional wisdom is that we are left holding the bag. We must accept that our dream does not align with our talent and is, therefore, beyond our reach.

Happily, the conventional wisdom is wrong. Dreams come in many different versions. You can work in a field about which you are passionate if you remember that your Natural is both that which you enjoy doing and that which you do well.

There are many ways to work in professional sports, entertainment, and publishing (or any other field for that matter), and it's those alternatives—coaching, producing and editing, for example—that can provide employment in your passion because they do draw on your inherent talent. You may not hold up an Oscar, a World Series trophy or a Pulitzer Prize, but you can still be a career champion.

You can have your dreams and work in positions where you will excel. You can do that which brings you happiness even if it's not in the way you first imagined it would happen.

When you work both at what you most enjoy doing and at what you are most capable of doing, you position yourself to reach a special zone of performance. It is an arc of excellence that lifts you up to a level of self-realization that cannot be reached in any other way. At the nexus of those two cardinal directions, you are empowered and enabled to be your personal best. And, only that high bar of behavior produces genuine and lasting happiness at work.

What Makes Happiness Possible?

Focusing our careers on what we most enjoy doing and do best is not, of course, a new notion. Career counselors have been urging it on us, at least in the United States, for a quarter century or more. For most of that period, however, it was the right idea at the wrong time. With the notable exception of extraordinary individuals—musical prodigies, theoretical physicists, grand chess masters, gifted athletes—most of us simply did not have the freedom or the capacity to pursue true happiness in our work.

Today, we do. Every single one of us has a life and the liberty to be fulfilled through our careers. We have achieved that freedom thanks to two historic and paradigm shifting developments.

The Installation Of An Accessible Internet

When times are good, most of us don't worry about our careers; when times are bad, however, we quickly realize how little we know (at least without study and practice) about how to plan, organize and direct our experiences in the workplace.

The reality is that effective career self-management cannot be accomplished by dilettantes, by those who practice it for a month or two every five or six years, when they look for a new or better job. Directing your career so that it achieves goals that are meaningful and rewarding for you requires genuine skill and in-depth knowledge, and the Internet has made both available to everyone.

Prior to the advent of the World Wide Web in 1991, most people did not have access to the information and resources necessary to direct their own careers. What was available was difficult to find, inconvenient to use, and often out-of-date. Today, however, anyone and everyone with a connection to the Internet can transform themselves into well informed and highly skilled captains of their own careers. You can do so right from your own home and desktop or, if you don't own a computer, right from today's wired and user-friendly public libraries.

You can investigate the latest salary surveys in your field or in any other career path; you can find job postings from employers in your hometown and anywhere else around the country; you can study tips on resume writing and interviewing and in how to network into the hidden job market; you can get advice on how to handle a prejudiced boss or acquire the latest skills in your field; and most importantly, you can explore your true interests and learn how to achieve your full capacity in the world of work.

> **Effective career self-management cannot be accomplished by dilettantes.**

This knowledge and insight are available to you:

- at the Web-sites and blogs of career counselors, coaches and other experts in occupational planning and development;

- in articles archived on job boards and at the Web-sites of professional societies and trade associations, trade schools, undergraduate and graduate alumni organizations, and affinity groups;

- through interactions with your peers—networking—at the discussion forums, bulletin boards and listservers on those same association, alumni and affinity group Web-sites and on social media sites such as Facebook.com, LinkedIn.com and Twitter.com;

- in articles and columns archived on the Web-sites of newspapers, professional publications, and trade and business magazines;

    and

- via studies and surveys conducted by government, academic and other research organizations and published on their Web-sites.

While not all of this information and expertise is accessible for free, much of it is. As a consequence, the Internet has democratized career self-management; it has brought the skills and knowledge required for the pursuit of Happiness—in the workplace at large and on-the-job for a specific employer—within the reach of everyone, including you.

The Outbreak of a Recognized War for Talent

A cataclysmic societal event occurred in the United States in 1994. For the first time in several hundred years, the rate of growth in the size of the job base exceeded the rate of growth in the size of the workforce. That inversion of the equation in labor economics began an inexorable shift in power in the American workplace. Employers no longer enjoyed their traditional surplus of labor—a market in which people chased jobs—but, instead, faced an unprecedented shortage of labor—a market in which jobs (and employers) had to chase people. The seeds of a War for Talent had been sown.

There was much made of this demographic shift in the press, but in reality, most employers scarcely felt its impact. Thanks to downsizing and layoffs, they had more candidates than they could manage for their openings; their postal and electronic mailboxes were filled to overflowing. A decade later, however—by 2004—they began to see hotspots of troubling shortages that were, in fact, affecting their operations and even threatening their bottom lines.

By 2006, they realized that they were not fighting for talent in general—they were not waging a War for Any Talent; they were battling for superior performers—they were engaged in a War for the Best Talent. And, when that kind of labor market challenge exists, there can be only two kinds of employers: winners and losers.

What is "the best talent" from employers' perspective? It is workers with the specific expertise that a specific organization needs to succeed. Today, the Best Talent encompasses two cohorts of the workforce:

- those individuals who possess certain critical, but hard-to-find skills. Currently, for example, "the best talent" includes pharmaceutical sales reps, engineers, experienced nurses, information technology professionals with the latest Web programming skills and machinists;

  and

- those individuals who deliver a rare contribution on-the-job. Employers consider these workers to be "the best talent" because they are experts in their profession, craft or trade AND they use that expertise to achieve consistently superior results in their work.

The competition among employers for workers in one or both of these cohorts has become so intense that it has changed the fundamental dynamic of the labor market. Those who have rare skills and those who are rare performers now have their choice of employers. They can (and should) select organizations that respect their talent and provide the necessary support for them to express and experience that talent at work.

In an era of intense global competition, the Best Talent are the key to organizational success. That's not a CEO slogan; it's a fact. And, that fact democratizes opportunity for each and all of us.

Every single person has the inherent potential to be a rare skill holder and/or a rare performer. When we elect to realize that potential, we position ourselves to apply the skills and knowledge of career self-management to our own benefit. We put the pursuit of Happiness not only within our reach, but within our ability to grasp, as well.

So, What's It All Mean?

Together, the Internet and the War for the Best Talent form the Emancipation Proclamation of the American worker. These two developments have recast the composition of our employment so that it truly offers genuine opportunity and the pursuit of Happiness to everyone.

For the first time in American history, every single person is now a full and free citizen of the American workplace. We can take charge of our careers and set a course that we will define and bring to fruition. We have always had the right, and now, we have the ability to be all of who we are.

Not everyone, of course, will achieve great wealth, fame or power, but every single one of us will be able to determine our own destiny and have the wondrous experience of being the best we can be in our work. We are free, free to claim our birthright and pursue employment wherever we can best earn the happiness to which we aspire.

As with our political freedom, however, career freedom comes with responsibility. It is up to us to exercise our rights, to invest ourselves in shaping our present and future in the world of work. We cannot depend on others or on our own good luck. We must set ourselves free and actively protect and preserve our liberty on our own.

If a democracy is only as vibrant and strong as the interest and participation of its citizens, our careers are only as rewarding and healthy as the dedication we each show and the efforts we each make to transform our rights into the reality we experience on-the-job.

How do you show that dedication and make those efforts? That's what Career Fitness enables you to do. Just as physical fitness is the way you nurture your body so as to achieve physical health and, ultimately, a sense of well-being, Career Fitness is the way you nurture your Natural so that you achieve career health and, ultimately, happiness. It involves exercising and conditioning your career to give it capacity, strength and endurance. It is achieved through your commitment to a regular, comprehensive regimen of activities that will vitalize and reinforce your freedom in the workplace.

The Career Fitness Regimen

There's never been any lack of career advice for working men and women. Career guides are available in virtually every bookstore, library and counseling center in the country. For many, however, these books are inadequate. Indeed, for the first time ever, sales of career books actually went down during the 2001 recession and have stayed at historical lows ever since.

Why? Because the advice these books offer is well meaning, but not practical. They describe good ideas, but provide no effective way to implement them in the push and shove of people's lives. As a consequence, the vast majority of us have yet to learn how to hone our skills of career self-management and, no less important, how to apply those skills in the day-to-day passage of our careers.

The Career Fitness regimen is designed to correct this situation. It provides a detailed, step-by-step plan for achieving Career Fitness day-in, day-out. At the core of the regimen is a uniquely powerful binary feature:

- **A set of seven practices**, called exercises, that will enable you to strengthen your career health in an orderly and effective way;

  and

- **A schedule** that will enable you to execute each of the seven practices with a frequency and duration that will deliver their maximum benefit to you and your career.

As shown in the Figure that follows, the Career Fitness regimen is composed of five discrete steps. Collectively, they are a way for you to take responsibility for your career health and to work on it every day.

Just as important, the five modules are organized to support your safely starting, effectively executing and fully recovering from strenuous career building activity. As such, they are analogous to the stages of a well designed physical fitness program:

STEP #1: UNDERSTANDING

To achieve the level of commitment and continuous effort required to build physical fitness, you must understand the core principles of human health and exercise philosophy. These concepts aren't complicated—they can be understood and effectively applied by everyone. They are important because they provide the rationale, guidelines and parameters for the physical work you will do.

The same is true with your career health. You must understand and, no less important, you must accept the core principles of Career Fitness and its exercise philosophy. These concepts aren't complicated, but they are real, absolute and must be learned. They lay the conceptual foundation for the activities you will perform to strengthen and tone your career. They are introduced in Chapter Five.

STEP #2: PREPARATION

Physicians and trainers agree that you shouldn't embark on physical activity without first taking a stress test to determine if you can safely engage in rigorous exercise. It's important that you know your limits so you don't exceed them and hurt yourself.

Similarly, you shouldn't embark on exercises designed to develop your career until you can do so in the right way. You must first know yourself well enough to recognize what will strengthen and enrich your well-being at work. Instead of establishing your limits, however, the Career Fitness evaluation seeks to remove them. It is designed to eliminate self-imposed (and other) constraints on what you can accomplish through employment so you can discover your Natural. For that reason, it's called a De-Stress Test. This assessment is presented in Chapter Six.

STEP #3: WARM-UP

The warm-up phase of a physical fitness regimen ensures that you have put yourself in a position where you can safely begin rigorous exercise. It involves setting goals for what you would like to accomplish in an exercise period and then carefully readying your body for that activity.

The Career Fitness regimen begins with a similar period of preliminary planning and benchmarking of personal success. Its purpose is to set goals for your career in the near and mid-to-longer term on-the-job and for the personal growth that will enable you to achieve those objectives. This goal-setting activity is detailed in Chapter Seven.

STEP #4: THE EXERCISES

In physical fitness, you "work out" to eliminate the toxins, excess weight and lethargy that sap your strength and overall health. The more rigorous and regular the periods of exercise, the greater the benefit to your body.

In Career Fitness, you "work-in" to put employment into your life in a meaningful way—to ensure it gives you the rewards and happiness your deserve. The seven constituent exercises of the Career Fitness Work-in are organized in a schedule that ensures you perform them with the requisite frequency and duration to affect your career both positively and permanently. And, here's the best part: it takes just nine percent of your work day to perform all of the activities in all seven of the exercises. That's a modest commitment of time for career-long fulfillment and success. This systematic program for career development is unique to Career Fitness and described in Chapter Eight.

STEP #5: COOL DOWN

In physical fitness, cooling down involves moderated activity that enables your body to recover fully from rigorous exertion.

In your career, cooling down is also a time of moderated activity. It is a regular, but limited resting state that refreshes the energy and enthusiasm you have for your career by giving you the opportunity to recognize what you have accomplished through your commitment to the Career Fitness regimen. You acknowledge and celebrate your success by creating a record of your "career victories" that are, in turn, the foundation of your career security in the 21st Century workplace. This period of reflection and regeneration is explained in Chapter Nine.

The Career Fitness regimen provides a practical, step-by-step plan for infusing the philosophy of Career Fitness into your job search and employment on-the-job.

- The philosophy details a comprehensive strategy for being the best you can be at work and, as a result, freeing yourself to enjoy a meaningful and rewarding career in the 21st Century workplace.

- The regimen provides the tactics—the readying steps and practical, day-to-day activities—that will enable you to implement your strategy effectively and, as a consequence, pursue and achieve genuine Happiness.

The Career Fitness Regimen

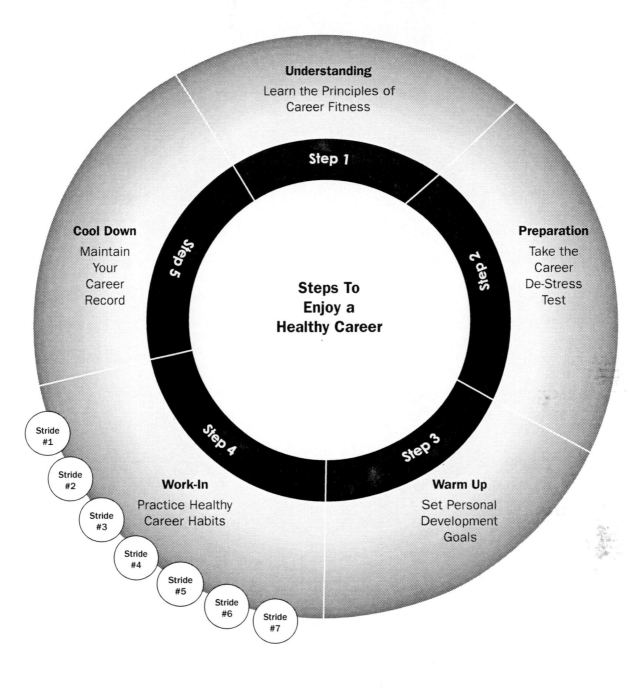

Understanding
Learn the Principles of Career Fitness

Step 1

Preparation
Take the Career De-Stress Test

Step 2

Step 3

Warm Up
Set Personal Development Goals

Work-In
Practice Healthy Career Habits

Step 4

Cool Down
Maintain Your Career Record

Step 5

Steps To Enjoy a Healthy Career

Stride #1
Stride #2
Stride #3
Stride #4
Stride #5
Stride #6
Stride #7

Career Fitness is a uniquely powerful system for organizing and sequencing the development of your career health. It ensures that nothing important is omitted and that everything involved contributes to a job search and a career that will serve your best interests and enduring success in the world of work.

Chapter Five

Step #1: Understanding
Learning the Principles of a Healthy Career

"As long as you're coaching, you have to always be thinking of getting better. As long as you're playing, you've got to always think of getting better. As long as you're doing what you're supposed to be doing, you've got to think about getting better."

Mike Krzysewski, Coach of the Duke University basketball team

While the challenges of the 21st Century workplace confront us all, addressing those obstacles is an individual endeavor. The key questions, therefore, are:

- How do you transform your work from an onerous obligation to an opportunity to serve someone special: you?

- How do you face up to the responsibilities and the potential of your career and face down the pressures and demands of the modern workplace?

At first blush, these questions may seem misconceived, for they indisputably link the practical with the philosophical, the get-it-done-in-the-real-world with the spiritual or inner journey of self-fulfillment. But, that is precisely the purpose and the potential of Career Fitness. It offers you a way to connect your work and your pursuit of Happiness so that you earn <u>both</u> a financial and a spiritual return on the time and talent you invest on-the-job.

To establish that connection, however, you must recognize and respect the principles that support Career Fitness. You must understand and abide by the fundamental rules for living a healthy life in the world of work. There are only four such principles; they are:

- **Principle #1: You are the captain of your career and the keeper of its health.**

- **Principle #2: You must exercise your freedom to experience the best of what's inside you.**

- **Principle #3: Stretching yourself to achieve a healthy career must empower not hurt you.**

- **Principle #4: Your best work never ends, nor does your responsibility for performing it.**

Understanding and accepting these principles is accomplished in the first step of the Career Fitness regimen because the value system they provide is the key to using that regimen effectively. Without this foundation of knowledge and commitment, you are unlikely to appreciate the role or the importance of the regimen's implementing exercises or to realize their benefit in your work. To put it another way, these principles form a credo—a belief set—that enables you to take your talent to work and use it effectively on-the-job. Without them, you are powerless to be the best you can be.

Career Fitness Principle #1

You are the captain of your career and the keeper of its health.

Career counselors and workforce experts believe that workers today—regardless of their age, occupational field or industry expertise—will experience a significantly greater number of changes in their employment than did workers in the past. They predict that the average will increase from the late 20th Century norm of three-to-five job changes in a career to an astonishing twelve-to-fifteen such transitions in the 21st Century workplace.

If you begin work at age twenty and work until age sixty-five, that means you'll be taking a new job every 2½-to-3½ years. Even more unsettling, you'll likely go from spending your entire career in a single occupational field to switching occupations at least once and maybe even twice or more during that period. In short, change is now the norm in the American world of work.

This dynamic new reality is driven by many factors, including:

- mergers and acquisitions among employers, positioning them to lower costs by eliminating redundant jobs and even career fields;

- technological advances in production and distribution, making some traditional jobs obsolete and creating others that are entirely new;

- shifts in consumer tastes, requirements and/or needs, leading to the introduction of new products and services and causing existing jobs that are tied to earlier products and services to be fundamentally redesigned and/or eliminated from the workplace;

- marketplace competition from foreign as well as domestic companies, triggering demands for ever greater productivity from those employed in an organization's "core" functions so that jobs involving other functions can be outsourced to cheaper providers;

- penetration of the U.S. labor market by overseas suppliers, sending jobs to other countries where they can (allegedly) be filled to the same standard, but more cheaply;

    and

- advances in healthcare and nutrition which enable people to spend more years in the workforce and thus be available for employment in a greater number of jobs during their career.

With all of these forces now in play, change in your employment situation—your job, your employer, your industry, your workplace or even your occupation—is all but unavoidable. It may not occur this year or next, but it definitely will at some point and probably in the not too distant future. It is not, however, a one-time-and-you're-done event; it will happen again, and then again, and again after that.

This reality confronts you (and everyone else) with a stark choice: you can either be in charge of these changes or you can be their victim. There are no other options. You can either give in to the chaos around you or give yourself the capacity to control it. You can decide to do nothing and ensure that you'll be the butt of change, or you can step to the head of your career and put change to work for you.

Sure, it's easier said than done. Absolutely, it is unsettling; change always is. But, who wants to leave their fortune and their future to chance? Or, to the machinations of an uncaring economy? Yes, you have a choice, and the only rational course is to take charge of what happens to you in the workplace. To protect yourself and those you care about.

> **You and everyone else now face a stark choice: you can either be in charge of the (inevitable) changes in your career or you can be their victim.**

To do that, however, you must accept another job, one at which you will work for the rest of your career. Whatever your title, seniority or profession might be, you will also and always have to serve as the "captain" of your own career. Not the coach, but the captain. The one who sets the direction and pace and, ultimately, steels you with the conviction to succeed.

This additional role is not a second job. It is not one that you take to supplement the primary work that you do for your employer. Instead, being your own career captain is actually your first job. It is your primary responsibility, your first priority. Why? Because it serves you and your family. It refocuses your career on being the best you can be for the people who matter most to you.

To accept that responsibility and to discharge it effectively, you must first accept a counterintuitive idea: a successful career in the 21st Century won't happen because you do good work for your employer. Rather, you can only achieve a successful career by doing work that is good for you. If your work engages and challenges you, it will stimulate your optimal performance, and it's the satisfaction you earn from your own peak performance that promotes a vibrant and rewarding career.

Equally as important, when you perform at your peak, you also serve your employer. You make a greater contribution on-the-job, but you do so with an important difference. Your commitment to self-excellence will enhance your stature—your perceived worth to your employer—and that distinguishing position puts you in charge of your workplace experience. You get to pick the organizations and jobs that work for you—that provide the platform for your own continuous improvement—and jettison forever the out-of-date notion that you work for an employer. In essence, you shift your allegiance from the source of your paycheck to the source of your happiness, from the organization to yourself.

Work At Your First Job

What exactly does accepting the job of career captain entail? What are you being asked to do?

As your career's captain, you take responsibility for the success of your career. It's up to you to define that success—it's no longer dictated by the next rung up on the corporate ladder—and it's up to you to make it happen. You have to decide which employers deserve the contribution you can make in your field, which jobs you will accept with those employers, and which course your career will take as a consequence. No one else will make those decisions for you. Only you can … and you must.

Why? Because the priorities and responsibilities of employers are different—very different—from yours. Most U.S. employers are for-profit companies, and according to contemporary business practice, they have a single, all consuming goal: to deliver a financial return on the investment of their shareholders. If that means adding new technology to eliminate jobs or making workforce cuts to reduce headcount or sending jobs to another state or overseas to slash expenses, then that's exactly what they will do.

We live in an era where the limits of corporate accountability end at the bottom line. The fate of an organization's employees—while a matter of concern at the human level (at least among good employers)—is not material to its economic performance. Its leaders are obligated—indeed, they have a fiduciary responsibility—to maximize the organization's, not their workers' wellbeing.

You, of course, bring a more personal perspective to the workplace. You see yourself as a contributor, as someone who provides the genuine capability and dependable commitment necessary for the organization to succeed. You believe you enable that success and, at least in part, determine its magnitude. You are certain that you deliver meaningful value to the organization that can and should be maximized. Not commoditized or treated as just another input to the business model.

This view, while rational and reasonable, has not influenced corporate behavior, at least until now. The historic relationship between an employer and a worker was not a partnership of equals; it was not a team of individual, but similarly valued contributors. And, it was not a joint venture for the mutual benefit of all participants. Most companies employed workers "at will" and their willingness to do so was based entirely on an economic calculation—on the impact it would have on their bottom line.

Today, this separate and unequal definition of employment is obsolete. Talent is the real energy source of the global marketplace, and in the U.S. today, talent is in critically short supply. So, if you are at the top of your game in your profession, craft or trade, organizations need you as much as you need them. If your view—that you deliver genuine value to the organization that can and should be maximized—is actually backed up with quality, dependable work on-the-job—then your perspective is now just as important to maximizing an employer's success as that of the employer, itself.

> **As your career's captain, you take responsibility for ensuring that the work you do works for you as well as your employer.**

The value you deliver to an organization, however, is only half of the picture. The other half is often overlooked, but no less vital. It is the value your work delivers to you. Sure, your effort should contribute to your employer—that's what you get paid for—but it's equally as important that it contribute to you, as well. To be an appropriate and responsible use of your talent, the work you do must benefit you—not only in your paycheck, but in the satisfaction and sense of accomplishment you bring home from the workplace each day.

Achieving this binocular view of the value of your work is your primary responsibility as the captain of your career. It is the essence of the job. And happily, all of us have the inherent capacity to do it and do it well.

You can be the captain of your career because you (and everyone else) are born with a "career genome." As with our human genome, it is composed of DNA, the DNA of a successful career:

 = our innate desire for development. Every human being wants purpose, challenge and meaning in their work because they are the building blocks of personal growth and excellence.

 = our innate need for nurturing. Every person wants to work in an environment where they will feel comfortable, engaged and supported in their quest to do their best work.

 = our innate drive for advancement. Every individual wants opportunities to expand their contribution at work and to extend their accomplishments and their success in their field.

Acting as the captain of your career, therefore, is actually a matter of being true to your own nature. It entails identifying, planning for, achieving and enjoying a certain kind of employment. Fundamentally, it means ensuring that you take work that benefits you. Such employment:

- supports your quest to be your personal best. That's the only way your time on-the-job will be both meaningful and fulfilling. It must stretch you to your limits so that you grow and gain the self-affirmation that comes from the development and expression of your innate talent, your Natural.

- enables you to provide for yourself and your family. That's the only way your time on-the-job will be worthwhile and rewarding. It must offer the realistic expectation of adequate compensation to sustain a standard of living that is acceptable to you and those who depend on you.

All jobs are designed to accomplish specific tasks, and these two tasks define the job requirements for a career captain. They are what you must do to act as the keeper of your career's health. You were born with the potential to perform these tasks, but you cannot realize that potential without personal growth. You must ready yourself to become your own captain by acquiring the skills of career self-management <u>and</u> the knowledge of how best to apply those skills in the 21st Century workplace.

That's a big first step. The 21st Century workplace is not the same playing field we knew in the 20th Century. The rules for career success have changed. Many, maybe even most of us, however, are still comfortable with the old rules. As unfair as they were (and are), we just don't want to part with them. And yet, we must.

The new rules—the ones that are actually shaping the present—are not voluntary or optional. We ignore them at our peril. They redefine the reality of our experience in today's world of work. They determine whether we will win or lose in our careers.

What are these new imperatives? There are just two:

- **Rule #1: Job security has become an historical artifact.**
  It is as relevant to the 21st Century workplace as a buggy whip or carbon paper. In the past, you could count on loyalty to your employer and superior performance on-the-job to provide the critical safety net of job security. Today, you can't.

  Employers are facing so many changes—in technology, competitors, marketplaces, consumer preferences and government regulations, to name just a few—that's it's hard for most of them to know what kind of talent they will need six months in the future, let alone two or three years down the road. As a consequence, even the most dedicated "A"level performers can now find themselves unemployed and out on the street looking for work.

- **Rule #2: Career security is the safety net of the 21st Century.**
  It represents the ability to be employed without lengthy or disruptive interruption. It is the capacity to keep working and to do so with employers and at jobs you select. It doesn't mean you won't change jobs—as indicated above, there are too many dynamics underway in the global economy to produce such stability—but it does ensure that you will always be able to find good employers that want to hire you.

  Unlike job security, however, career security is not something an employer provides; it is a state of being in the workplace that you create and sustain. It requires that you transform yourself from a career couch potato to a career athlete. Career security is a commitment to yourself to build occupational strength, agility, endurance, and reach for yourself. How? With Career Fitness.

These changes to the rules of work leave you with no choice but to alter the game plan for your career. What delivered success in the 20th Century will not do so in the 21st Century. You have to devise an approach that is synchronized with the reality of the challenge you face.

That approach must have two elements: first, you have to be good at what you do and second, you have to be good at deciding where, when, and how you will do it. To put it another way, you must now be an expert in two jobs: the one you share with your employers—the position in which they employ you—and the one that's all yours—the role in which you act as the captain of your career.

Career counselors, of course, have been promoting the notion of career self-management since at least the early 1990s. They have been urging us to take charge of our careers, to take responsibility for their direction, content, pace and progress. What Career Fitness offers is a way to do it. A way to own and operate the one-third of our day we spend at work.

Career Fitness provides the means by which you can successfully perform your first job: serving as your own career captain. Career Fitness provides the skills and knowledge you need and the practical steps you must take to direct your career toward employment experiences that work for you. And when they do, they will also work for your employer, as well. You become the star of your own career and an all star for the organization.

Career Fitness Principle #2

You must exercise your freedom to experience the best of what's inside you.

Career Fitness is a regimen that exercises your Natural so that the work of your career remains meaningful and rewarding for you, regardless of the job you hold or the organization which employs you. It provides a way for you to overcome the four risk factors that can weaken and even mortally wound your career:

- lethargy—being indifferent to what happens in your career or too lazy to do anything about it;

- habit—being so comfortable with the routine and the familiar in your career that you refuse to move beyond where you are;

- fear—being so obsessed with the difficulties and the challenges of change that you avoid doing anything new or different;

  and

- self-satisfaction—being so enamored with what you have already accomplished that you stop striving to do more.

These four factors put your career at risk because they make you immobile. They cause you to stand still, to hold back, to remain where you are. And, when you do that—when you accept inaction—you remain unfinished, unfulfilled. When you stop moving forward, your career grows flabby and your reach falls short of the best that's inside you.

Fortunately, today's career jungle gym presents you with more opportunities for action than most of us have ever had in the workplace. Unlike the situation on the old fashioned career ladder, there is no prescribed path to success in your work, no lockstep route to advancement, and no single way to enhance your standing in your field. In effect, you now have options—alternative courses you can take—each with different prospects and challenges. Progress may be achieved by moving up, but it might also be accomplished by shifting sideways or even back a step or two. It all depends on your vision, your reach and on what you decide to strive for.

As the captain of your career, you determine which direction you will take and you are responsible for implementing that decision. You can:

- stick with your current job with your current employer;

- convince your current employer to redesign your current job by redefining its responsibilities (e.g., adding, modifying or deleting tasks);

- convince your current employer to accept a different working arrangement with you in your current job (e.g., allowing you to move to part time or contract work);

- convince your current employer to change the conditions under which you work in your current job (e.g. allowing you to move to a flexible schedule or telecommuting);

- seek a different job with your current employer;

- seek a new job offering new responsibilities with a different employer in the same industry;

- seek a new job with a different employer in a different industry;

- seek additional education in your field and use your enhanced capabilities to pursue one of the courses described above;

  or

> **As the captain of your career, you are able to determine which direction you will take and you are responsible for implementing that decision.**

- switch career fields and change the composition, purpose and/or opportunities of the work you do.

There are undoubtedly other options, as well, but what's important is that it's up to you to decide which course you will take <u>and</u> to act on that decision. You have to make it happen. Not wait for your employer to act. Sure, that organization has the power to hire or fire you and to promote or demote you, but those actions—as consequential as they may seem at the moment they occur—cannot trump the actions you take for the long term health of your career. But, only if you take them.

If you do nothing—if you leave a vacuum in your career—then external actions by your employer, in the industry where you work or as a result of the economy will inevitably take precedence. They will significantly influence (and likely even determine) your employment experience. If, on the other hand, you act according to your own vision for your career, you will shape your work to reflect your own interests and goals. Everything may not work out exactly as you plan—this is life, after all, not a fairy tale—but you will establish what's important in your work and how you will reach for that goal.

An Active, Not A Passive Concept

The actions that employers take influence individual jobs, but not which jobs an individual takes. That's why the notion of job security is now obsolete. It's a 20th Century idea that's been overtaken by events in the 21st Century. Wikipedia defines job security as "the probability that an individual will keep his or her job." Today, however, employers face such intense competition in both their domestic and global markets and, for public companies, such single-minded pressure from Wall Street that they can no longer provide an employment guarantee to any employee, whether they're the Chief Executive Officer or the mailroom clerk.

This new reality can't be changed by an employment contract, a collective bargaining agreement, the loyalty that's shown to an employer, or even the highest level of on-the-job performance. In effect, companies now operate in a disruptive environment, and that disruption can and probably will affect everyone's employment, including yours.

When you adopt a laissez-faire approach to your career, therefore, you make yourself vulnerable to potentially destabilizing and even harmful disruptions. When you take control of what happens, on the other hand, you influence far more than your employment. When you set the course and take the actions necessary to implement it, you determine the quality of your career. You decide how good it is for you and to you.

No less important, you also create an alternative definition of security. You transform the idea from something based on a job—a position designed to serve an employer—to something that is centered on your career—an experience that serves you. Your proactive involvement eliminates the shifting sands the global economy places beneath your career and replaces them with a foundation you can trust and count on.

At that point, however, you have a decision to make. Economists define "employment security" as the ability always to find work. So, you can elect to manage your career according to that standard—you can take those actions which will ensure that outcome. Or, you can choose to manage it to an even higher standard called "career security." It involves taking those actions which will ensure that you can always work and that you will always work at what's important to you.

Career security is employment security with fulfillment. It is the ability to stay gainfully employed in your Natural. You achieve it by using Career Fitness to do all the right things for your career at the right time, in the right way and for all the right reasons.

A commitment to career security is the defining attribute of the rational and responsible working man and woman in the 21st Century. It is based on quintessential American values: individualism, a can-do work ethic, and a profound belief in one's right to Life, Liberty and the pursuit of Happiness.

That may sound melodramatic, but it's actually more grounded in reality than the naive notion that you can expect career stability in a disruptive economic environment. Long term employment with a single employer still happens, of course, but it is increasingly the exception to the rule. As noted earlier, change is the new norm in the American workplace. Therefore, building a career that ensures those changes benefit you is now the only realistic and appropriate goal for a working person.

Career security accomplishes that goal by changing the central focus of your work. It transfers your focus from something over which you have little control—a paycheck—to something over which you have total control—the satisfaction and pride you derive from your work. That is your personal act of emancipation. It is the liberation of your occupational persona.

Committing yourself to a proactive agenda that will develop and express your fullest capacity in the field of work that you most enjoy doing and do best recreates you as a full-fledged citizen in the American workplace. In essence, you free yourself from the separate and unequal employment experience of the past and claim the integral and equal status of a person of talent.

Making that claim, however, is only the first of the two essential building blocks of career security. In the United States of America, you have the right to pursue happiness, but the success of that pursuit is not similarly guaranteed. Centering your career on your Natural is the foundation of career security. Its superstructure is amassed with the decisions and actions you take to realize that self-commitment.

The course you select may or may not involve a change in employment. It may or may not shift you from one assignment to another in your current job or move you from your current job to another with your current employer or take you from working for that employer to working for another. What's critical is that you make the claim and you make the claim happen. You act. You take the steps that produce change, a change in and for you. You initiate and perpetuate your own personal growth.

Such proactive self-development is essential because managing your career in today's workplace is a lot like riding a bicycle. When you first got up on a two-wheeler, you learned a very simple rule of physics: either you kept moving and, therefore, made progress on your ride or you came to a dead stop and toppled over.

The same is now true with your career. Either you keep growing in your Natural and, therefore, make progress in your quest to be the best you can be or you come to a dead stop and see your career crash, causing damage to both your present and future in the world of work.

A healthy career, then, is a journey, not a rest stop. It is not defined by going to work for as long as possible in a single job or for a single employer. In most cases, that's stasis. It is the career equivalent of standing still. And in today's ever-changing workplace, motionless is a form of desperation and, ultimately, self-defeating.

> **A commitment to career security is the defining attribute of the rational and responsible working man and woman in the 21st Century.**

Career vitality is built with aspiration. It is a commitment to continuous self-improvement. It is non-stop personal progress. That progress is achieved with momentum—a constant force of action which you provide. Momentum isn't speed; it is steady, unceasing movement forward.

Momentum in sports is the competitive advantage that occurs when an individual achieves a rhythm of peak performance that propels them to victory and positions them for future success. Momentum in careers is the personal advantage that occurs when your work achieves a rhythm of peak performance that produces superior results and creates meaningful opportunities for you at work.

Momentum on the playing field or on the court often begins with an extraordinary event—a big play. In careers, momentum begins with an extraordinary development—an act beyond what is expected of you on-the-job. What is that act? It can be any one of the following:

• Improving your capabilities for performing your current job;

• Acquiring new capabilities in order to secure a new job;

    or

• Reaching for a more challenging position that will enable you to express all of the capabilities you have improved and acquired.

These self-improvement actions expose you to new ideas, alternative perspectives, additional knowledge, and greater insight. They, in turn, enable you to draw on more of your Natural and express it more fully in your work. They capture the energy and imagination that are available outside the limitations of your current job description and transform those assets into capabilities you can employ to excel at your work and enhance your contribution on-the-job. In short, these momentum-building actions set you up to be the best you can be, not the minimum specified for satisfactory job performance.

As on a bicycle, you can also coast in your career for limited periods of time—say, to care for young children or for elderly parents—but the longer you do, the less momentum you have and the harder you must work to reaccelerate your career. Indeed, it's best never to halt your personal progress altogether, even when you've stepped outside the workforce.

A dead stop, no matter how seemingly important or justified, can leave your career just as dead and literally force you to begin all over again. Moreover, in today's wired world, it's easier than ever to stay connected with both your colleagues and your field of work. (For more information on how to restart a career after a period of coasting, please see the Appendix entitled Rookies & Comeback Pros.)

The pursuit of Happiness through the proactive development of personal excellence is a key contributor to career health. In the past, it was a state that only a few lucky or extraordinarily gifted individuals could attain. In the 21st Century workplace, it is a Life that is open to all of us. You no longer have to endure a job you dislike or an employer that holds you back. Today, you have the Liberty to determine what work you will do and where you will do it in order to make steady, genuine progress in your pursuit of Happiness. All you have to do is exercise that right and act.

Career Fitness prepares you for exercising such initiative. If physical fitness is a form of preventive medicine, then Career Fitness is a form of preventive action. One wards off physical ailments and disease; the other wards off career cardiac arrest or the painful, debilitating and potentially fatal trauma of unemployment.

Career Fitness Principle #3

Stretching yourself to achieve a healthy career must empower not hurt you.

In the 20th Century, many coaches and physical trainers used a trite, but powerful message to urge athletes on to ever higher levels of performance. "No pain, no gain" was the conventional wisdom. Push yourself until it hurts, and then, push yourself some more. That was the way you achieved athletic success, or so they thought.

Physical fitness experts have now determined that this notion is a surefire way to do lasting damage to your body. Forcing yourself to endure acute physical discomfort does not enhance your physical prowess; doing so actually weakens and eventually destroys it.

The same is true with your career. "No pain, no gain" implies that you should work at whatever maximizes your paycheck, even if you hate every moment you spend on-the-job. It suggests that you should endure unpleasant working conditions as long as they permit you to earn a living. And, that view is also completely wrong.

A dull or unpleasant job transforms your working life into the daily grind or, worse, into an experience that grinds you up. It leaves you feeling wasted and even abused. It doesn't enhance the health of your career: it profoundly weakens and eventually destroys it.

Career Fitness, on the other hand, encourages you to see your work in a very different way. Any job that seems dull and unpleasant to you should be done by someone else who finds it interesting and exciting or, at the very least, satisfying. For both of you, the employment experience should be a chance to "play" at something you enjoy and get paid to do.

A healthy career unfolds like an adult game; it is a series of challenges—the jobs at which you are employed—that enable you to dream bigger, reach further, and achieve more than you ever have before. Your work, in essence, becomes the way you discover more about the champion who lives inside you and, as you come to know that person, to raise the level of your performance on-the-job.

That achievement of your personal best, in turn, unleashes a chemical reaction in the brain that humans are hardwired to seek. It produces a cognitive state that every person craves. Psychologists call it happiness.

Pushing yourself to develop a healthy career, therefore, should not be a form of torture, but a pathway to something invigorating and, ultimately, beneficial. It is the way you transform the single largest segment of your life—the time you spend at work—from a painful passage into a journey of self-exploration and self-fulfilling expression.

You are not competing with others on a race up the corporate career ladder, nor are you competing with yourself to see how much unhappiness and dissatisfaction you can endure on-the-job. Instead, Career Fitness is based on two simple, but powerful ideas:

- First, work can and should be good for you on the inside as well as on the outside;

  and

- Second, achieving the full measure of such goodness is an exercise in developing and using your Natural, the special talent that is an integral part of your being.

Accept those two ideas and you put happiness within your reach at work. You move it from a dependency on what happens outside of you to an "independency"—to what happens inside of you. Your career may play out in the workplace, but your play occurs within your mind and spirit. The pursuit of Happiness is an inalienable right; the feeling of happiness is the inner experience of the right work.

> **Seeking to achieve your personal best unleashes a chemical reaction in the brain that humans are hardwired to seek. It produces a cognitive state that every person craves. We call it happiness.**

No Happiness, No Synergy

In today's anxious and often cynical workplace, this notion of working at your happiness is sometimes ridiculed as naïve, unrealistic, even dangerously sentimental. The critics say that it is wishful thinking or, worse, ostrich-like behavior in the face of a tough job market and demanding work environment. And yet, there is ample proof that centering one's career on a mental and spiritual paycheck is actually what most of us would prefer to do and, absent outside influences, is the way most of us will naturally go to work.

That proof is best articulated in a 1990 book entitled *Flow, The Psychology of Optimal Experience,* written by Mihaly Csikszentmihalyi. His conclusions are derived from interviews with thousands of working men and women all over the world. The subjects included those who were clearly working at their Natural—professional athletes, entertainers, and grand chess masters—and those who were working simply to earn a living. All were asked the same questions:

- When, during the day, did they most enjoy themselves?

- What were they doing when they most enjoyed themselves?

- And, how did they feel—what was the experience like—when it happened?

The findings of this research are as startling as they are counterintuitive (at least in a workplace defined by Dilbert). The vast majority of the people in the survey reported that:

- they most enjoyed themselves during the workday;

  and

- they achieved the strongest feeling—a deep and lasting happiness—when they were engaged in interesting and meaningful work.

Contrary to the mythology of our consumer-based, pleasure-centric culture, we aren't happiest when shopping or on weekends loaded with leisure pursuits. Luckily, we achieve our greatest sense of satisfaction and well-being where we spend the greatest part of our lives ... at work.

Why? Csikszentmihalyi surmised that it's because *"On the job, people feel skillful and challenged, and therefore feel more happy, strong, creative, and satisfied."* Work, in other words, provides that rare opportunity for self-exploration which brings us to a new realization of who we are and what we can be. It, alone, gives us a way to search for and express the full dimensions of our natural talent—to see and experience the best we can be. That expression of our own magic leaves us profoundly fulfilled. It is the source of true happiness.

> **Research reveals that work—not your job—is the one best way to discover your personal best.**

No one pretends that work is all fun. Quite the contrary. The most fulfilling work confronts you with difficult, even demanding challenges. Those goals may be set by your employer, but they can—indeed, they must—also have purpose and meaning for you. They can and must provide a course—a physical, psychological or intellectual "lane"—where you can stride toward the realization of your Natural.

That kind of work enters you in a race, not with others, but with yourself; not up a career ladder, but across a career jungle gym; not for a job that holds you back, but to a finish line that demarks a victory for you. The resulting sense of accomplishment—the extraordinary feeling of being the best you can be—is both unique to work and the true meaning of a fit career. It comes not from the position you hold in an organization, but rather from the work you do in the position.

Is this "career satisfaction" identical to the "job satisfaction" employers spend so much time trying to optimize among their workers? There have been countless surveys probing the catalysts for job satisfaction. Employers believe that if you feel satisfied with your job, you will also be satisfied with your employment. And, if you're satisfied with your employment, you will work harder and better than you otherwise might for their business objectives.

As rational as this point of view may be, however, it is not the experience of working men and women. In fact, you can be satisfied with your job and still unhappy in your work and unfulfilled in your career. Your employer can provide adequate compensation, benefits and physical security—which are among the top components of job satisfaction identified in employee surveys—and you can still feel as if your work is an unpleasant even onerous aspect of your life.

What's behind this disconnect between job satisfaction and career satisfaction? There are several root causes:

- A job is transitory and so too are its benefits. In the 21st Century workplace, you will work in multiple jobs for multiple employers. Your career, on the other hand, may not be forever, but it is certainly a long term endeavor. Hence the benefits it provides—at least when it is healthy—are stable, dependable and enduring.

- The purpose of a job for an employer is not employment, but output. It must contribute to the mission of the organization. The purpose of a job for you, on the other hand, is not to advance the organization's mission (although that should also happen), but to advance your own career. It must enable you to express and experience your Natural.

- The elements of job satisfaction (e.g., pay, benefits, work schedule) are determined by employers. They are provided by employers at their discretion and necessarily based on their financial capacity and expertise. The elements of career satisfaction (i.e., self-respect, self-knowledge, self-expression and, ultimately, happiness) are determined by you. They are created by you at your discretion and based on your capacity and expertise at work.

Should you care about the elements of job satisfaction? Of course. Should you be satisfied with job satisfaction? Absolutely not. To do so is to sell yourself short. Job satisfaction provides the conditions for you to do your best work on behalf of your employer. Career satisfaction expands those conditions to ensure your best work works for you, as well.

If you use a job to stretch your skills and knowledge, if you use it to strengthen your occupational capacity and endurance, then your work transcends that job and becomes a step forward, a step along the journey to being the best you can be. It is transformed from simple labor into a quest for self-fulfillment. From working for a monthly paycheck into working for genuine and sustained happiness.

Csikszentmihalyi's research reveals that work—not your job—is the one best way to discover your personal best. For that to happen, however, you must focus your work on your Natural and its application to the challenges that hold meaning for you. As he writes, *"The best moments usually occur when a person's body or mind is stretched to its limits in a voluntary effort to accomplish something difficult and worthwhile."*

That stretching doesn't hurt, but rather empowers you. It enables you to go beyond external expectations or requirements and reach for inner possibilities. In essence, the optimal experience—the time when you feel most satisfied and happy—is something that you make happen inside yourself at work.

Does that make your career more important than your family, your friends, or your life outside the workplace? Of course not. There are two kinds of fulfillment, and both are essential to living a rich and rewarding life.

Happiness is a cognitive state. It is an experience of the mind that is achieved when the mind is fully engaged, meaningfully challenged and completely realized. As Csikszentmihalyi discovered, it is most likely to occur at work.

Joy, on the other hand, is an emotional state. It is an experience of the heart that is only possible when we are surrounded by those whom we love and who love us. As we all know, joy occurs in our relationships—in the bonds we build with others—and through the lives we lead in the world at large.

Career Fitness transforms your natural potential for happiness into reality. It enables you to feel fulfilled in the one-third or more of your day that you spend at work. Its benefit, however, does not end there. By helping you exercise your inalienable right to the pursuit of Happiness at work, Career Fitness also provides a foundation for the joy you deserve to feel in the rest of your life. It removes the distractions and stress of unhappy work, so that you can feel fulfilled among family and friends. That's not work-life balance. It's work-life synergy.

Career Fitness Principle #4

Your best work never ends, nor does your responsibility for performing it.

Working people today spend forty, fifty, sixty hours per week or more at work. Given that huge commitment of time and effort, it only makes sense to devote your career to that activity from which you derive the greatest benefit. Said another way, the time you spend on-the-job is just as important as the time you spend off-the-job, and the quality of all those hours and minutes is just as important as the quantity.

To ignore the quality of your workday is akin to seeking joy from the time you spend with family and friends while accepting despair from the time you spend at work. It is the equivalent of giving up on and giving away a third or more of your existence.

Career Fitness is based on your determination to seek a real and lasting benefit from the whole of your life—your time on-the-job as well as your time off. To do that, you must know how to define quality time.

While employers have always measured the quality of your work time—they call the process "performance appraisal"—most of us have never determined what quality time on-the-job means for us. We assume that work is a four-letter word and not meant to be personally meaningful or we accept the notion that quality employment is a job that demands the least of our time and effort.

The first step in achieving our own quality time at work, therefore, is to understand how it is achieved. Since work is the single best place to realize your optimal experience or happiness, then quality employment is the activity which provides that experience. It is the collection of tasks and responsibilities that make you happy on-the-job.

That activity—work where your *"body or mind is stretched to its limits in a voluntary effort to accomplish something difficult and worthwhile"*—only occurs when you are seeking an ever-increasing level of mastery in your profession, craft or trade. Quality time at work moves you through successive stages of self-improvement, enabling you to redefine yourself continuously as an ever more realized expression of your Natural—the achievement of the best you can be.

> **Quality time at work moves you through successive stages of self-improvement, enabling you to redefine yourself continuously as an ever more realized expression of your Natural—the achievement of the best you can be.**

Continuous self-betterment, then, is the only pathway to a meaningful and rewarding career. Your recognition of this precept positions you to perform a key task in building Career Fitness. It enables you to evaluate the substance and opportunity of different jobs.

How? By providing a single, unequivocal metric for your assessment: What's In It For Me (WIIFM). That's the criterion you should use to judge your current job and any new positions that you're considering. It is, in essence, a form of "employer appraisal." The WIIFM factor ensures that your employment experience is as good for you as it is for your employer.

This perspective, however, is not a new idea. Ironically, employers have been using a kind of employer appraisal for years. They call it "fit."

To them, it means answering this question: "Do you fit in with them?". They assess whether there is a good match between your skills, values and personality and the requirements, values and culture of their organization. Employer appraisal, in their view, is actually an exercise in determining WIIFT—What's In It For Them.

Employer appraisal in Career Fitness not only has a different intent, but it reshapes the lens through which we see our careers. The old way of looking at career events was to see them as a series of endings. Graduation was the end of your education. Finding a job was the end of your job search. Reaching your goal on the climb up an employer's career ladder was the end of your growth and advancement.

This perspective caused you to see your career as:

- an experience shaped by outside forces that were beyond your control;

   and

- a series of disconnected events, each of which led to its own final and discrete conclusion.

It was this point of view that gave job change a bad name. It laced every move in your career with a negative feeling. There was no sense of passage, no feeling of progress because success meant only that you were done.

Without an overarching rationale or vision, nothing tied the changes in your career together. They all just happened. And often, they happened to you. There was no recognition of your needs or dreams, no personal development, no ultimate vision for you.

The result of this incoherent movement was a deep and dispiriting feeling of helplessness. Your career made you feel like that shiny little ball in a pinball machine. You were pushed and flippered from post to post and, while the lights would occasionally flash and the bells might go off, you were never in control and never had the chance to establish a pattern or purpose for your work.

And, as if that weren't bad enough, each unconnected event also came to its own conclusion. You did, of course, get some satisfaction from the advancement you were able to achieve, but the happiness it created was transitory and disappeared at its conclusion. You had reached your goal. You were done. The engagement and energy that were stimulated by striving to reach it quickly faded. All you were left with at the end, was the memory of that exclamation point of achievement and the hungry sense of disappointment at its fleeting presence.

Career Fitness, in contrast, enables you to see career change as a continuum. Each event is connected to the one that preceded it and to the one that follows it and to those that will follow it, as well. They are all stepping stones along the journey you are taking in your pursuit of Happiness. What sets them in place and holds them together is the exploration and expression of your Natural.

To put it another way, the changes in your employment experience should all have the same purpose: to advance your development and use of the unique and special talent within you. When you ensure that happens, you are the best you can be for:

- your employer—which maximizes your performance, your perceived contribution and your paycheck;

and

- yourself—which maximizes your self-esteem, your sense of fulfillment and, ultimately, your happiness.

This perspective—the lens of WIIFM—transforms career events from endings into beginnings. While the outcome is clearly important, it is the ongoing experience of moving forward—the taking of the next step, rather than where the step lands—that is your penultimate reward.

Graduation, a successful job search and the advancement of your career through promotion or job change can be seen for what they truly are, at least in the new world of work in the 21st Century. Graduation is not the end of your professional development, but rather the beginning of your quest for professional expertise. Landing a new job doesn't mean the hard work is over in your career, but rather, that it is just beginning. And, earning a promotion or taking a better job isn't your reward for what you have already done, but instead your single, best opportunity to do even more.

Each event, but especially each job, is a platform for both performance and preparation. It is a crucible in which the challenge of your work draws out the dimensions of your best self, and that expanded capacity, in turn, positions you to advance to yet another and greater employment experience which then draws out even more of the best within you and prepares you for still another challenging opportunity.

These serial accomplishments are the only career victories that matter because they, alone, maximize the WIIFM aspect of your work—What's In It For Me.

The Power of Beginnings

The beginnings in your career enfranchise you in the opportunity of the American Dream. The changes that occur in your work when you acquire new knowledge, accept greater responsibilities or aim for higher levels of performance are never-ending second chances. They are "do-overs" for your shortcomings and "do-betters" for your successes. They are events with the power to refresh you and reenergize your commitment to yourself and your goals.

These events produce a positive, hopeful feeling—a sense of capacity and capability—that empowers you to be the best you can be. Beginning again (and again) gives you an endless supply of fresh starts—the unconstrained opportunity to start out on new quests. The freedom inherent in these commencements—unlike the captive closure of an ending—makes it possible for you to be better than you have been. It positions you to stand on your own shoulders and reach further across that career jungle gym than you have ever reached before.

As with all accomplishments of any magnitude and meaning, the experience will take you outside your comfort zone. The challenges will be great, the work will be hard, and that's exactly how you should want it. A person who sees the events in their career as beginnings may come home from work feeling dead-tired, even completely drained, but a person who sees such events as endings will go off to work that way. The beginnings reward your hard work with exhilaration; the endings only produce exhaustion.

Beginnings, by their very nature, aren't easy. Developing your Natural and expressing it on-the-job will push you to your limits and beyond every day. There is no free lunch in the workplace, and there is no free happiness in your work. Pursuing it, therefore, can sometimes feel onerous, overwhelming or simply more than you want to do. Your life is likely already complicated with webs of obligations and challenges; the last thing you need is a career that calls for you to work harder and better than you ever have before and to do so each and every day you're in the workplace.

It's that reality which causes many of us never to get started on our careers—to give in, give up and simply stand still—to do just enough to get by. Whatever our capabilities, we work down to the minimum level that our employer will accept. We don't want to be thought of as mediocre—and, indeed, usually have a much higher opinion of ourselves—but we also don't want to break a sweat with our Natural. As a consequence, we avoid new jobs with heavy responsibility, we limit the responsibilities of the jobs we have, and we ignore the responsibility for keeping ourselves up-to-date and at the state-of-the-art in our field and industry.

The excuses for such behavior are legion:

- My job is boring;

- My employer doesn't deserve any better;

- My supervisor is holding me back;

- They aren't paying me enough;

- And on and on and on.

Whatever the rationale that's used, the basic idea is the same: hard work interferes with my happiness, and I have a right to happiness, so I'm not going to work hard.

And, there's the blind spot in the view of many American workers today. No one has a right to happiness. We all yearn for it, of course, but happiness is something you have to achieve. And, the United States of America is the only country on earth specifically founded to give you and everyone else the right to pursue it.

All Americans *"are endowed by their Creator with certain unalienable Rights, that among these are Life, Liberty and the pursuit of Happiness."* That right to seek happiness, however, means that your beginnings are not only opportunities, but also duties. They are an obligation to use the freedom you are guaranteed to strive for real and lasting happiness.

Contemporary culture eschews such duties; Career Fitness requires that you embrace them. If you want a healthy career, you cannot be satisfied with a job you can tolerate until the weekend. You must seek more than a short commute or a convenient work schedule. You must reach higher than the minimum requirements to earn more than an unsatisfying paycheck.

To achieve Career Fitness, you must strive to find and experience that which gives you deep self-knowledge and genuine self-fulfillment. You must accept nothing less than the contentment that comes from having completely lived.

That is Happiness—happiness with a capital 'H'. It is the essence of the American Dream. And, it can only be approached one way. With work. Work that engages and challenges you, work that enables you to express the very best of yourself, work that represents your ceaseless drive to become who you are and were meant to be. That is the sole source of Happiness, and it is the foundational duty of your first job—your employment in a career that serves you with the boundless opportunity of beginnings.

To Be or Not to Be

That famous question was posed over 500 years ago by William Shakespeare. Every student learns it at one time or another and then forgets it as soon as they enter the world of work. Yet, the question precisely expresses the dilemma facing those who seek career success in the 21st Century. It represents, to use a more modern metaphor, the tipping point in your career. It is the choice you must make in your pursuit of Happiness.

You can choose to listen to your calling—to seek out the natural talent with which you have been blessed—or you can ignore that voice and listen, instead, to whatever screams at you in the workplace.

Those external voices come in many forms. They create an insistent cacophony that urges you to:

- chase after whatever will pay you the most money, give you the most power or shower you with the most fame;

- commit your career to whatever work you happen to stumble into as you leave school;

  or

- listen to whatever others believe you should be doing based on their experiences and beliefs.

The resulting din is a distraction, to be sure, but it does not prevent you from listening to your own voice. All too often, we accomplish that feat all by ourselves. There are many ways <u>not</u> to pay attention to your calling, many ways to avoid or work around your Natural, and sadly, that's exactly what many of us do. We ignore the voice calling within us to be the best we can be and relegate the expression of our special interest and ability to a hobby or outside-of-work activity. Sadly, some of us reject it altogether and banish it and the happiness it creates from our lives.

> **Your job is not to spend eight or more hours per day satisfying your employer, but instead, to invest that time in working at your own happiness.**

Why do we accept such limitations on our pursuit of Happiness? Because the pursuit involves effort, and that effort not only demands more of us, but it also feels awkward and even uncomfortable. Undoubtedly, this out-of-step, out-of-synch feeling is, at least in part, a normal reaction to something that's unfamiliar in our lives. It's only unfamiliar, however, because we haven't been doing it. And, now we can. There's nothing to prevent us from embarking on our pursuit of Happiness and every reason that we should. Once we do, what seems abnormal will come to feel less out of the ordinary and much more like what is and should be normal.

Getting comfortable with listening to your calling is only half the challenge, however. Of equal importance is finding the will to hear what it's saying. It takes courage to recognize what will enable you to be the best you can be because, for many of us, doing so will involve a fundamental break with what we have known in the past. It will require that we set aside what we believed about work in the 20th Century and envision a new purpose and role for work in our lives—one that is consistent with the realities and possibilities of the 21st Century.

Traditionally, we have been conditioned to believe that the workday belonged to our employer, and the rest of the day belonged to us. Career Fitness, in contrast, is based on the radical notion that the entire day—all twenty-four hours of it—is yours. Your job, therefore, is <u>not</u> to spend eight or more hours per day satisfying your employer, but instead, to invest that time in working at your own happiness.

The irony, of course, is that doing so is the most effective way to serve the interests of your employer. Being the best you can be assures the organization that you are providing a full and sufficient return on its investment in you. The converse, however, is not true. If you devote your work to serving your employer's benefit—the traditional view of an employee's role in the 20th Century—you will almost never achieve genuine and lasting happiness for yourself.

That realization is what is most discomforting about Career Fitness. It obliges you to accept a new definition of loyalty in the workplace. Seeking your own happiness at work requires that you be loyal first and foremost to yourself. It reorders priorities and makes <u>you</u> the center of your career, not your employer.

Yes, of course, you are still loyal to your employer. That loyalty, however, is not expressed as a commitment to work in the organization, but rather, as a pledge to do your best work for the organization. It is not the willingness to sacrifice all for the good of the organization, but instead, a determination to do your best by the organization all of the time.

Getting Ready & Set to Go

Committing to a program of Career Fitness can feel like trying to get in shape at the beginning of a new year. Your intentions are good, your resolve is genuine, but you know from experience that it will be hard—maybe almost impossible—to stick with it over time. The pressures and obligations of day-to-day living can overwhelm your determination to do what you know is in your own best interest.

So, how can you make a meaningful start on building Career Fitness? How can you make it the resolution that you keep?

While there is no simple solution to this dilemma, it is helpful to give yourself credit for what you are setting out to accomplish. When facing a big challenge, we oftentimes play tricks on our mind; we don't focus on the enormity of the task in order to keep ourselves from being intimidated and eventually paralyzed by the prospect of doing it. With Career Fitness, however, it's important to realize just how big a step you are taking.

Making Career Fitness an integral part of your life requires great bravery. You must put aside the familiar methods for achieving career success—the ones you have likely been taught, if you are just entering the workforce, and the ones on which you likely have relied, if you are a seasoned veteran of the workplace—and replace them with a fundamentally different view of work and your career. There is nothing easy or inconsequential about that.

Stepping up to the philosophy and regimen of a healthy career is a stupendous personal undertaking. Doing so, therefore, represents an extraordinary act, a bold declaration of your own potential and independence.

So, give yourself credit for that. Recognize the momentous nature of your act. Celebrate the courage it took to get even to that point. Because when you do, you will reinforce your commitment to go on. You will create an expectation of success. Within you and for you.

In a world that is addicted to taking the easy way out, saluting yourself for accepting the course of the "harder right" gets you ready and set to go … to live up to your own expectation.

Chapter Six

Step #2: Preparation
The Career De-Stress Test

"Champions aren't made in the gyms. Champions are made from something they have deep inside them—a desire, a dream, a vision."

Muhammad Ali, Champion boxer

Finding Your Natural

Understanding the challenge involved and still summoning the courage to address your career health is the first step in the Career Fitness regimen. It is a significant accomplishment, in and of itself, and achieving it provides the foundation for moving ahead. The next step in the regimen, the Career De-Street Test, will help you find your Natural, the greatness you can be in the world of work, the champion you are destined to be if you are true to your unique talent.

Most of us believe that we are very familiar with the side of ourselves we bring to work each day. We spend a lot of time in this role, and that longevity, we assume, produces an intimate knowledge of our interests and capabilities in the workplace. Some of that insight comes from others—the evaluations of our supervisors and peers—and some of it comes from our own, private observations of what we do and how well we do it in the workplace.

These observations are meaningful, however, only if you are working at what you most enjoy doing and do best. If you have aligned your career with your Natural, they are an accurate picture of what you have to offer in the world of work.

If, on the other hand, you are in a career that does not position you for your best work, these perceptions will not only be inaccurate assessments of your capability, but they are likely to lead you to incorrect conclusions about the potential inherent in your career. They will be based on a distorted image of who you are and have the capacity to be. To put it another way, you can't truly know how well you are doing in your work, if you first don't know yourself well.

And that's a problem. Most of us wander into one career field or another, gain a little expertise, have a little success, and then conclude that where we are is where we ought to be in the workplace. Experience, however, is not necessarily the pathway to a fulfilling and rewarding career. It may provide a modicum of comfort—a familiarity that enables us to perform at an acceptable or even superior level—but it does not reliably lead us to satisfaction and a sense of accomplishment in our work. It does not make us feel fulfilled. To achieve that state of being—to be happy—we have to probe inside ourselves. We have to listen to the inner voice calling out to us, telling us what we were meant to be.

> **Most of us wander into one career field or another, gain a little expertise, have a little success, and then conclude that where we are is where we ought to be in the workplace.**

Performing that task isn't simple or easy, particularly in our modern capitalist society. The complex pressures and dynamics of today's environment often make it difficult to listen to our calling and, even if we pay attention to it, to hear its message.

- **Some people never even make the effort to know their inner voice.** They believe that work and happiness are incompatible. They ignore their calling to excuse themselves from having to acquire the skills and expertise necessary to work at it. As a result, they spend most of their waking life going off to some job each day without any expectation or any hope of being happy in their work. Not surprisingly, they aren't. For them, the experience of work is the same as it is for beasts of burden; it has no redeeming value other than as a way of securing food, shelter and an occasional rest.

- **Others don't have the self-confidence to accept what their calling is telling them.** Instead, they labor away in a dissatisfying field because that's what their parents, family, spouse, colleagues or friends tell them they should be doing. Alternatively, they model their careers after those of the iconic figures in American business whose sole measure of success is American culture's fascination with wealth and the lifestyle it affords. In either case, they aren't living the lives they were meant to live, but rather someone else's rendition (or perversion) of it. For most of these individuals, achieving happiness on-the-job is either an unfulfilled wish or an accident. They aren't following their own inner light, but the shadowy illumination of external sources.

- **Still others are too impatient to pay attention to their calling.** They rush headlong into a career because it caught their eye or piqued their interest when they were a teenager or a young college student. Years later, however, they are likely to have learned a lot more about themselves and find they are stuck in an occupational field that neither challenges nor excites them. Their early infatuation, based as it was on an impulse, turns out to be less than an enduring passion. While they may be competent or more in their work, it does not fulfill them or make them truly happy.

These dynamics create the set of outcomes arrayed in Figure 3. Its four cells summarize the most prevalent kinds of careers among those in the workforce today.

Some people simply put up with a career. For them, there is no hope or expectation that they will be the best they can be at work. They convince themselves that they can't be successful or happy at their work because they just aren't good enough. They don't have what it takes to be a winner at work. As a consequence, they accept employment with no goal other than to endure the experience.

Others are puzzled as to what they can do in the workplace. They are often book smart, but not career smart. They go off to school and get educated, but do not learn how to nurture their own talent and thus grow in the world of work. They wander into their profession, craft or trade on a whim or by happenstance, so they may or may not be engaged and rewarded by their work. The outcome, good or otherwise, is simply a matter of luck.

Figure 3: Career Dynamics

Puzzled May Be	Positive Must Be
Put Up Can't Be	Pushed Should Be

Still others are pushed into their careers. They may be book smart and even career smart, but they are not self-smart. They don't know what they can do in the world of work and aren't willing to invest the time and effort to figure it out. They are capable and energetic, but lack personal insight, purpose and direction. As a consequence, they let others call the shots in their career. They don't listen to their calling, but instead, let teachers, mentors, bosses, spouses, friends or parents tell them what they should be in order to achieve success.

The final and tragically the smallest cohort of the population is book smart, career smart and self-smart. They know what they must be in the workplace because they have determined what they most enjoy doing and do best. They are positive about their career choice because they have listened to and heard their calling. They recognize their Natural and devote their work to developing and expressing it. These men and women are the career athletes of the 21st Century. They are the champions of the modern workplace.

Comprehending Your Calling

The purpose of this step in the Career Fitness system is to enable you to identify what you must be in the world of work. It will help you to determine the talent that is your defining and enduring gift. To do that, however, you must first understand how a calling actually works. You must recognize what it will and will not tell you. In other words, if you know what to listen for, you are much more apt to hear it and assimilate its message. So, what does a calling sound like? And, what does it say?

First, as its name implies, a calling is an inner voice—it is the conscience of your working self. It is the knowledge that you were born with, but must acknowledge to acquire. And, it is the emotional connection between your identity—the essence of who you are—and your work—what you do on-the-job. This inner voice articulates your Natural. Your calling is, in essence, a description of your talent spoken softly. It is the quiet spokesperson for the best person you can be in the world of work.

Second, your calling does not articulate a job title. It will not whisper civil engineer, trial lawyer or sales executive. Instead, a calling is an insight, a cognitive discovery that illuminates your capacity for excellence. It might quietly speak to you of your ability to disaggregate large initiatives into more manageable tasks or to communicate complex ideas so they can be understood by everyone. It doesn't point to a career field, but to the kind of work you love to do and do best.

For example, your calling might express your innate compassion for those who are suffering from illnesses. That message, however, does not mean you are destined to be a physician. There are many ways—a wide range of careers and jobs—which would enable you to accomplish that calling. You could, of course, be a nurse, a physical therapist, a home health aide or even a hospital administrator. The choice of an occupation depends on your ability and interests. That's what a healthy career does: it integrates your passion <u>and</u> practicality.

Third, your calling doesn't envision you as a finished product, but rather as a work-in-progress. It encourages you to express your Natural at work so that your workday:

*   reinforces the foundation of who you are and thereby enables you to build the person you hope to be;

*   tests you and stretches you in ways that are aligned with what you value and respect;

    and

*   pulls the best you have within you out into the world where you and everyone else can experience and enjoy it each and every day.

In short, your calling is a private, personal sage. It knows you and your capability better than anyone else—even better than you. If you listen to and hear its wisdom, therefore, you will come to know the uniquely talented human being you truly are. You will know your Natural.

> **A calling is an inner voice—it is the conscience of your working self.**

Without that self-awareness, you are far more likely to spend a lifetime chasing career goals that bring you little or no happiness in their accomplishment. They may move you up the corporate hierarchy and they may even make you wealthy, but they will never make you happy.

Whatever the external measures of success, work that feels unnatural to you inflicts real and lasting damage inside you. It traumatizes your spirit and fills you with anxiety and despair. You aren't doing what you are naturally good at, and the dysfunction of your workday gnaws away at you. You know—you comprehend at some level of consciousness—that you are not being the best person you can be. Whatever your employer's appraisal of your performance, your own assessment is bleak. Your work defines a pale shadow of the vigorous, capable individual—the all star—within you.

This absence of self-awareness also makes you vulnerable. While some of us can still earn our employer's accolades despite our dysfunction, most of us cannot. An internal disconnect prevents you from doing your best work. This sub-par performance is visible to those around you—your colleagues and your boss—only they don't know that it's not the real you. They see your diminished contribution in the workplace and assume it's the best you can be. And, in an increasingly unforgiving workplace, being less than your best stresses your career and ultimately sabotages its health.

The Pursuit of Happiness

Career Fitness enables you to hear your calling by temporarily reorienting your focus from the external to the internal passage of your life. It does so by immersing you in a concentrated experience of self-exploration.

This guided process of discovery triangulates you to that singular intersection of what you most like to do and do best. For that reason, you should perform the diagnostic before you set out on your career and, then, repeat it from time-to-time, just to make sure that your work is actually strengthening your satisfaction and happiness on-the-job. This self-assessment can, of course, be supplemented with more formal personality tests, such as the Myers-Briggs Type Indicator or the Strong-Campbell Interest Inventory, but the ultimate goal remains the same: to determine what powers you to excellence.

Such initial evaluations are routinely prescribed in physical fitness to ensure that you exercise safely and in a way that will improve your health. Called stress tests, these assessments are performed before you set out on a regimen of physical activity so that you can pinpoint your physical limits. That knowledge is important, of course, because if you exceed your limits in a physical work-out, you can badly hurt yourself.

In Career Fitness, this initial stock-taking is called a "de-stress test." Rather than preventing you from hurting yourself, it enables you to make yourself happy. It does that by helping you remove the limits you've consciously or unconsciously imposed on or accepted in your career. In other words, if a stress test determines what you can't do, a de-stress test identifies what you can. If a stress test is a way to listen to your body; a de-stress test is the way you listen to and hear your calling.

The de-stress test is composed of three exercises that, together, bring you to the unique locus of talent that is your Natural. They incorporate a procedure originally developed in competitive athletics. It involves "visualizing" the goal you seek by using your imagination.

Research shows that great athletes are gifted with both extraordinary physical skills and with the ability to imagine or visualize their best levels of performance. Before the contest ever begins, they can picture in their minds the record race they want to run or the winning shot they seek to make. This visualization is much more than pleasant daydreaming, however; great athletes use it to fix a detailed image of a specific outcome in their minds and to rehearse the accomplishment of that goal in their imagination until they get it right.

In a similar way, your de-stress test will enable you to fix an image of your Natural in your mind so that you can imagine your star performance in the workplace and practice it throughout the course of your career. In essence, you "hear" your calling by enhancing your self-perception. The assessment removes the boundaries that clutter and constrain your sense of yourself and stimulates your consciousness of the champion within you.

How is that self-recognition achieved? The three exercises of the de-stress test probe the three dimensions of genuine and sustained happiness at work. These dimensions are summarized in the following formula:

$$\text{Happiness}^{\text{Work}} = E + R + C$$

where

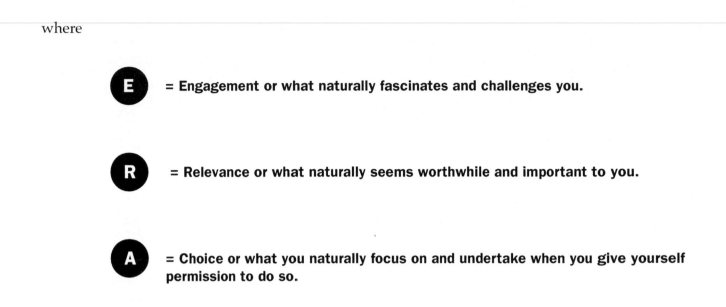

E = Engagement or what naturally fascinates and challenges you.

R = Relevance or what naturally seems worthwhile and important to you.

A = Choice or what you naturally focus on and undertake when you give yourself permission to do so.

These three factors are the building blocks of individual happiness at work. They are present in all of us and unique to each of us. Discovering them is the single best way to listen to and hear your calling.

The three exercises of the Career Fitness De-Stress Test are:

- **Exercise #1: Recalling My Best Memories**
  This component of the self-exploration yields a vision of the activity that most engages you.

- **Exercise #2: Writing My Own Tombstone**
  This component of the self-exploration yields a vision of the activity that is most relevant to you.

- **Exercise #3: Winning the Lottery**
  This component of the self-exploration yields a vision of the one activity you would choose to do most often, if you could.

The following guidelines will ensure that you get the maximum personal insight and understanding out of the exercises.

- First, complete all three of the exercises in the order they are listed above;

- Second, don't undertake more than one of the exercises in a single session;

- Third, don't move on to the next exercise until you have completely finished the one before it; and

- Fourth, separate each of the exercise sessions by at least one but no more than three days.

In other words, give yourself sufficient time to focus on each exercise and use it to open yourself up and peer inside. Take a deep breath, close your eyes and follow wherever the exercise takes you. Don't judge, don't argue, and don't hold back. Just let yourself go.

To deepen and accelerate the insight you gain, control the conditions around you. Do the exercises in a quiet room, when you're alone and not likely to be interrupted. Don't sandwich them in between classes or shuttling the kids to soccer practice and don't try to complete them while you're watching television, surfing the Web or texting someone on your cell phone.

Instead, pick a period in the day when you can cordon off at least several consecutive hours. Modest as this commitment of time may seem, it is usually more than most people have ever devoted to discovering the nature of the work they most enjoy and the direction of their career. So, give yourself that gift: the richness of personal time.

In the solitude of this interval:

- Clear your mind. Put aside your deadlines and crises, your job, your upcoming tests, the errands you have to run, and everything else that's tugging at you for time and attention.

- Concentrate on yourself. A career de-stress test is just about you, the real you. It is a way to spend some quality time with the quality person you've been ignoring.

- Exercise your imagination. Peel away the limits you've imposed or let others impose on you and see whatever it is that interests and challenges you.

That's how you take the stress out of your career and open it up to the pursuit of Happiness at work. You listen to the voice inside that's calling you to be the best you can be.

The Career De-Stress Test

The Career Fitness De-Stress Test begins on the next page. Each of its exercises includes a visualization scenario followed by a number of worksheets. Read the scenario slowly and then let your mind run free. There are no correct or incorrect responses so the possibilities are limitless. They are anything and everything you can imagine.

Exercise #1: Recalling My Best Memories

In this exercise, you're going to return to another time in your life: your childhood. This period has some very special characteristics that can still be helpful to you today.

- First, kids feel free to try on roles. They spend hours playing at being captains of spaceships, major league baseball players, doctors, cowboys, bankers, and lemonade-stand owners. This occupational exploration is unconstrained by the "should be's" of parents, peers, or spouses. Instead, it's being something for the pure joy of the experience. Sure, we may model our play after what we see our mothers or fathers doing, but we are just as likely to imitate the work of a relative, neighbor, family friend or fictional character.

- Second, the make-believe roles we play as kids are serial explorations. They are our mini-journeys of self-discovery, seeking to uncover those activities that are the most fun for us. If something doesn't quite connect or feel just right, there is no "adult baggage" to worry about. We simply move on to the next role and try it on for size. As a result, we are often able to identify the kinds of things we most enjoy doing, even though we have absolutely no experience in the world of work. We discover our Natural by playing at it.

This exercise is designed to help you remember what you learned about yourself as a child. Its purpose is to reacquaint you with your "best memories," your recollections of what you most enjoyed doing at play.

If you feel as if you need some prompting, something to jog your memory, use a scrapbook, a family photo album, home videos or the pictures stored on your computer. Then,

(1) let your mind wander back to your childhood;

(2) recall as many of your favorite roles at play as you can;

    and

(3) identify those that you seemed to repeat most often, the ones to which you seemed most attracted and in which you always were happy.

Try to recreate each of the best experiences by picturing it in your mind. Visualize everything you did in playing the role from start to finish, just as if you were doing it again. Using the worksheets that follow, describe the role, itself, and pinpoint the activity it involved which made it so enjoyable for you.

For example, if you could hardly wait to get up on a summer's morning to set up your lemonade stand, what was it about that experience that you recall most fondly? What seemed to be the most fun: preparing the lemonade, setting up your stand, talking to your customers, or counting your money? What aspects of this "Best Memory" still bring a smile to your face even today?

Recalling My Best Memories Worksheet

When I think back to my play as a child, what make-believe roles do I remember making me happy? What occupational games did I find particularly interesting or feel drawn to most strongly? List each of the roles that you remember as a childhood favorite. *Describe this role in as much detail as you can recall.*

Of all the favorite roles I can recall, which one did I seem to enjoy the most? Which specific occupational game seemed more interesting, more comfortable, more fun than any of the others? *Describe this role in as much detail as you can recall.*

Work Strong

Of everything I did while playing at my favorite role, which specific activity (e.g., making the lemonade, setting up your stand, talking to the customers) stands out most in my mind? What element of the role did I look forward to the most and have the most fun doing? *Describe this activity, being as specific as possible.*

As I think back to my favorite activity in my favorite role, what was it about the activity that made it enjoyable? What aspect of the activity—what responsibilities, challenges, decisions, actions or outcomes—made it so much fun, so engaging and so memorable even today, years later? *Describe this aspect of your favorite activity as completely as you can.*

Exercise #2: "Writing My Own Tombstone"

Most of us have heard the age-old adage that no one ever inscribes his or her tombstone with a memorial to their employment. You'll never find a grave marker where the departed's final words are "I wish I had spent more time on-the-job." The point being made by the adage, however—the message it is meant to convey—is often misunderstood.

We do, in fact, spend most of our adult lives in the workplace, and the conventional interpretation of the message is that we should spend less. We ought to take time away from our work and invest it somewhere else. And, most of us assume that this alternate commitment of our time and attention should be directed toward our families and our leisure time pursuits.

No one can argue with trying to spend more time with family and friends, but that is not the lesson this adage is teaching. Its message is not that we should replace work with something else more important, but rather that we should engage in work that is more important to us.

No one wishes they had spent more time on-the-job because most of the time we spend there fails to fulfill or satisfy us. The adage, therefore, is reminding us that we get just one life with which to pursue happiness—one opportunity to make our life's work worthwhile—and the only way to do that is to work at something that is personally relevant and meaningful. Without a sense of purpose, there can be no lasting expression of our best selves, and without that expression, there is little worth remembering about our work, on our tombstone or anywhere else.

The goal of this exercise is to figure out that sense of purpose—to discover what you would be proud to have inscribed about your career on your tombstone. It is to answer the question, "What do I want to have accomplished with my life's work?"

When you strip away all of the circumstances and excuses, all of the reasons "why not" and all of the rationales for "how come," what do you truly want to be the lasting testament to the one-third or more of your life that you will spend on-the-job?

To make this discovery, you'll have to embark on an out-of-body experience. In this exercise, you'll visualize your life's final hour. Just before you walk into the bright light of what lies beyond, however, you're going to stop and imagine the life you've led. You're going to extend all of your current workday activities and habits, good and bad, to their final, logical conclusion, to how they are most likely to look at the end. This experience is your baseline. It's what you think will form the dimensions of your career when it is over. It is what will be inscribed on your tombstone ... if nothing changes.

In this exercise, however, you're going to be given a Scroogian replay. You're going to get a second chance, another shot at doing it right. You will be offered the opportunity to re-write your epitaph by reshaping your career as you would truly like it to be.

You're going to ask yourself what you would do differently. Which decisions would you change? Which priorities, values or perceptions would you adjust? How would you alter the course of your career to feel good about its goals and accomplishments? How would you re-imagine your work in order to cherish the way your employment goals and accomplishments are remembered?

Writing My Own Tombstone Worksheet

If nothing significant changed in my work between now and the time I passed away, what would my career look like? What is likely to be the sum and substance of the time I've spent in the workplace? *Describe the way your career would look at its conclusion if everything continued just as it is today.*

What would I most regret about the course of my current career? If my work ended just as it is right now, what opportunities would I have missed? What challenges would I have avoided? What contributions would I have failed to make? *List these disappointments, being as specific as you can.*

If I got a second chance to chart the course of my career, what would I do differently? How would I change my priorities and activities on-the-job to make my work more relevant and important to me? *Describe these adjustments to the course and content of your career as completely as you can.*

Work Strong

What would be the high points of my new career? What specific elements of my work—which responsibilities, challenges, decisions, actions or outcomes—would I want to be my legacy? How would I rewrite the testament of my work on my tombstone? *Describe these hallmarks of your best work in as much detail as possible.*

Exercise #3: Winning the Lottery

Who hasn't, at some point, day-dreamed about winning the lottery? We hear the ads touting the latest jackpot, we read the newspaper stories describing that lucky person who won the big check, and we think to ourselves, "What would I do if that were me?". "What would my life be like if I suddenly became a multimillionaire?"

This exercise enables you to answer those questions. You're going to visualize picking the lucky ticket. You're going to see yourself turn on the evening news, pick up the newspaper or check the lottery Web-site and discover that you've just won $20 million. All by yourself. It's all yours.

You now have enough money to live comfortably for the rest of your life. Car payments, house payments, college tuition bills, business debts, bank loans—they're all taken care of. Even better, you don't have to go to work to put food on the table, gas in the car or clothes on your back. Now, you can focus on what most pleases you. You don't have to worry about a paycheck or the boss's approval. You get to choose what you want to do.

Sure, you may take some time off for that around-the-world cruise you've always dreamed about and, of course, there's probably a top-of-the-line car and maybe a new house to buy. Eventually, however, spending money, even lots of it, is going to get routine and boring. At some point, you're going to realize that you want to do something more substantive with your life. You will decide that you have a greater purpose, a more important role to play. You will conclude that you have a contribution to make that draws on and expresses your best self.

So, what would you choose to do?

Maybe there's a community activity, a business venture or a social service program that you've always thought about pursuing, but couldn't, given the pressures and obligations of day-to-day employment. Maybe it's an abiding interest or activity to which you've always been devoted—as a hobby or an avocation or a ministry—but never as your job. Or, maybe it comes to you as a new idea, something you don't even remember thinking about before, but suddenly, it pops into your head as the one thing that you really want to do with your life.

The goal of this exercise is to determine that purpose. It is to answer the question, "What work would you do if you were independently wealthy?". What Life would you choose if your Liberty was secure and you could pursue whatever it is that brings you the most Happiness? Your newfound financial freedom enables you to dream, so go ahead, let your imagination take you where it will.

What have you always wanted to do (whether you knew it or not)? What activity has previously been beyond your reach (for whatever reason), yet holds a special attraction or fascination for you? Is it tinkering with cars, arranging flowers, teaching English to non-English speakers, or designing new board games? Would you help sick kids or take up carpentry; would you learn landscape design or become a community college instructor? Whatever it is, now's your chance to recognize and celebrate it.

The Winning the Lottery Worksheet

If I won $20 million in the lottery today, what would I like to do with my life? What activities would be dreams come true for me? How would I fill my days now that the size of my paycheck doesn't matter? *List all of the activities that come to mind.*

What's kept me from pursuing these activities before now? Why haven't I been working at one (or more) of them in my career? What's held me back? *Describe these impediments as completely as you can, remembering to look inside as well as outside yourself.*

Work Strong

If I could transform just one of those activities into reality and make it a part of my life, which would I choose? What single activity would I most want to perform over and over again? Which would provide an optimal experience for me? *Describe this activity in as much detail as you can.*

What elements of the activity I selected—what responsibilities, challenges, decisions, actions or outcomes—make it feel so compelling, so important to me? What is it about the activity that captivates and inspires me? *Describe these elements with as much specificity as possible.*

Work Strong

Learning What You've Discovered

After you've finished the three de-stress exercises, review the notes you took. You've uncovered a lot about yourself. You've probed your instinctive preferences, your enduring hopes, and your most fulfilling dreams. Now, it's time to analyze these personal factors, to explore how they come together to form the special talent that belongs to you. The next step is to learn what they tell you about your Natural.

This insight will be acquired by detecting what's similar or shared across your answers to the exercise questions. You are looking for the common factor that brings you to the intersection of your preferences, hopes and dreams. Although the words or images may be different in each of the exercises, you are trying to identify the one kind of behavior that you have repeated (perhaps even unconsciously) in all three of them. You want to know which single activity seems to engage, stimulate and reward you unlike anything else you experience?

To find this common factor, study the notes you took during each of the exercises and answer the following questions:

- What activity seems always to be present when I think about my instinctive preferences, my enduring hopes and my most fulfilling dreams?

- What activity seems always to make me feel as if I'm doing what I was meant to do, what comes naturally to me?

- What activity seems always to tap into my strongest interests and my innate skills and abilities and thus enables me to perform at my best?

Now, analyze your answers. If they are the same or essentially the same for all three questions, your evaluation is complete. You've made your acquaintance with your Natural. You've identified the specific activity—the work—you are called to do in the workplace. You can proceed to the development of your Intention Commitment—your pledge of allegiance to your Natural—that is introduced in the section which follows.

If, however, your answers reveal two or even three different activities—a not unusual occurrence— you will have to continue your investigation. The key in this follow-up step is to look for connections or links that tie the seemingly different activities to one another.

To accomplish this additional analysis, you must deconstruct the activities and look at their constituent actions and circumstances. You're going to examine the building blocks that produce the experience you have with the activities. You want to know:

- The conditions under which the activities were performed;

- The tasks involved in performing the activities;

- The kinds of people with whom you interacted during the activities;

- The materials, machines, technology or tools you used in performing the activities;

    and

- The outcomes of the activities.

Use these factors to find the single aspect or dimension of an activity—the function—that engages you, is important to you and which you would choose to do if you could. In fact, the dictionary defines a function as "the action for which a person or thing is specially fitted." It doesn't matter if you've never worked a day in your life at this function. It doesn't matter if you studied something else in college, community college or trade school. It doesn't matter if you've never even thought about the function as a career. All that counts is that this function is the only verb than can complete the following statement:

> **I am happiest when I ...**
>
> _____.
>
> **That verb—that activity or function—is your Natural. It is the secret your calling is whispering.**

The Purpose of Your Work

What you hear when you pay attention to your calling is an internal celebration of your Natural. It's what your inner being—that totally liberated, self-aware person inside you, that joyous performer craving to act out the best of you—really wants to do with your life. And, if you're like most people, it's not the work you're doing on-the-job.

Oh sure, it may be a hobby or a weekend avocation, but it is not the focus of the one-third or more of your waking life that you will spend in the workplace. Instead, it's quietly there inside you, buried under a mudslide of misperceptions about work and missteps in your career. Until this very minute, your calling has probably been unrecognized, unacknowledged, and, as a consequence, unappreciated. And that's why so many of us consider our work our least favorite time of the day.

Your calling, therefore, is not only a sage—the wise spirit of your being—but a "career scout"—a guide to the work that will bring you happiness. Without it, happiness happens only by happenstance, if it happens at all.

Listening to your calling, but more than that—hearing it, as well—is the one sure way to discover your Natural. It alone has the personal fidelity to reveal what you most enjoy doing and have the potential to do best. And, only your Natural enables you to step over the quagmire of humdrum employment and devote your workday to that which liberates your spirit and gives you a genuine and profound sense of accomplishment.

A healthy career, then, is one in which <u>you</u> align your work with your Natural by listening to and hearing your calling. Each and every job that you take in a healthy career echoes your calling by enabling you to work at the development and expression of your unique talent. When you do that, you position yourself to do your best work. That is the first accomplishment of a career athlete: to empower yourself to excel. To put yourself where you can be the champion who lives inside you.

Achieving that objective—to be the best you can be by working at your Natural—is your employment intention. Any other purpose or any other direction in your work denies you the chance to reach your personal apogee, to be on the outside the champion you are on the inside. And, a career without that ambition denies you your right to the pursuit of Happiness. The guarantee you acquire as a citizen becomes null and void in your work because you fail to follow the instructions imprinted within you.

A career athlete, therefore, pledges to establish and preserve this work-calling connection in their career. It is a promise they make to themselves. It must, however, be more than the best of intentions. It must be a code of behavior. It must become a reference point and an obligation. For that reason, it must be written down.

To align your work with your Natural, you must record your pledge in a statement, a personal testament called your Intention Commitment. That statement is the final outcome of your Career De-Stress Test.

Your Intention Commitment memorializes your Natural. It's not unlike a personal version of an organization's mission statement. Employers use a mission statement to articulate their purpose. It enables all members of the organization:

- to understand why the organization has been formed—the goal they are seeking to achieve through their employment;

   and

- to use that knowledge to align the talent they provide at work with the accomplishment of the organization's goal.

Similarly, your Intention Commitment enables you:

- to understand your purpose at work—the inherent talent you are trying to develop and express through your career;

   and

- to employ that talent in an occupation that will position you to do your best work and thereby advance your pursuit of Happiness.

Unlike an organization's mission statement, however, your Intention Commitment is not a statement to or for others; it is an oath you swear to yourself.

An Intention Commitment is a personal promise to align the work you do with the natural talent you are. You write it down so you recognize and understand it <u>and</u> so you won't forget or ignore it. Your Intention Commitment is there to help you shape your career with your Natural and to remind you to devote your workday to that which you most enjoy doing and do best.

> **Your calling is not only a sage—the wise spirit of your being—but a "career scout"—a guide to the work that will bring you happiness.**

It is the way you achieve the fulsome self-expression that is so well described in Robert Frost's poem, "Two Tramps in Mud Time."

> *My object in living is to unite*
>
> *My avocation and my vocation*
>
> *As my two eyes make one in sight.*
>
> *Only where love and need are one,*
>
> *And the work is play for mortal stakes,*
>
> *Is the deed ever really done*
>
> *For heaven and the future´s sakes.*

Write It Down Right Now

Your Intention Commitment need not be poetry, but like poetry, it must capture the pure essence of the matter: the talent you are and were meant to express at work. To do that, it has two parts:

- The first completes the following phrase, "I am committed to developing and expressing my special gift for ...." It is a description of your Natural.

- The second connects your Natural to the workplace. It identifies the type of employment you will use to develop and express your special talent. It connects what you most enjoy doing with what you have the potential to do best.

The Career De-Stress Test provides the knowledge necessary to articulate the first part of your Intention Commitment. Many of us, however, lack the expertise to describe the second part. We do not know the range of occupations that can potentially bring our Natural to life. To fill that gap—to learn how you can work at what you do best and most like to do—research your options with the following sources:

- *The Occupational Handbook*, published by the U.S. Department of Labor. It lists hundreds of types of occupations and, for each, describes what workers do on the job, typical working conditions, the workplace prospects for the occupation, the pay it provides and the education and training necessary to do the job. The book is available in most public libraries or it can be ordered for a fee from the Bureau of Labor Statistics in the U.S. Department of Labor.

- The Occupational Information Network (O*Net Online). This online resource provides free access to a large database of occupations which can be searched by knowledge, skills, abilities, work activities, interests and work values. The database can also be searched by job family (e.g., architecture and engineering, personal care and service), high growth industries (i.e., those deemed "economically critical [and] projected to add substantial numbers of jobs" in the years ahead) and STEM Discipline or the science, technology, engineering and/or mathematics education required for successful job performance.

- The list of occupations at Wikipedia, the free, online encyclopedia (www.wikipedia.org). Although entries vary widely in detail, many provide exhaustive descriptions that include the history of the occupation; its responsibilities; its educational, training and certification requirements; notable figures who have worked in the field; and a list of references where additional information can be acquired.

Work Strong

Your Intention Commitment should draw a clear-sighted line between what you hear from the voice calling within you and the occupation which enables you to express that voice—your unique and natural talent—in your work. As such, it is a roadmap for you to follow in your pursuit of Happiness.

You might, for example, write:

I am committed to developing and expressing my special gift for using technology to organize information by building a healthy career as a database administrator.

or

I am committed to developing and expressing my special gift for persuasive verbal communications by building a healthy career as a pharmaceutical sales rep.

or

I am committed to developing and expressing my special gift for organizing and leading others in accomplishing difficult tasks by building a healthy career as a noncommissioned officer in the military.

or

I am committed to developing and expressing my special gift for describing important but complex issues in a logical, easily understood way by building a healthy career as a litigation attorney.

There are, undoubtedly, other vocations that you could pursue in each of the examples above and still be aligned with your calling. That range of opportunity, however, is both a blessing and a challenge. It gives you options and the chance to make a mistake. That's why the first part of your Intention Commitment is so important.

The memorializing of your Natural is your compass through those fifteen-to-twenty job changes and two-or-three occupational changes that you're likely to experience in the 21st Century workplace. It's your guide across the career jungle gym. It is the true north of your career.

If what you are doing in the workplace brings love and need together, as Frost describes it, then you are fulfilling your commitment to yourself. If, on the other hand, love and need are not one—if those two essential but individually insufficient elements of happiness have diverged in your career—then your Intention Commitment will help you to redirect your work and realign them. That continuous calibration is the essence of effective career self-management. It is the first job of a career athlete. It is the way you ensure progress in your pursuit of Happiness.

Your Intention Commitment

Use what you've learned about yourself in the Career De-Stress Test and describe what would bring "love and need" together in your career. Create your pledge to yourself in your Intention Commitment below.

I am committed to developing and expressing my special gift for ...

_____

by ...

_____.

Yes, You Can!

Now that you've memorialized your Natural, you've probably begun to hear another voice inside you, only this one is not natural. Unlike your calling, it is not an inherent part of who you are. It is not calling to you; it is yelling at you. This second voice always originates outside you. And, it's saying, "No, you can't. No, you can't. No, you can't."

So many times in life, in so many endeavors, in subtle and not so subtle ways, we're told that we can't do something. We're not strong enough, fast enough, smart enough, good-looking enough to do that which our calling tells us we should. Or, what we want to do—what we feel compelled to do—doesn't somehow measure up to someone else's expectations; it's not what they would do, or it's not what they are comfortable with, or it's simply not right … in their judgment. Whatever the reason, whatever the circumstance, the conclusion is always the same: "No, you can't!".

This nay-saying voice is, more often than not, the first obstacle we face in living up to our Intention Commitment. We experience it as a seemingly insurmountable roadblock to our recognition and enjoyment of our Natural because it's often expressed by those whose opinions we value and care about most. Our family. Our friends. Our teachers. Our boss. People who often mean well, but who experience the world of work differently than we do. They (usually) want what's best for us, so they spare no effort in expressing their view. They want to be helpful, but to us, their voice seems insistent, implacable and in violation of who we truly are.

Ironically, this clamor from the outside is often easier to hear than our own voice within. If you listen to it, however—if you let the external cacophony overpower your calling—you'll put yourself at a terrible disadvantage. You will experience the workday equivalent of being "psyched out" in sports, of being defeated before the contest even begins. You'll be blocked from doing what you truly want to do—from what you do best—not by the limitations of your own talents, but by the limited vision of those around you, by those who say, "No, you can't!".

This obstacle, however, is not the insurmountable barrier it may, at first, seem. You can overcome it. How?

- With the knowledge you've acquired about yourself in the Career De-Stress Test. By knowing what brings you happiness;

  and

- With the courage and resolution you articulated in your Intention Commitment. By staying true to the promise you made to yourself.

With that foundation, you have what it takes to turn your promise into reality. For example, you may not have the talent to be an astronaut, but if you love the stars, yes, you can work in space. Your Natural may be in any of a multitude of other fields—engineering, logistics, planning, information systems—that are the building blocks of space exploration.

Similarly, you may not have the talent to be a professional basketball player, but if you love the competition of that game, then yes, you can work in professional sports. Your Natural may be in any of a myriad of specialties—sales, promotion, personnel, operations—essential to successful team and club management.

And as well, you may not have the talent to be a published author, but if you love the printed page, then yes, you can work in the field of publishing. Your Natural, however, may be in editing or commercial art, in marketing or any of dozens of other occupations which help to bring a book to print and into the local bookstore.

Whether you're taking your first job or your seventh, whether you're at the midpoint of your career or just starting out, you will inevitably hear a chorus of advice and opinions from well-meaning friends, relatives, and colleagues. Many of these voices express constructive, helpful views that you should consider. Your career plans and goals, however, are not a group sport. They are yours and yours alone. And, the very best guide to what's best for you is your own voice inside you.

It's the counsel you hear in quiet moments when you're alone. It's the sage who knows you best. It's the guide who calls you to your Natural. And, it's the voice that always and forever says, "Yes, you can!".

Listen to that voice, and use the insight it provides to guide your experience in the world of work. Make it the foundation on which you build your career. A healthy career. One that is based on what you can do, not on what you can't.

Work Strong

Chapter Seven

Step #3: Warm Up
Your Career Fitness Plan
How to Stay True to Your Calling

"Good, better, best. Never let it rest. Until your good is better and your better is best."

Tim Duncan, Professional basketball player

The key to progress is to move from thinking to doing, from contemplation to action, from understanding to undertaking a mission. The next step in the Career Fitness system will help you develop a proactive plan for implementing your Intention Commitment, for powering up your job search and reshaping your career so that it engages and nurtures your Natural. Making such a plan isn't all that difficult; sticking with it is the challenge.

We are all familiar with this kind of situation. Every New Year's day, millions of us make resolutions that we hope will improve the quality or meaning of our lives. We commit to losing weight, to visiting a museum regularly, to learning how to speak another language, to being kinder to our neighbors, to paying more attention to our kids, to _____

_____

… you've probably done it too, so you can fill in the blank.

The problem with these commitments is that we seldom act on them for any extended period of time. Oh sure, for the first week or two, maybe even during the first month, the determination to follow through—to adhere to what we have resolved—is top of mind, and as a consequence, we work at it regularly. But then, as time goes by, we lose our focus.

Life's events begin to put new pressures on us and what was once a priority becomes an afterthought. The goal is still there, but we are unable to stick to our plan. And then, finally, we forget about our New Year's resolution altogether and lose the benefit—the improvement in ourselves—that we sought to gain.

An Intention Commitment changes that dynamic. It's the resolution you won't overlook and don't forget. There are two important reasons why that happens:

- **First, you wrote your Intention Commitment down.**
  Simple as that act may sound, it has a powerful impact on what you subsequently do. Now, you've got to deal with something that is real and tangible. It's more than a whim or a fleeting fancy. A commitment is a pledge, and because that pledge has been memorialized in writing, you're either going to live up to it or you will have to choose not to.

  Sure, you can still shove the document into a desk drawer or lose it under everything else behind the magnets on your refrigerator door. But, doing so takes on more meaning—it is a conscious act of self-betrayal—because your written obligation is a contract with yourself. It is a pledge that has both physical substance and moral weight and thus cannot be easily ignored.

- **Second, you're going to make that commitment an integral part of living your life.**
  You're going to refer to it constantly and rely on it regularly during your workdays. You see, an Intention Commitment is a living creed in that it initiates and sustains a set of career enhancing actions. That set—the Career Fitness Work-in—will alter the way you work at your job search or the job you have. It will also change your approach to every job you take in the future.

  This resolution is not a one-off event that is accomplished (or not) and then forgotten; rather, your Intention Commitment transforms you into a "work-in-progress," a self-improvement project for the rest of your career. That project can only be undertaken successfully, however, if you follow a plan—an orderly, progressive and dynamic strategy that serves as your daily reference point. It is the way you keep yourself on track to be the best you can be.

How do you start building this plan? By defining success. What will Career Fitness look like once you've achieved it?

Career Victories

Your Intention Commitment defines the maturation of your Natural as the long-term objective of the work you do in your career. It's how you describe the spot at the apex of the career jungle gym—the apogee of your unique talent—the point at which you will truly be your personal best.

Each of the bars beneath that spot represents an opportunity for you to develop and express your Natural further. Reaching up or out or even down to those bars will enable you to expand your limits toward that ultimate experience of the talent within you. This contribution to your personal growth is what gives those rungs their value to you, not their location within a corporate hierarchy and not the wealth they may (or may not) generate.

As a consequence, you will use your Intention Commitment:

- to evaluate alternative rungs for their potential value to you—their capacity to extend your understanding and use of your Natural;

  and

- to identify and select rungs as employment goals for yourself—objectives that will enable you to advance your work-in-progress.

In some cases, these rungs are the employers for which you decide to work. In other cases, they are the jobs you are willing to accept. And, in others, they are discrete assignments or even a specific responsibility for which you might volunteer or on which you might decide to focus. In all cases, however, the attainment of the rung begins the work that stretches you to produce an accomplishment that expresses and refines your Natural. That feat is, in a very real sense, a "career victory" for you. It is a personal achievement that you set out to realize and that you respect and value.

The key to building Career Fitness, then, is to achieve these career victories on a regular, continuous basis. They are the goals you establish for your best work and the outcomes you achieve with your best performance in the workplace. They forge the link between your Natural and your day-to-day employment. Different jobs and employers provide different pathways with which to reach that link, and your progress depends upon your evaluating and selecting the optimal course for you.

Using your Intention Commitment as a guide, you must:

- find options in the workplace that hold the prospect of advancing your work-in-progress;

- assess those options and compare their relative potential for enabling your success at a particular point in your career;

    and

- select the option with the greatest potential and then proactively strive to realize it.

You must execute these steps dispassionately and with all of the courage you can muster. Such is the essence of being a career athlete and the responsibility inherent in being loyal to yourself.

If you cannot achieve a career victory by working for a specific employer or in a specific job, then that situation is obstructing your pursuit of Happiness. No matter how much it pays, no matter how prestigious the role, no matter how much pressure you feel from your boss, your peers or the organization, staying put is putting you off course. It is preventing the alignment of your talent with your work and, as a consequence, weakening and, in all likelihood, harming your career.

> **The key to building Career Fitness is to achieve career victories on a regular, continuous basis.**

The concept of focusing your career on the achievement of personal victories at work changes the dynamic of your workday. It replaces the ultimately unsatisfying notion of getting ahead (of others) with the inherently fulfilling credo of moving ahead (in your own development).

In the 20th Century, the career ladder held workers back by forcing them to compete with one another; in the 21st Century, you can advance by challenging yourself. The purpose of reaching for each rung on the career jungle gym is no longer to step over someone else, but, instead, to take a step forward that has meaning and purpose for you—to race to the peak of your natural capabilities.

That achievement is a victory because it enables you to develop your talent, to excel at your work, to better your own personal best. It is the way you build up yourself, rather than beat out the other person. It is the way you live the career you want, not the career you stumble into or put up with.

When you run a race with yourself, there are only winners. There are no losers. That's why a career victory is a genuine "optimal experience." More than any other kind of achievement, it conveys a profound sense of personal satisfaction and fulfillment. It is a chance to recreate yourself—to improve who you are and what you can do—and to enjoy that success at no one else's expense.

There are two steps involved in developing a Career Fitness plan that produces such career victories:

- First, you set specific, finite, achievable goals for yourself and always work at them. The effort required for you to achieve those goals forces you to stretch your limits and develop a greater capability in your Natural. It is the way you advance to being your personal best.

- Second, you conduct a personal, private and unflinching evaluation of your performance on a regular basis. This evaluation ensures that you stick with your plan, that you make progress in your work, and that you acknowledge and reward yourself for your achievements.

Setting Goals

The pathway to being the best you can be is always being better than you were yesterday. To build lasting Career Fitness, you have to set three sequential goals that are continuously iterated. They are cycles of progress for your work:

- **One cycle focuses on Achievement.**
  It sets a goal that you can accomplish in the near term, say within the next six-to-twelve months. It identifies an outcome you can achieve in your current job or employment situation, such as a step-up in your performance, the completion of a special project, the solution to an especially tough problem or the resolution of an issue that has degraded your work. This short term cycle recognizes that Career Fitness is something that must happen regularly by providing a requirement that demands and produces your personal best in the work you're doing in the present.

  By acknowledging the importance of what is happening in your current work, Career Fitness delivers two important results. First, it ensures that you deliver the best level of performance that you can on-the-job—that's the 21st Century definition of loyalty to your employer. It's doing your best work to help an organization accomplish its goal.

  Second, it gives you a chance to be successful. It provides a way for you to optimize the application of your talent in the phase of your career that you're experiencing right now—that's loyalty to yourself. It's not sublimating your career to the organization, but instead, aligning your talent with it—with the accomplishment of its mission. Doing so enables you to provide a fair return on your employer's investment in you and achieve a work goal that is meaningful to you.

  The resulting sense of accomplishment is, quite literally, a "career victory," a recognizable and important step forward in your quest to be your personal best. It is a milestone along the pathway to the penultimate expression of your Natural, and reaching it stimulates both a justifiable pride in your own work and a continuing commitment to your Career Fitness regimen.

- **A second cycle focuses on Advancement.**
  It is a goal that you can accomplish in the mid-to-longer term, say in the next three-to-five years. This cycle identifies the next job you want to hold or the next level of work you want to be able to perform. It may involve your current employer or it may require that you move to another work situation, but it will always represent a major leap forward in your effort to develop and express your Natural.

  The Advancement cycle recognizes that building Career Fitness is a never-ending process. A healthy and rewarding career is not an end state, but a continuous quest. Therefore, even as you are working in your current job—even as you are stretching to be your personal best in the present—you must be aware of what you should do in the future in order to continue to advance yourself. It is the "career victory" that you aspire to, but cannot yet reach.

  An Advancement goal should be carefully set. It is a stretch to be sure, but one that pushes you forward, not down. It must represent a clear and genuine challenge—a significant new expression of your Natural—but not so great a leap forward as to be unachievable within the mid-to-longer term.

  Why set three-to-five years as the horizon for this goal? Because in a growing number of fields today, that is the half-life of your expertise. It is the boundary to your peak performance. You cannot sustain your maximum contribution in the workplace beyond that limit. To advance, therefore, you must force yourself to move forward to a new level of performance. You must strive to do more than what you can already do.

> **The pathway to being the best you can be is always being better than you were yesterday.**

- **The third cycle focuses on Development.**
  It is the bridge that connects your Achievement goal and your Advancement goal. It enables you to build on the success you accomplish in the present by adding the supplemental capabilities and knowledge that prepare you appropriately to conquer each of the challenges you've selected for your future. Hence, establishing this goal requires a candid assessment of:

  o what you will be able to do as a result of your career victory in the Achievement cycle;

  o what you must be able to do to achieve a career victory in the Advancement cycle;

  and

  o what you must accomplish in the interval—the next two-to-three years—to close the gap between those cycles.

  The development goal might involve your acquiring a new skill through training or a formal educational program; it might require that you achieve greater stature in your field through participation in your professional society or trade association; or, it might mean that you gain more insight and understanding about certain aspects of your work through discussions with a mentor.

Whatever the activity, your Development cycle transforms you from a resting to an active state, from a worker-in-place to a worker-in-progress. It propels your career from the finish line you've already crossed to the successive starting lines you've yet to reach. It primes you to be constantly developing and growing so that your personal best is always getting better.

Your Achievement, Advancement and Development goals give your career direction and momentum. They keep you progressing, but unlike in the past, you define the nature of your passage. You decide what your next level of performance or your next job will be. You lay the course, and you set the pace. And, when you do, you position yourself for an endless string of personal accomplishments, a continuous cycle of career victories.

Those victories benefit you in two ways. They provide both the satisfaction that comes from enjoying a healthy and rewarding career and the perpetual, positive reinforcement that keeps you motivated and moving forward in the realization of your Intention Commitment. They are the reward you earn with your Life and Liberty in the workplace. They are the mile markers in your pursuit of Happiness.

Develop Your Plan

The Achievement, Advancement and Development cycles form the structure of your Career Fitness Plan. They are separate endeavors, but established and accomplished as an integrated whole and then iterated over and over again to continue and expand your success.

In a sense, each three-cycle set is a stage in your own championship season. Each is a formidable test and a liberating opportunity. Each defines a personal victory and adds to a winning record that enlarges both your own satisfaction and your stature in the workplace.

Using the following worksheets, develop your plan for the first iteration of your Achievement, Advancement and Development cycles. Remember that your guide in establishing these goals is your Intention Commitment. Each of them should relate to that promise you made to yourself, and all of them should help you achieve genuine and sustained progress in making it come true.

To help you keep that focus, restate your Intention Commitment here:

I am committed to developing and expressing my special gift for ...

_____

by ...

_____.

And then, remember one other thing ... Yes, you can!

Achievement Cycle Worksheet

In the next six-to-twelve months, I will…

Advancement Cycle Worksheet

In the next three-to-five years, I will…

Development Cycle Worksheet

In the next two-to-three years, I will...

Evaluating Your Performance

Setting goals that stretch you to ever higher levels of personal performance and capability tests your self-knowledge and your self-confidence. Reaching those goals—making them come true—is no less demanding. It requires determination, concentration and resilience. It demands personal fortitude.

To help you find, use and, if necessary, reinforce those qualities within yourself, the Career Fitness plan also includes continuous self-evaluation. This personal assessment enables you to:

- measure the progress you've achieved in your career;

- take appropriate remedial steps, if necessary;

  and

- acknowledge your accomplishments.

Measuring your own progress is a performance review without office politics, individual personalities, and the imperfect perceptions of bosses. This self-assessment enables you to measure the day-to-day execution of your workplace activities—to be your own personal career captain—so that you don't slip from your goals. It's a way to check up on yourself and make sure that the pressures and obligations of daily life and work haven't overwhelmed your Intention Commitment or your adherence to the principles of Career Fitness.

Taking appropriate remedial steps acknowledges that we all slip up from time-to-time. We make mistakes or we get side-tracked, and our progress slows or stops altogether. Such situations only harm your career, however, if you let them continue uncorrected. If you revise and reset the conditions of your employment, if you realign your work with your Natural, then even missteps can advance you. They become yet more rungs of personal growth on your journey across the career jungle gym.

Acknowledging your accomplishments reminds you to reward yourself for each and every career victory. It expands the definition of self-loyalty to encompass taking stock of your achievements. It ensures that you give yourself the most important kind of payout you'll ever earn in life: self-respect for meaningful work well done.

To have the optimum impact, you should evaluate your performance against your plan every three months. At the end of each quarter, pull out your Achievement, Advancement and Development goals and give yourself a "personal performance review." This review is an occasion for private, candid reflection on the health of your career. It involves asking yourself two questions:

> ### #1: Am I staying on course?
> Have I remained true to my Intention Commitment or have I wandered away from my Achievement, Advancement and Development goals? Am I—unconsciously or even consciously — moving in a direction that will interfere with my determination to be the best I can be?

> ### #2: Am I moving forward?
> Have I acted to implement my goals? Did I make decisions, take actions—did I do anything—that would help me to accomplish those objectives? And, if I did, were the steps I took positive and helpful to me? Am I, in fact, making progress?

If you can answer "Yes" to both of these questions, pat yourself on the back. Give yourself credit for the distance you've covered in your quest to be the best you can be. If you've achieved a career victory during the time since your last review, congratulate yourself and then reward yourself by memorializing your success. Detail that accomplishment on one or both of two separate and very different documents: your Career Record so that you can enjoy and remember it, and if appropriate, on your resume so that others will recognize and respect it. (See Chapter Nine for instructions on how to write a Career Record and a resume that reflect your Career Fitness.)

If your progress moved you closer, but not all the way to a career victory, celebrate the good you are doing for yourself. You are eliminating career flab and adding career muscle. You are building career security—the capacity to be in charge of the change in your career rather than its victim. And, you are doing work that will enable you to pursue happiness successfully—to realize, in full measure, your version of the American Dream.

If, on the other hand, the answer is "No" to either or both of these questions, you must embark on a two-step personal counseling process. First, you have to convince yourself that there's a problem. You must be willing to acknowledge that you've let yourself down. Second, you must stop the work you're doing—take a full day off from your job—and have a serious conversation with yourself about how to fix the problem.

- "No" to the first question means that you've lost your focus. You are not visualizing the goals that will engage and empower your Natural. You have, in a sense, taken your eye off the ball in your career. Whatever led to this misperception—however important it may have seemed to you at the moment—it is inevitably undermining your ability to succeed at that which you most enjoy doing and do best. The necessary remedial action is to return to the Career De-Stress Test and retake the exercises. Rediscover the healthy center of your career.

- "No" to the second question means that you are falling behind in your quest to be your personal best. Your work generates a paycheck, but is not delivering an enduring reward. It does nothing to advance you toward your personal best. You're simply coasting (or worse, standing still), and as a consequence, you're jeopardizing the growth and happiness inherent in your best work. The necessary remedial action is to return to the goal-setting step and reexamine your plan. Redefine your Achievement, Advancement and Development goals so that they stretch you toward a more complete expression of your Natural.

Your "personal performance review" is simply a way to keep yourself honest. It is a career self-management technique that will help you make sure that you're always in the "Yes" zone. It will perpetuate your ability to say "Yes, I can" and translate it into progress with your commitment to saying "Yes, I will."

Maintaining that connection between your ability and commitment is critical because it alone sets you up for career success. Only by saying "Yes" to both do you put yourself within reach of the career champion inside you. Unlike any place else, in the "Yes" zone:

- you're working at what matters most to you;

  and

- you're working to be your personal best.

As a consequence, each and every day, your work is one of your "best times." It is transformed from what your job requires you to do into what you want and are destined to do. It offers you the kind of experience that heretofore you could have only after work or in your leisure time. Work becomes an activity that is engaging, meaningful, and profoundly rewarding. For you.

Each task at work, each assignment, each project, even each problem to be solved becomes an occasion for you to experience your Natural. These situations are contests that stretch your special talent and push you to ever higher levels of performance. They are passages of personal growth and accomplishment that strengthen your muscles of self-understanding and self-respect. They are challenges that, time and time again, give you the satisfaction and sense of fulfillment that come from doing what you do best and most like to do. In short, when you're in the "Yes" zone, you are living the American Dream … you are not just in the pursuit of Happiness, you are achieving it.

Use the following worksheets to conduct the first four of your personal performance reviews.

Personal Performance Review #1

Am I staying on course?

If so, restate the goals you've set for yourself and rededicate yourself to achieving them. If not, describe what you did or didn't do that got you off track. Then, return to the Career De-Stress test and either confirm your Intention Commitment or develop a new one that serves you better.

Am I making progress?

If so, describe the actions you've taken to advance toward your Achievement, Advancement and Development goals. If not, describe the obstacles you encountered that prevented your progress. Then, return to the goal-setting step and either confirm that your goals can move you forward or revise them so they will.

Personal Performance Review #2

Am I staying on course?

If so, restate the goals you've set for yourself and rededicate yourself to achieving them. If not, describe what you did or didn't do that got you off track. Then, return to the Career De-Stress test and either confirm your Intention Commitment or develop a new one that serves you better.

Am I making progress?

If so, describe the actions you've taken to advance toward your Achievement, Advancement and Development goals. If not, describe the obstacles you encountered that prevented your progress. Then, return to the goal-setting step and either confirm that your goals can move you forward or revise them so they will.

Personal Performance Review #3

Am I staying on course?

If so, restate the goals you've set for yourself and rededicate yourself to achieving them. If not, describe what you did or didn't do that got you off track. Then, return to the Career De-Stress test and either confirm your Intention Commitment or develop a new one that serves you better.

Am I making progress?

If so, describe the actions you've taken to advance toward your Achievement, Advancement and Development goals. If not, describe the obstacles you encountered that prevented your progress. Then, return to the goal-setting step and either confirm that your goals can move you forward or revise them so they will.

Personal Performance Review #4

Am I staying on course?

If so, restate the goals you've set for yourself and rededicate yourself to achieving them. If not, describe what you did or didn't do that got you off track. Then, return to the Career De-Stress test and either confirm your Intention Commitment or develop a new one that serves you better.

Am I making progress?

If so, describe the actions you've taken to advance toward your Achievement, Advancement and Development goals. If not, describe the obstacles you encountered that prevented your progress. Then, return to the goal-setting step and either confirm that your goals can move you forward or revise them so they will.

Chapter Eight

Step #4: The Career Fitness Work-in
How to Build a Healthy Career Every Day

"Spectacular achievements are always preceded by unspectacular preparation."

Roger Staubach, Former All Pro quarterback

Once you understand the Career Fitness philosophy and have completed your preparation and warm-up, you're ready to begin the program of exercises that will empower your career and enrich the happiness you derive from it. These exercises comprise the Career Fitness Work-in. Its purposes are to shape and tone your career so that:

- you work in jobs that enable you to develop and express your Natural;

   and

- your work in life is meaningful and rewarding to you and thus makes you happy.

Regularly performing the regimen's exercises is an effective way to build a healthy career. It's a short program. There are only seven exercises. But if you stick with them, they'll improve the effectiveness of your job search, if you're in transition, or the quality of your performance if you're employed. And, in both cases, you will deepen the sense of accomplishment you derive from your work.

The Career Fitness exercise will strengthen your muscles of self-understanding and self-respect and extend your reach and agility in the pursuit of Happiness. Why? Because in a very real sense, the time and attention you devote to these exercises is fundamentally an investment in yourself. And, making such an investment is the only way to build a career with enduring meaning and value in your life.

The work-in helps you plan and execute the steps that will bring you to a healthy occupational state. It is the way you transform yourself from a career coach potato—the victim of what happens to you in your work—to a career athlete—the captain who takes charge of your career and directs it toward ends that are relevant and important to you.

That doesn't mean you flit from one job or employer to another, without purpose or principles. Career athletes do, of course, change jobs and employers because, from time-to-time in their careers, they determine that doing so is the best way to accomplish their Achievement, Advancement and Development goals. At other times, however, they may decide that the best course of action is to be active in place. They can move forward in their career through their current position or through another with their current employer. The key is their commitment to progress, not their location. And, the Career Fitness Work-in is a systematic way for you to achieve that progress regardless of where you are employed.

The work-in is a structured, integrated set of occupational exercises that ensures:

- The most important activities are recognized. There are hundreds of different ways to develop your career. The work-in has been designed to include the right activities—those that will have the most lasting effect on your career in the 21st Century workplace.

- The most important activities are prioritized. There are hundreds of responsibilities calling for your attention in and outside the workplace. The work-in has been designed to ensure you recognize and plan for the right activities to derive a genuine benefit—a positive outcome—from performing them.

- The most important activities are performed most effectively. There are many different approaches to performing the right activities; some are effective, some aren't and some are less effective than others. The work-in has been designed to help you execute the right activities in the right way so that you derive the maximum benefit from your investment of time and effort.

Unlike its counterpart in physical fitness, this set of activities is not a workout, but a "work-in." It is a way to put meaningful work into your life. Simple as that sounds, it represents a profound shift in the experience most of us have each day in the workplace.

A life based on meaningful work empowers you to raise your expectations about what your career can and should do for you. It gives you the conviction and the capability to remove the uncertainty many of us feel on-the-job today—an uncertainty caused by doubts about our security, our employability and our prospects—and replace it with a real and lasting happiness—a happiness that comes from doing what you most like to do and do best.

As introduced in Chapter Five and summarized in the following table, this transformation takes you through three stages of personal development. Each stage of growth represents a profound change in the nature of your work and the benefits it provides to you. The more advanced the stage of work you achieve, the greater the happiness you are able to experience.

> **Unlike their counterpart in physical fitness, the Career Fitness exercises are not a workout, but a "work-in." They are a way to put meaningful work into your life.**

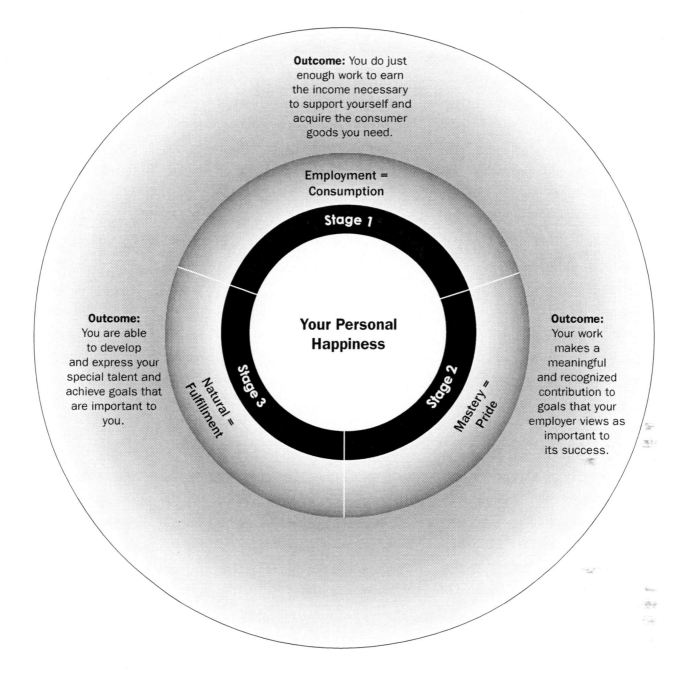

Outcome: You do just enough work to earn the income necessary to support yourself and acquire the consumer goods you need.

Employment = Consumption

Stage 1

Your Personal Happiness

Stage 2

Mastery = Pride

Stage 3

Natural = Fulfillment

Outcome: You are able to develop and express your special talent and achieve goals that are important to you.

Outcome: Your work makes a meaningful and recognized contribution to goals that your employer views as important to its success.

Conventional wisdom has long recognized this progression. We are all told, at one time or another, that money won't buy us happiness. And yet, many people never move beyond the first or consumption stage. They begin and end their entire working lives with only the most basic expectation of their work: they are simply laboring for the income that enables them to purchase goods and services.

Any form of Employment is important, of course, because it produces a critical outcome—the ability to meet our basic needs of food, shelter and clothing. When we get stuck in or addicted to that consumption, however, we force ourselves to earn far more than we need. When that happens, our work experience is diminished. It becomes our occupational drive—a drive that is totally disconnected from the work we perform.

Our employment is not directed at the development and expression of our Natural on-the-job, but rather at supporting our compulsion to acquire products and services outside the workplace. As a consequence, we don't bother with self-improvement or personal growth, but instead, focus on simply doing our job adequately and nothing more. We work only when, where and how our employers require and only for the paycheck they provide. Consumption work enables us to meet our basic needs and it may even afford us a lavish standard of living, but it leaves our spirit impoverished.

When we strive to do more than the bare minimum in our employment, when we upgrade our performance beyond what's adequate, we move from consumption to work in which we can take pride. This higher level of work involves our acquiring a skill set that our employers need and attaining mastery in its application on-the-job. That commitment to personal growth gives us the expertise necessary to accomplish goals that are recognized as worthwhile and important by our employers. We become savvy in the way our employers want our work to be done, and we measure up to that standard.

Mastery work positions us for personal achievement on-the-job. It enables us to feel satisfied through the accomplishment of tasks that are valued in the workplace. As a result, our income (usually) goes up, but more importantly, so too does the pride we feel in what we do and the organization for which we do it.

We feel as if we have contributed to the success of the organization, so we share in the recognition and stature it earns. We wear hats and shirts emblazoned with its logo, and we pour ever more time and effort into ensuring it continues to perform well.

That devotion to organization progress, however, does not necessarily provide an equal measure of progress for ourselves. Indeed, a singular focus on the success of our employer can actually weaken the health of our career by interfering with our own development. And when that occurs, ironically, not only are we disserved, but so too is our employer.

Natural work is the penultimate stage of employment. It applies our inherent talent to tasks we find challenging and worthwhile. Natural work enables us to express and experience our unique capacity for excellence and to do so in endeavors that leave us feeling fulfilled. It is, in effect, our commitment to pursuing Happiness.

With that philosophy as our north star, we continuously achieve our optimum employment experience. We make the choice to share the benefit of our work with our employers, but the focus of our time and effort on-the-job is to reach and then extend the best we can be. That drive for excellence both stirs us to perform at our peak and to raise that peak over and over again so we are always climbing to ever higher echelons of capability.

Our superior performance, in turn, will often increase our paycheck, but will always increase the happiness we bring home from work. Natural work delivers its benefits by continuously expanding our self-knowledge, self-commitment and self-respect.

Natural work is not egocentric, however. The benefits it produces also have an external beneficiary. They are the pillars on which we erect the superstructure of our contribution to our employers. Said another way, by serving our own best interests first, we are able to serve the best interests of the organizations that depend on us, as well.

Work, then, is only fulfilling when it is seen as a progressive experience in personal development—in the maturation of the champion inside you. How does this growth process unfold? How do you reach the fulfillment stage of work and keep yourself there? With the Career Fitness Work-in. To ensure you achieve this state, however, it's important to adhere to certain guidelines. These conditioning parameters combine and summarize much of what you've learned so far about career health, and enable you to get the best possible results from your developmental effort.

One, Two, Three ... and One, Two ...

Adhere to the following guidelines when performing your Career Fitness Work-in.

1. Exercise every day

The workplace of the 21st Century demands an ever increasing and often changing array of skills, knowledge, and experience. As a result, you must be constantly building new occupational capacity or your career will atrophy.

Exercising and stretching your occupational competence every day is the best way to ensure that you stay abreast of the constantly shifting requirements for peak performance on-the-job. It's a way of building career strength and endurance by acquiring "just-the-right" capabilities all of the time.

There will, of course, be impediments and distractions that can sap your commitment to daily exercising. Crises that come up on-the-job, business travel, responsibilities at home, even an illness can make it difficult to stick to the Career Fitness Work-in. Building career health doesn't require that you ignore such matters, only that you manage them.

You should:

- Establish a routine so that the completion of the work-in becomes an integral part of your daily schedule and not the exception to it. Make the regimen a priority in your work and your career and give it the attention it deserves.

- Whenever disruptions do occur, reinforce the habit of your routine by doing as much as you can, even if it involves only a modest investment of time and effort. It's better to do something than nothing at all.

- Don't let lapses linger, but instead limit the duration of any unavoidable breaks in your regular routine and get back to the work-in as soon as you can. Perfect participation is less important than continuous participation.

Exercising every day is an imperative of good career health. It is also a feat of dedication. It is the allegiance that you pledge to yourself and to the very best that's in you. No less important, it is the courage you show in helping others to understand and respect that commitment. If Lance Armstrong taught us to Live Strong; Career Fitness enables you to Work Strong.

2. Stop if it isn't fun

This guideline is the career equivalent of the physical fitness maxim, "If you feel faint or dizzy when exercising, STOP." In physical fitness, you shouldn't push yourself so hard that you hurt yourself. In career fitness, the same principle applies.

You never want to push yourself into work or into a job that is unsatisfying and unrewarding simply because you think that it will advance your career. Indeed, the only way to be your personal best is to work at a job that interests, challenges, and fulfills you. To do otherwise hurts your career

> **Exercising every day is an imperative of good career health.
> It is also a feat of dedication.**

because you will not be able to sustain or even reach your best level of performance. And, when you cannot achieve your best level of performance, you cannot reach the optimal experience that is the true essence of a healthy career.

There are danger signs that will tell you when you've gotten off track. If you're bored at work, if you feel tired or worn out before you even get to work, if every challenge on-the-job seems more like a disaster than a chance to flex your knowledge and creativity, then the work you're doing is hurting your career, not strengthening it. You are endangering your happiness because you are not working at your Natural. If that's your employment experience, you should stop.

Difficult as it may be to do, you should take a break and return to the warm-up stage of the Career Fitness system. Re-take the Career De-Stress Test and pinpoint what it is that will enable you to be the best you can be on-the-job. This reassessment will bring you to one of two conclusions:

- You may discover that your career is headed in the wrong direction. Somehow, you've wandered down a path that takes you to work where you can't hear your calling. The time you're spending in the workplace is unfulfilling because you're accepting employment in the wrong field.

  If that's the case, re-center your career on your Natural. Change your occupation. Yes, of course, that can be difficult and stressful. Admittedly, it could lower (at least temporarily) your standard of living or impose changes on your lifestyle that will require adjustments both by you and, no less important, by your family.

  Despite all of that, however, you must take this step—you must realign your work with your Natural. Why? Because failing to do so is an act of disrespect to yourself. It abuses who you are and who you can be—the champion living within you. The only healthy course of action, therefore, is to embark on a new career, one that enables you to work at that which you most enjoy doing and do best.

- Alternatively, you may discover that your current job has taken you away from your Natural. Your career is still focused correctly, but somehow you fell into a position or an employment situation that is impeding your progress.

  You may have misjudged what your job involved or misunderstood the culture and values of your employer. You may have misread the responsibilities and requirements of the position or misinterpreted what was said about them by the employer's representatives. Whatever the reason, the end result is the same: you are working in a position that is undermining the health of your career.

  If that's the case, change jobs. You can take on a different role with your current employer (if its environment is conducive to your success) or move to another organization altogether. In either case, your goal is to re-center your daily work on your Natural. You want to be employed in a job that enables you to do your best work each and every day.

  Once you've completed the reassessment—once you've made sure that both your career and your employment are centered on your Natural—then it's safe and appropriate for you to return to the Career Fitness Work-in. With that foundation in place, the exercises will refresh and energize you and infuse you with excitement.

3. Be your own peak performer

Strengthening your career in the 21st Century is not a competition with others. Unlike the norm in the 20th Century, your advancement does not occur at the expense of your coworkers. It's not a race up the corporate ladder or a contest with your colleagues to see who's got the biggest muscles of organizational influence and power. Instead, building a healthy career in today's workplace is a "self-competitive" sport.

The Career Fitness Work-in is designed to help you challenge yourself to be better at your work. Building a healthy career is, in essence, a rivalry with yourself for yourself.

The work-in, therefore, prepares and encourages you to move beyond your comfort zone, to reach beyond the limits imposed by others (no matter how well meaning) and by yourself. Developing a strong and vibrant career is a test of your ability to be the best You. Not in comparison to others, but in comparison to the champion you were meant to be.

The experience is analogous to the way people run a marathon. Only one person can "win" the race, and only a very small and elite group of runners have even a chance of doing so. Most marathons, however, attract hundreds, even thousands of runners. They do so because they are viewed as a "competition" in which everyone has the opportunity to achieve a victory. Not for simply participating, but for pushing to personal excellence.

Zoe Koplowitz provides an instructional case in point. She's run the New York City marathon a number of times, and in every race, she's finished dead last. In 2007, she crossed the finish line more than 24 hours later than the "winner." Her time was 28 hours and 45 minutes. Her performance, however, was both meaningful to her and inspiring to everyone else who watched. Why? Because Zoe has multiple sclerosis. She braves the 26.2 mile course with crutches and back and knee braces. Her goal isn't to beat the other runners or to set a world's record. She knows she never will. Instead, Zoe runs the marathon to stretch and improve herself. Her goal is to be her personal best.

All of us can do what Zoe does. Maybe not in a marathon, but certainly in our work. We can test our limits, reach for a higher level of performance, and stretch ourselves to realize more of our inherent capabilities. That's the way you build physical fitness, and it's also the way you develop career fitness. You strive to be your personal best in meaningful and rewarding work each and every day.

> **Building a healthy career is a rivalry with yourself for yourself.**

The Career Fitness Exercises

There are seven exercises in the Career Fitness Work-in. They are:

> **I. Pump up your career cardiovascular system.**
>
> **II. Strengthen your career circulatory system.**
>
> **III. Develop all of your career's muscle groups.**
>
> **IV. Increase your career's flexibility and range of motion.**
>
> **V. Work with winners.**
>
> **VI. Pace yourself.**
>
> **VII. Stretch your soul.**

The complete work-in is detailed in the following pages. The description of each exercise is organized into three sections:

- The Exercise Strategy—your game plan for success;

- The Exercise Strides—the specific activities or "plays" you execute for success;

  and

- My Exercise Record—a "trophy case" for your career victories.

The Exercise Strategy section describes how the exercise contributes to your career health, so that you understand why you should devote your time and effort to doing it. Most of us want to see our careers progress and flourish, but we're mystified about which developmental activities will best achieve our goal. That's because it's not always easy to see a direct link between the actions we're taking and the outcome we want to achieve. We don't recognize the connection between our dedication and a gain that's important to us. So, that's what The Exercise Strategy section provides—a rationale for the effort required to build and maintain a healthy career.

The Exercise Strides are designed to help you:

- acquire the necessary information to plan for career enhancing activities on your own;

  and

- execute those activities in a timely and effective way.

In some cases, the acquisition of information and the execution of one or more activities occur within a single exercise stride. In other cases, information acquisition occurs in one stride and the execution of the activity in a second. The outcome, however, is always the same: informed, proactive career self-management, because that is the prescription for a healthy career.

This comprehensive guide to execution is unique to the Career Fitness system. In effect, you're told:

- how to perform each stride or activity in each exercise—what to do;

  and

- how frequently each stride in each exercise should be performed—when to do it.

The work-in schedules the appropriate repetitions of healthy career-building activities to ensure that you perform them as often as you should in order to see real results—to have a positive impact on your career.

In addition you are asked to think about how to implement each stride in your career—where to do it. You must move beyond the stride as it's described on paper and, using The Exercise Strategy, transform it into a specific action or set of actions that you can perform in the workplace. You must take the potential inherent in the stride and determine the best way to realize that potential in your own work experience.

You will then detail this personalized plan of application in writing so that it:

- guides your execution of the stride;

  and

- ensures you actually benefit from it.

Each of the strides helps to prepare you for your next career victory (and for those after that) by upgrading and refining your performance at work and/or by reinforcing and augmenting your capability in the workplace. Every stride, therefore, is a critical component of its exercise. That's why Career Fitness is first and foremost a test of your resolve. There is no cherry-picking those activities that are convenient or most easily accomplished. All of the strides must be executed, and they must all be executed according to the prescribed schedule.

The Career Fitness Work-in is also not a "checkmark in the box" kind of endeavor. The quality of what you do is just as important as the quantity of that activity. You must not only perform all of the strides, but you must perform them correctly and with as much energy and diligence as you can muster. Otherwise, the benefit you derive from the exercises will be diminished or even completely eliminated. You will have invested time and effort but not strengthened the health of your career.

The third section of each exercise—My Exercise Record—will help you keep track of your execution of the work-in's activities on a daily, weekly, monthly and quarterly basis. As with physical fitness, Career Fitness takes a certain "stick-to-itiveness." The work-in requires dedication and constant monitoring if progress is to be made.

The My Career Record section shows you where you are on a regular basis. It provides a way for you to:

- reward yourself by noting how far you have come;

  and

- remediate yourself by indicating when and where you have fallen behind.

While the seven exercises of the Career Fitness Work-in are a full and sufficient developmental program for career health, they are not exhaustive. There are other activities that you can and may want to perform to strengthen your career. It's perfectly acceptable to include these supplemental efforts in your regimen after you've tested them out.

Add them to your routine for 60-90 days and then assess the results. If they yield the outcome you expect, include them in your work-in and monitor their execution with your Exercise Record. Only do so, however, if they will not interfere with your Career Fitness exercises—those activities are the most important for the health of your career—and if you intend to perform them with sufficient frequency to achieve the benefit they can provide.

Finally, it's best to acquaint yourself with all of the exercises in the work-in before beginning to execute any one of them. Make sure that you understand the totality of what you are setting out to do and why. The big picture may initially seem off-putting and even intimidating. It may strike you as unrealistic or even naïve, given all of the pressures and demands you face in the workplace. Such a reaction is absolutely understandable.

The legacy of 20th Century biases—that your work is the penalty you must endure for your paycheck—is not easily removed from our systems. If you fail to exorcise it, however, the harm it does will metastasize throughout your career in the 21st Century. It will sap the strength you need to stand up for yourself and realize your full potential. It will constrict your work and cripple your performance on-the-job. It will debilitate your Natural and, ultimately, devastate your quality of life in the workplace.

Throwing off that view, therefore, is the critical breakthrough you must achieve in order to embark on the Career Fitness regimen. It is the curative self-empowerment that liberates and launches you toward the epitome of your work self. Equally as important, it reveals the pathway to your experiencing the extraordinary talent with which you have been endowed. With these two bits of knowledge you have everything you need to direct your career toward the pursuit of Happiness.

Career Counselors & Coaches: Personal Trainers for Your Career

Some of us can take charge of our career on our own. Others of us will need assistance. Seeking such help doesn't signal a lack of resolve, however, nor does it indicate a deficit of character or talent. Rather, it is an act of supreme self-confidence and self-respect. It acknowledges the existence of personal roadblocks, but refuses to be bound by them. Therefore, if you find yourself unable to begin the process of career development, don't be intimidated or put off by the situation. Get some help, but get it from a professional.

In physical fitness, that professional would be a personal trainer. In Career Fitness, it is a career counselor or coach. These individuals are experts in helping working men and women achieve engaging and rewarding careers. They may or may not use the concepts and terminology of Career Fitness, but in almost every case, they will provide the insights and assistance that will help ready you for it. They will bring you to the starting line for the Career Fitness Work-in and ready you for the race of your life.

Using a career counselor or coach isn't usually free. While some of these experts are available in state or federal counseling centers or the career services office of your college, university or trade school, most are private professionals who provide a service for fee. The money you spend, however, buys you their knowledge and something more. It makes a commitment to your future. It is, in a very real sense, an investment in your career.

To get the most out of that investment, you should select a counselor or coach with whom you are comfortable and who has bona fide credentials in their field. As with other types of service providers, there are excellent career counselors and coaches and those who aren't so good. While some of the best are independent practitioners, they are also often members of one or more professional organizations. These include:

- CareerDirectors International;

- International Coach Federation;

- and

- National Career Development Association and the National Employment Counseling Association, both units of the American Counseling Association.

If you do engage a career counselor or coach, however, take advantage of their expertise and insights, but do not relinquish your commitment to the Career Fitness system. It, alone, can give your career the strength, reach and endurance to find a great job and hang onto it—to achieve career security that will increase both the paycheck and the satisfaction you bring home from work.

The Career Fitness
Work-In

I. Pump Up Your Career Cardiovascular System

Exercise Strategy

The heart of your career is the currency and scope of your expertise in your profession, craft, or trade. Simple as that statement sounds, this fundamental fact of life at work is often forgotten or ignored. You have a job that demands a lot of time, your boss is happy with your work, and you have an active family or social life outside the office—basically, you already have a full and probably hectic schedule—so why should you even consider taking on the extra obligation and pressure of acquiring the latest skills in your field?

Besides, the experience you're gaining on-the-job certainly enhances your ability, and that's important too. The work may get to be a bit repetitive, and it may not involve the most advanced techniques or the newest developments in your field, but it is providing you with a genuine store of wisdom which any employer would be foolish to discount.

But discount it they do. Being wise in outdated and less efficient or effective processes and procedures will never trump state-of-the-art expertise. And, cutting edge knowledge and skills are what employers want to hire in today's competitive, global business environment.

They rightly believe that up-to-date competence is the key to success in a knowledge-based economy, not familiarity with how things get done in the organization or experience doing the same old things over and over again. In fact, they often come to see an understanding of "standard operating procedures" as a handicap because it prevents those who have it and the organization that employs them from tapping into new and potentially more innovative approaches to work.

From an employer's perspective, the "way we've always done it" crowd is unable to think outside the box, and the box confines, limits and holds them and the organization back. In effect, worn out occupational expertise weakens the heart of your career, and that prevents you from performing at your peak and developing career security.

Career Fitness, therefore, ensures that you acquire the most advanced capabilities available in your field and deliver them on-the-job. That's the definition of talent in the 21st Century workplace.

It cannot be achieved with longevity of employment or even with loyal and steady service. Valuable as those attributes are and as deserving of recognition and reward as they may be, they do not give you the occupational strength and durability necessary for long term health in your career.

From an employer's perspective—and they're the ones that make the hiring and firing decisions—only the latest knowledge and most complete skill set applied at work enable them to compete effectively in the marketplace. Therefore, only those who can deliver that expertise on-the-job are worthy of employment.

That's why you simply cannot afford to engage in a career diet that is starved for the nutrition of continuous development. Occupational stagnation—falling behind the state-of-the-art in your field—is the cholesterol of your career. Eventually, it will kill it. How? By diminishing the flow of your contribution to your employer, even as others in the workforce are able to provide a more fulsome stream of value.

Every year, our colleges and vocational schools graduate men and women who are schooled in the latest techniques and concepts in each profession, craft and trade. Others who are already in the workforce go back to the classroom to improve their knowledge in the field. Some of these people will want your job, and in today's hypercompetitive business world, their occupational muscle is stronger than yours.

Whether you've just taken your first job or are comfortably ensconced in your fifth or sixth one, they have a greater capacity to apply expertise in the workplace. So, what happens? You are given your walking papers and your career goes into cardiac arrest.

How do you protect yourself from dying of obsolescence? The statin, the cholesterol-reducing drug of Career Fitness is learning—the continuous expansion of occupational competency. As you push out the dimensions of your knowledge in your field, you simultaneously extend the potential range and depth of your contribution to your employer. The greater that contribution—the closer you are to being the best you can be—the greater your capacity to play a meaningful role in your employer's success.

Potential contribution, while necessary, is not enough, however. To be truly helpful to your employer and thus too valuable to lose, you must transform that potential into performance on-the-job. In other words, you must increase your capability and deliver it to the organization.

State-of-the-art knowledge is not enough. State-of-the-art knowledge that is withheld or limited in application is not enough. Only state-of-the-art knowledge and state-of-the-art performance provide value to the organization. And that value, alone, is what gives you career security in the 21st Century workplace. Jobs may come and go, but you will always have employers seeking to hire you for jobs that are meaningful to you because you have genuine occupational value, and you bring it to work each day.

And, that's no different from how we all act. When we have an illness, for example, we don't want to be treated by a physician whose understanding of our ailment hasn't been updated since they graduated from medical school twenty years ago. Not unreasonably, we want the services of a physician who is at the cutting edge in medicine, in general, and in the illness we have, in particular. We want that doctor to have the latest knowledge and to be able to apply that knowledge to help us get well. Their expertise is critical to our health, but only if it is effectively applied to diagnose and treat our illness.

A lack of applied expertise is why there are so many job openings that go unfilled today even as so many people are looking for work. Employers want top talent—not mediocre, barely good enough or has-been talent—but more than that, they want top talent who can and will commit their expertise to the mission of the organization. And, if they can't find that kind of talent where you live, they'll move their facility to where they can find it or ship the job offshore. That doesn't make them heartless corporate citizens or disloyal U.S companies; it makes them smart consumers. They're shopping for talent the same way we all shop for an accountant or car mechanic. We keep looking until we find someone who can do the job right, and so do they.

Today, however, the half-life of your expertise has never been shorter. New knowledge is being created at an accelerating pace in virtually every field of work. As a consequence, your ability to deliver value on-the-job is relentlessly growing obsolete.

In addition, the kinds of knowledge that employers need are changing rapidly, as well. As previously noted, the shifting dynamics of the global marketplace, the introduction of new technology and other factors now force continuous adjustments in employers' talent requirements. They may need your skill today, but there's no guarantee they will need it tomorrow or the day after that.

The only way to protect yourself in this hostile environment is to develop the occupational heart of a champion. You must hone your skills constantly, not only with experience—what you learn on-the-job—but with continuous education and training—what you learn for-the-job. In short, you must always be learning in two distinct, but equally important ways:

- You must seek formal learning opportunities that will expand the knowledge and skills on which you can draw while you are at work;

and

- You must seek employment opportunities that will enable you to stretch and strengthen your ability to apply that expertise in the workplace.

Traditionally, this need for continuous self-improvement was recognized in only a relatively small number of select occupational fields, such as medicine, accounting and engineering. Typically, those who pursued a career in these fields were not considered qualified (or licensed) to work unless they accrued a certain number of continuing education credits each year and were periodically re-certified, sometimes even with a formal exam.

The public will not tolerate physicians or tax advisors (or any other critical service providers) who are obsolete, so every physician and every tax advisor understands that their ability to work, to earn a living, to pursue a career in their chosen field depends upon their unwavering dedication to occupational excellence.

Today, that same commitment is a nearly universal requirement. Because the U.S. economy is based on ever expanding knowledge and reliant on ever more sophisticated technology in order to prevail in an ever more competitive and global arena, virtually every occupational field is undergoing constant, high speed change. That's true for manufacturing workers as much as it is for office workers. And, it's true for workers in the Silicon Valley of California as much as it is for workers in the Rust Belt of Pennsylvania and Ohio.

Whether we like it or not, we're competing for employment with the workers in the next town over and with workers in other states and regions. We're competing with workers who live where the cost of living is cheaper than in our hometowns and with workers who live in India, China, Brazil and other developing countries. While tax breaks and lower labor costs have an effect, however, the greatest single factor in an employer's decision to send jobs to one place or another is the skills and knowledge of the workers living there.

This reality presents you with a choice: you can either strengthen your occupational competence or you can watch as your career grows weak with heart disease. You can either adopt a healthy diet of continuous knowledge acquisition and regularly exercise your expertise on-the-job or you can permit your capabilities to grow stagnant and see your contribution at work decline. You can either change the dynamic of your career to a competition with yourself—you can, in effect, challenge yourself to maximize the value of your work to potential employers—or you can see your ability to be selected for engaging and rewarding employment opportunities steadily, even precipitously decline.

The first exercise in the Career Fitness Work-in enables you to choose the healthy course. It enables you to pump up your career cardiovascular system by building capacity—personal knowledge and skills—in two key areas:

- for performance excellence in your current job—your Achievement goal;

    and

- for performance potential in your next job—your Advancement goal.

Actively performing this exercise erects a bridge between those two goals. It is, in effect, a critical element in meeting your Development goal. And each time that you do, the resulting excellence—the championship caliber of your work on-the-job—becomes your new baseline, and that new baseline, in turn, becomes the foundation on which you can stand and reach for your next bar of progress on the career jungle gym.

For Your Current Job

The first objective of this exercise is to acquire the occupational strength that will enable of you to achieve a baseline of sustained excellence in the work you're doing now, so that:

LEVEL 1
You make the maximum contribution you can to your employer on-the-job;

LEVEL 2
You enhance the value of that contribution to your employer, thereby increasing both the monetary reward you receive and the career security you establish; and

LEVEL 3
You free yourself to feel truly, deeply happy by virtue of the optimal experience you've had in developing and expressing your Natural through your work.

For Your Next Jobs

The second objective of this exercise is to acquire the baseline of occupational strength that will enable you to move, at your discretion, to positions requiring excellent performance with more advanced skills and knowledge, so that:

LEVEL 1
You make an even larger contribution to your current employer or a superior contribution to a different one;

LEVEL 2
You multiply the value of your work and thus the paycheck you can earn and the career security you will enjoy in the workplace; and

LEVEL 3
You extend and reinforce the happiness you achieve on-the-job by expanding the dimensions of your optimal experience— the application of your Natural in ever more challenging and important occupational roles.

When you exercise at continuous education and training for your current job, your goal is to be your personal best in that position. When you exercise at continuous education and training for your next job, your goal is to be your personal best in a position that will move you beyond the status quo. In some cases, that can mean preparing for the very position that will eliminate your current job. In other cases, it will involve outgrowing what you do today and "graduating" to more complex and responsible positions in the future. The effect, however is the same: you strengthen your career security. You enlarge the capacity of your work to sustain a vibrant and rewarding career.

How do you acquire the right expertise for each of those two situations?

• **First, identify the skills you need.**

   To determine which skills will enhance your performance in your current job, talk to your supervisor and/or your employer's Human Resource Department. Target those capabilities that will enable you to work with your employer's newest technology, on-going or planned process improvements or changes in work practices.

To determine which skills will best prepare you to be selected for and succeed in your next job, talk to your mentor, if you have one; to other workers who already hold the kind of position you seek; or to recruiters or executive search consultants who specialize in your field. Focus on those capabilities that will either enhance your level of perceived professional competence or upgrade any certifications or licenses you may currently hold.

- **Second, determine where you can acquire the skills.**

Investigate what courses or programs are being offered by your current employer. According to the Business Roundtable, U.S. companies spend more than $70 billion annually on training for their employees. While much of this investment is made by large organizations, smaller employers are increasingly providing educational opportunities, as well.

Such instruction has a number of benefits:

(1) it costs you nothing;

(2) it's normally offered on-site so there's no travel involved;

(3) it's often provided during the business day so you don't have to give up your evenings or weekends;

and

(4) it delivers skills and/or knowledge that your current employer needs and values.

Alternatively, identify the best academic programs, training courses and other educational resources for acquiring the skills you seek. Check your professional society and trade association as well as the colleges, community colleges, and commercial training companies in your area. Compare the options you identify by assessing their cost, duration and the reputation of both the institutions that are offering the programs or courses and the instructors who are delivering them.

Also, consider doing your learning online. Today, many graduate and undergraduate academic institutions as well as a growing number of community colleges and commercial training companies are delivering instruction over the Internet. Not everyone is suited for these programs, however, as they require considerable self-discipline and the ability to manage your time effectively. That said, they are also extraordinarily convenient and provide instruction that is often just as rich as that received in a traditional classroom.

To determine if the skill or knowledge you seek can be acquired online, check the following sources:

- o DirectoryofSchools.com

- o DistanceStudies.com

- o Peterson's Online Learning Programs Directory (www.petersons.com/distancelearing/code/ search.asp)

- o WorldwideLearn.com

- o Yahoo! Education Directory/College and University Distance Learning Programs (www.yahoo.com/Education/Distance_Learning/Colleges_and_Universities).

Finally, check with your employer to see if it will cover the cost of some or all of the tuition for any of the programs you take. A 2006 survey, conducted by the Society for Human Resource Management, found that almost six-out-of-ten employers (59%) offer undergraduate tuition assistance and almost five-out-of-ten (48%) offer graduate-level tuition support. However, be sure that you understand any restrictions (e.g., paying only for select programs) and/or post-education obligations (e.g., a requirement to stay with the company for a fixed period of time) that your employer might impose for such financial aid.

• **Third, acquire the skills you need and put them to work.**

None of us lives or works in a vacuum. Distractions are likely to come up, both at home and work, during your educational program or training. Don't let these interruptions—no matter how pressing they may seem—deter you from your goal. The learning you're doing isn't optional. The skills and knowledge you're acquiring aren't nice-to-have. They are essential to your career health.

Prepare your family, your boss and your colleagues in advance; invest the time to help them understand what you're about. Enlist their assistance in minimizing the distractions and, as much as possible, dealing with them quickly when they do come up.

Whatever happens, however, don't stop. If you must, slow down, but never come to a total halt. Regardless of how long it takes, complete each and every course or program you begin so that you actually strengthen your competency in the workplace.

Then use what you've learned. Just as you must exercise your heart to strengthen your physical capacity and endurance, you must exercise your new expertise to strengthen the prospects and rewards of your career. Equally as important, expertise that is not practiced quickly expires. It must, therefore, become an integral part of the way you express your Natural in the workplace.

If you acquired a new skill to enhance your performance on-the-job, make sure your supervisor knows you have it and look for opportunities to use it in your work. If you acquired the expertise in preparation for your next job, make sure you add it to your resume, inform others in your field that you've acquired it, and begin your search for positions where you can apply your expanded capabilities in your work.

How do you implement this strategy for strengthening your career cardiovascular fitness? Exercise the following strides.

Exercise Strides for Career Cardiovascular Fitness

Stride 1: Join your professional, technical or trade association and attend its local and/or national conferences, seminars and other educational events. Learn from your peers who attend these meetings and from the formal instruction that is provided.

Repetitions: Attend at least 1 session every 2 months.

Use these events to:

- stretch and strengthen your skills and knowledge in your career field;

- access the experience-based insights and lessons learned of your peers; and

- expand your understanding of how best to apply your expanding expertise in the workplace.

Where will you perform this stride in your work?

Stride 2: Identify a social media community or employment Web-site that specializes in your field and offers an online platform (e.g., discussion forum, bulletin board or list server) for professional interaction and discussion. Join the peer-to-peer dialogue that occurs at such venues and draw on the knowledge that is shared.

A social media community might be a LinkedIn group, Facebook group or individual or corporate blog. An employment site might be a job board or career portal operated by a commercial enterprise, association and affinity group. (For the most complete listing available, see *WEDDLE's Guide to Employment Sites on the Internet* at www.weddles.com or your local library.)

Repetitions: Spend at least 30, but no more than 60 minutes per session, 2 times a week interacting with your peers online.

Use the time you invest to:

- stay on top of and conversant with the latest developments in your field;

- tap the expertise of your peers in resolving questions and/or issues that have arisen in your work;

 and

- share your knowledge and experience with the other participants.

Where will you perform this stride in your work?

Stride 3: Using the medium with which you're most comfortable (i.e., print, online, audio), subscribe to and read one or more of the leading professional or trade publications in your field.

Repetitions: Spend at least 2 hours per week reading and/or listening to such resources.

Use the literature to:

- keep track of trends and developments in your field and industry;

- assess the impact of economic, political and social events on your field, industry and employer;

  and

- gauge what currently constitutes the state-of-the-art in your profession, craft or trade and what it is likely to be in the next 3-5 years.

Where will you perform this stride in your work?

Stride 4: Using whatever medium is most effective for you (i.e., traditional classroom or online learning), take a class in your field that will optimize your performance on-the-job in the present and/or prepare you for moving to a more challenging and rewarding role in the future.

Repetitions: Finish at least 1 course every 2 years.

Continue your education in order to:

- Ensure that your professional knowledge and skills are current and commensurate with what's required for peak performance on-the-job;

- Expand the range of positions and situations in which you can work and contribute;

   and

- Refresh your passion for your work and the happiness you derive from it.

Where will you perform this stride in your work?

Other Strides

The preceding exercise strides are the minimum essential for healthy career cardiovascular development. If you are interested and able, you can supplement them with the following additional activities:

- Research and write an article for one of the professional or trade publications in your field.

- Start up and attend a study and networking group among your professional friends and colleagues.

- Identify the thought leaders in your field and make the effort to get to know them.

- Find someone who is more senior than you in your field and willing to act as your mentor; consult with them regularly.

- Explore with your employer whether it would be possible for you to take a sabbatical in order to go back to school full-time in your field.

What additional acitivies will you add to your Career Fitness strides?

My Exercise Record

Use the following worksheet to:

- Plan the time you are going to devote to each stride in the exercise and to set up a schedule for that activity in the upcoming months.

- Record your plan for and actual repetitions of each stride. Make sure your entries are accurate and up-to-date.

- Monitor your commitment to the work-in and to this exercise, in particular. Make corrective adjustments, as necessary.

The record is organized as an annual progression of monthly activity. Not every stride in every exercise is performed on a monthly basis, but the planning for and monitoring of your performance is. That continuous preparation and review optimizes the impact of your activity and ensures that you derive the maximum benefit from your effort.

Plan / Actual	Step 1	Step 2	Step 3	Step 4
Month				
Month				
Month				
Month				
Month				
Month				
Month				
Month				
Month				
Month				
Month				
Month				

II. Strengthen Your Career Circulatory System

Exercise Strategy

The lifeblood of your career is your network of friends and colleagues in your profession, craft or trade. The number and vibrancy of those contacts will often determine the range and quality of the employment opportunities you have available to you.

Why is that? Because many vacancies aren't visible to the general public. To find them, you have to know someone who will tell you about the job and point you toward the organization where it's located.

It's an old adage of the job market—and never more true than today—that over one-third of all open positions are never advertised and thus remain unknown to many, probably even most potential candidates. Career counselors even have a name for this trove of invisible employment opportunities. They call it the "hidden job market."

Employers "hide" their available jobs for two reasons:

- many employers now receive so many applications for their advertised openings, particularly those posted online, that they can't evaluate all of the candidates effectively;

    and

- many recruiters believe that the best candidates are those they reach by personal contact, either through their own networking or through their employee referral program (which is, itself, a form of networking).

Ignoring these two factors can diminish your ability to realize your Intention Commitment. When you conduct a job search that is limited to answering employment ads in the newspaper and responding to job postings on the Internet, you set yourself up to compete against a large number of people for only a subset of the available openings. In effect, you make it more difficult to attain your employment goal, and the position for which you're applying may not even be the one that's perfect for you. Your optimal job—the one that will enable you to do your best work—is just as likely to be stashed away in the hidden job market.

Additionally, when you limit your circle of contacts in your profession, craft or trade, you limit access to career development opportunities. Even when you're not actively looking for a new or better job, you want as many people as possible to know you and be aware of your work credentials. That's the best way to ensure that you'll be "top of mind" and seriously considered when a great job does come open, but isn't advertised.

So, whether you're actively looking for a job or actively engaged in your Advancement cycle, the question is the same: how can you increase your visibility in the world of work and thereby maximize your odds of finding a special employment opportunity? In short, how can you tap into all or at least more of the opportunities to develop and express your Natural, including those that you will never see advertised in print or online?

In the 21st Century world of work, these questions can be answered only one way: your career has to have a strong circulatory system. You have to enrich your career's lifeblood by strengthening your relationships with the people you know and by extending your relationships to people you don't yet know. That's the only way you can make sure that:

- You are widely recognized and respected among your peers and other professionals in the workplace who may be aware of employment opportunities that are right for you;

and

- Those peers and professionals will be inclined to tell you about those openings and/or feel comfortable passing your name along to the employers that have them.

Many of the best vacancies—and certainly the vast majority of high-paying, career enhancing jobs—are filled just that way. People who know other people connect you with employers that have open positions, and one or both of two good things happen: you will be included among a very small number of people who are seriously considered for the position and, if there is a good fit between your skills and outlook and the employer's job and culture, you will be offered the position.

From administrative roles to the seat in the corner office, a sizable segment of today's employers fill their most sensitive and important jobs through referrals made by employees, friends of the hiring manager and/or key professionals in the field. They limit the competition to those whom they know or those who are known by others known to them.

That's called networking. It's the key that opens the door to the hidden job market and, while almost everyone is aware of the practice, it is, unfortunately, done poorly almost all of the time. As a consequence, few of us see the full extent of the employment opportunities for which we are qualified, and almost none of us uncover what we would consider to be our dream job.

Most people network beneath their capabilities because they harbor one or more misconceptions about how networking is done:

MISPERCEPTION #1: Many of us fail to realize that the word says exactly what it means; it's netWORK, not net-relax or net-get-around-to-it-whenever-you-can.

To be effective, you must network as an integral part of your workday. It must be done regularly and energetically or it will not strengthen your circulatory system among peers and friends.

In an active job search, a weak circulatory system limits the openings you see to those that employers are advertising to everyone else in the job market. If you're a career athlete but not engaged in an active job search, a degraded circulatory system diminishes your reach in the workplace and the range of opportunities to which you can aspire and for which you can prepare.

In fact, the nature of today's workplace makes networking when you aren't looking for a job as important as networking when you are. Persistent, aggressive peer-to-peer interaction enables you to meet important people in your field and to tap into new ideas and information that will strengthen your performance in your current job. That will position you for success with your Achievement goal. It is also an essential element of your Development goal, helping you gain a more balanced and well rounded understanding of the preparation required to achieve your Advancement goal.

Most importantly, however, it is a fail-safe device for dealing with the uncertainty and unpredictability of the modern workplace. A strong circulatory system ensures that you have immediate, diversified access to the hidden job market should your employment situation change and throw you into transition. In essence, you've already "warmed up" for your job search and can, as a result, accelerate quickly to the pace necessary for a positive outcome.

MISPERCEPTION #2: Many of us think that networking is an exercise in generating more contacts.

We limit our efforts to the rapid collection of more and more names and addresses. It's a lot of activity, but it's not networking. In fact, this frenetic accumulation of contact information is best described as "notworking." The contacts you identify are nothing more than strangers, and strangers are seldom good connections. They don't know you or your capabilities or your track record, so there are plenty of unanswered questions about what you would be like in the workplace.

Are you dependable? Do you deliver quality work? Will you be a good team player? Would you pose a physical or psychological risk to your coworkers? Without that kind of insight into your qualities and qualifications, most of these contacts will neither share the information they have about openings of interest to you nor open private doors to the hidden job market for you.

The purpose of networking, therefore, is not to collect contacts, but to build relationships. It's not an exercise in bulking up your address book, but a process of developing familiarity and trust with other people.

If you've ever been in a relationship, and most of us have, you know that achieving that level of personal engagement takes time and effort. Hence, networking is not an activity that can be turned on and off as it's needed.

You can't start networking when you launch a job search and stop it when you find a job and expect that you will have a wide circle of people ready and willing to help you out. Instead, you must make a continuous investment in getting to know others and getting them to know you. You must work at your networking continuously if you want it to work for you.

MISPERCEPTION #3: It's O.K. to ignore the Golden Rule of Networking.

The rule is a very simple, but ironclad guideline: You have to give as good as you get. In other words, if you want others to be helpful to you in your career, you have to help them in theirs.

Networking works because you share your knowledge and insights with others who, in turn, do the same for you. It's the quintessential two-way street that promotes mutual performance improvement, mutual problem solving and, of course, mutual assistance in transition.

However, since you never know when you are going to need support in a job search or with a problem on-the-job, it's essential that you practice networking to help others all of the time. If they can count on you whenever they need your advice or assistance, you'll be able to count on them whenever you need theirs.

This shared propensity to aid and support one another creates a safety net that is one of the most effective defenses against the uncertainty of the 21st Century workplace. Networking takes the loneliness and trepidation out of confronting the unfamiliar and unknown. It makes each of us part of a team that is (or can be) our backup when dealing with changes, challenges and new opportunities. It is a kind of personal reinforcement which ensures that we aren't alone or without the resources we need not just to survive but to prosper, as well.

Work Strong

We set our sights low because we believe that networking can only involve our current coworkers or those who live where we do or people in the same profession or industry. Relationships, however, are not constrained by such artificial barriers, especially since the advent of the World Wide Web.

Life offers us a broad array of actual and potential interactions with others. The more of them we develop—the greater the number of strangers we turn into people with whom we share familiarity and trust—the stronger our career circulatory system.

Who are these relationships-waiting-to-happen? The conventional wisdom, perpetuated most recently by social and business networking sites on the Internet, is that they are people who know people who know other people who know you. In other words, your contacts are best defined by their degrees of separation from you. According to this view, the more degrees of separation you plumb, the more high powered your networking.

It's a plausible theory, but misses altogether the reality of our relationships with others. The truth is that most of us fail to tap all of those who are separated from us by a single degree of separation. Said another way, we are not making full use of our contacts among the people we know best, let alone among all of those to whom we are "connected" through someone else once, twice or more removed.

Since networking effectiveness (and efficiency) declines with each degree of separation, it only makes sense to focus your efforts on those who are closest at hand. The more members of that group with whom you develop and sustain a relationship, the more likely you are to see meaningful results from your networking.

These one-degree-of-separation connections are people you know personally. They include:

- All of your current friends;

- All of your friends with whom you have lost contact over the years;

- The mentor you have today and any mentors you may have had in the past;

- All of your former bosses;

- All of your current coworkers;

- All of your former coworkers;

- If you're a member of a professional, technical or trade association or society, all of the members whom you've previously met;

- If you've ever served on a task force, special project team or select group of any kind (for your employer, academic institution or association), all of those with whom you served;

- All of your former high school, trade school, college and graduate school classmates and those in the classes ahead of and behind you whom you knew;

- All of your former high school, trade school, college and graduate school teachers;

- If you're in a trade school, college, or graduate school (whether it's to earn a degree or to update your expertise—see Exercise I), all of your classmates and teachers;

- If you played competitive sports during your education or after it, all of your former teammates and the opponents whom you got to know;

- If you are or were involved with clubs, affinity groups or social organizations, all of the members of those groups with whom you've interacted;

  and

- If you have children, all of the parents of the other children in their classes and extracurricular activities whom you met.

The more of these one-degree-of-separation relationships-waiting-to-happen that you turn into actual relationships, the larger the team you develop and the greater the number of career enhancing opportunities you are likely to see. Yes, that takes some effort. No, it's not an unrealistic expectation.

You can now interact efficiently with all or most of these proximate connections—no matter how geographically separated they may be from you—thanks to the advent of electronic networking. Discussed below, this form of networking enables you to build relationships online, via the Internet and to do so whenever and wherever it's convenient for you. Traditional face-to-face networking remains important, but today, it can be augmented with virtual interactions.

MISPERCEPTION #5: Many of us think that networking methods and techniques never change.

Despite all of the commentary about online networking, some still believe that networking can only be performed the old fashioned way: in person. Traditional networking is clearly effective, but it's also extraordinarily time consuming. It involves meeting or speaking with another person one-on-one.

You might chat with a former coworker at a seminar sponsored by your professional association or call a neighbor who works for an employer in which you're interested. However you do it, the key to this form of networking is "who you know." If you know the right person, your networking is likely to serve you well.

Even at its most effective, however, such traditional networking is no longer sufficient, in and of itself, to keep your circulatory system functioning at peak levels. It does not enable you to build a large enough number of relationships to:

- see the full range of opportunities for which you are qualified;

  or

- ensure that your qualifications are seen by those who determine whether you will be considered or selected for the jobs you want in the future.

Networking to connect with "who you know" is still beneficial, but in the 21st Century workplace, networking to increase the number of people "who know you" is equally as central to career success. A large and continuously expanding circle of relationships is the pure oxygen of career progress, and it can only be fully tapped with technology.

You must extend your traditional networking with state-of-the-art networking on the Internet. You must bolster in-person networking with out-of-body or electronic networking.

What is electronic networking (also called e-networking)? It is both an active and a passive form of building relationships that is accelerated by online research:

- **Active e-networking** involves using the power of mass one-to-one communications online to interact with peers who have knowledge and connections that may be helpful to you;

- **Passive e-networking** involves the archiving of your work credentials on the Internet where they can be seen by employers and recruiters who have job openings that are appropriate for you;

   and

- **Online research** involves using Internet-based sources to collect background and/or contact information on select individuals with whom you have connected through your active and passive e-networking.

These three activities will increase the number of people from whom you are separated by only a single degree. Instead of connecting you with more and more people who don't know you, they expand the number of people who do. As a result, they augment both the efficiency and the effectiveness of your career's circulatory system.

Active Electronic Networking

Active electronic networking is accomplished by engaging in an online conversation that unfolds by posting messages in a trusted venue. It involves meeting new friends, new peers, new colleagues on the Internet and building relationships with them through regular online interactions.

Why is that so important in the 21st Century workplace?

- If the goal of in-person networking is to develop relationships one person at a time, the goal of electronic networking is to build relationships with dozens, even hundreds of people, all at the same time.

   Every message you send to the other members of the group with whom you are e-networking helps you build familiarity and trust—the twin pillars of a relationship—with each and every one of them. In effect, you are using the mass one-to-one communications capability of the Internet to increase the number of people who know you.

- If in-person networking often requires that you meet someone at a professional meeting or in an office somewhere, electronic networking offers the convenience of virtual (i.e., nonphysical or not-in-person) interactions that can occur anywhere you have an Internet connection and a computer.

   You can e-network while comfortably sitting on the sofa at home and you can do so sitting at a desk in your hotel room while you're on a business trip. In effect, there are no physical limitations to where you can reach out to others and help them get to know you.

- If in-person networking is usually limited to the interactions you can schedule during the business day (or evening), electronic networking provides the convenience of asynchronous conversations (i.e., the participants don't all have to be there at the same time).

   You can e-network whenever it's convenient for you 24 hours a day, 7 days a week and so can everyone else with whom you're communicating. In effect, there are no time constraints or scheduling conflicts with e-networking, and that increases the level of participation and expands the number of people who can potentially get to know you.

- If in-person networking typically involves getting dressed in business attire for a meeting in public, electronic networking is a comfortable activity that can be accomplished at home while you're wearing a bathrobe and your fuzzy slippers.

    There are no social conventions or dress codes in e-networking. It is a private activity that only becomes public when you hit the Send button and post your message for others to read. In effect, there are no appearances to keep up, and no lengthy sartorial preparations that can diminish your commitment to engaging with others who might like to get to know you.

Electronic networking is performed in two places online:

- at Web-sites that offer discussion forums, bulletin boards or list servers (also called listservs); and

- on your own blog or Web-log, should you have one.

Social Media Sites, Discussion Forums, Bulletin Boards and Listservs

These venues are specifically designed to help individuals with similar professional interests, industry backgrounds or career experiences interact with one another. They are normally hosted by professional societies and associations and by commercial sites of two kinds: social media sites designed expressly for professional networking (e.g., LinkedIn.com, Ryze.com, Ziggs.com) and employment Web-sites (e.g., Dice.com, Net-Temps.com, MeetingJobs.com).

For example, the Institute for Electrical and Electronics Engineers operates a traditional job board called the IEEE Job Site and a virtual community, where those with similar professional interests and training can network online. For the first time in history, an electronics engineer living in Houston, Texas can get to know an electronics engineer living in Honolulu, Hawaii by simply sitting in front of his or her computer and having an e-mail conversation via a forum on the IEEE Web-site.

Similarly, a human resource professional can visit the career portal known as EmployeeBenefitsJobs. com and interact with other individuals specializing in employee benefits administration. There is no membership fee to pay or occupational criteria to meet in order to participate. In most cases, a career portal is a public meeting place especially designed for those who work in the same career field or profession. They are operated by commercial organizations that rely on site advertising to support their online educational and networking services.

A newsgroup, in contrast, is a hosted site that supports e-networking by anyone with a shared interest, background or affinity. There are over two million newsgroups operating on the Internet today, all of which can be accessed through a directory at Google.com. While many of the topics discussed by newsgroup participants are work-related, many more are not. All, however, provide a way to connect and build relationships with others.

For example, a newsgroup that focuses on archeology permits those with a passion for that subject to come together online and interact. While some members of the group may actually work in the field of archeology, most are likely to be engaged in other occupations. For the latter subgroup, the sharing of knowledge and news related to archeology is actually an avocation—a leisure time pursuit—rather than a vocation or career.

Site Operated By	For Example
Professional societies and associations (see *WEDDLE's Guide to Association Web Sites*)	• American Society of Association Executives (ASAEnet.org) • American Society of Civil Engineers (ASCE.org)
Alumni groups	• Columbia College, Columbia University (http://www.college.columbia.edu/alumni) • Duke University, Fuqua School of Business (www.fuqua.duke.edu/alumni)
Affinity groups	• Baby Boomers (RetirementJobs.com) • U.S. military veterans (VetJobs.com) • Women In Technology International (WITI4Hire.com)
Newsgroups (see Google.com for a complete directory)	• For professional nail technicians (NailTech) • For those interested in ITIL (information technology infrastructure library) (ITIL Community Forum)
Career Portals (see *WEDDLE's Guide to Employment Sites on the Internet*)	• CareerBuilder.com • CollegeRecruiter.com • Dice.com • HigherEdJobs.com • LatPro.com • Monster.com
Publications	• The Chronicle of Higher Education (Chronicle.com) • FINS from The Wall Street Journal (www.fins.com) • InsideHigherEd.com
Social Media Sites	• BranchOut.com • LinkedIn.com • Ryze.com

This diversity of participants actually enhances the networking power of the newsgroup. There are those who can help a member of the group find a job in archeology and there are those who can be just as helpful in the other fields in which they work. For example, if an opportunity opened up in electrical engineering, a professional engineer with an interest in archeology might network with their professional peers at the IEEE Job Site and with those who share their interest in archeology in the archeology newsgroup.

As shown in the Table on the previous page, electronic networking occurs at sites operated by many different types of organizations.

To take full advantage of these sites, you must netWORK and practice the Golden Rule of Networking. You must participate regularly and share your knowledge and expertise with others. That may seem like an outsized commitment in your already full workday, but the return on that investment delivers three significant benefits:

- First, your contributions are seen and read by the other participants in your hometown and all over the world. As a result, you expand the number of people who know you and, thanks to the generous nature of your participation, many of them are likely to be predisposed to help you find a new job or advance your career, whenever you need and ask for such assistance.

- Second, the crisscrossing strands of personal recognition created by electronic networking help to make sure that you're never left out or overlooked when new opportunities are created in the workplace. By participating regularly in one or more online discussion groups, you are "top of mind" with a broader range of people whenever an organization reaches out to find top talent for its openings.

- Third, your participation will promote and enhance the personal growth inherent in your Development goal and the progress you are able to make in meeting your Achievement and Advancement goals. It exposes you to new ideas and insights that can upgrade your performance on-the-job and extend your capability in preparation for the next challenge in your career. It pushes you outside-the-box in your thinking by transporting you (virtually) outside-the-circle of your local friends and colleagues.

Your Own Blog or Web-log

Electronic networking can also be performed when you write your own blog or Web-log. This activity unfolds as a "public journal," an online expression of your thoughts and opinions which you invite others to read and comment on. If you then nurture that interaction into an ongoing conversation, you effectively create a relationship with everyone who participates.

Anyone can start a blog; it requires no expertise beyond the ability to think and type. Collectively, the entries that bloggers post are known as the "blogosphere," an unconstrained articulation of personal views on just about every topic the human mind can conjure up. To become a blogger, therefore, you simply have to determine the subject on which you will comment.

Many blogs are written because their authors are especially interested in politics, sports or the foibles of public figures. For e-networking, however, the key to creating an effective blog is to pick a subject:

- about which you have enough expertise and information to be able to discuss it intelligently;

- in which you have sufficient interest to explore it regularly (i.e., at least twice a week);

  and

- with which you think you can build and nurture relationships among others who share your knowledge and interest in the subject (but not necessarily your views on it).

There are numerous sites that will help you launch a blog at no cost or for a very low fee. These include:

- Blog.com (free and fee)

- Blogger.com (free)

- BlogIt.com (fee)

- TypePad.com (fee)

- WordPress.org (free)

- Xanga.com (free and fee)

The mechanics of the process are simple and straightforward. In fact, the easiest part of blogging is getting started; the real challenge is in the writing. It takes commitment and courage to sit down and express your views about a topic, knowing that they will be read by countless others around the world. Basically, you're strutting your stuff—for good or ill—on a global scale.

While blogs are often associated with extreme views and highly charged verbiage, blogging for the purpose of e-networking is not. You aren't trying to shock or insult the readers of your blog; you're writing to build a positive relationship with them. That will only happen if you express the same opinions and employ the same vocabulary that you would use in a more conventional face-to-face networking situation.

You must be genuine and insightful—who you are and the best you can be. Hence, you should treat every post on your blog as a chance to introduce the champion inside you, from the caliber of your thinking to the editing and proofreading of your grammar and syntax, from the wisdom you share with others to the respect you show them whether they agree or disagree with you. Your blog contributes to your career when it enables others to get to know the real you, not some fictitious persona that exists only online.

Passive Electronic Networking

Passive electronic networking involves archiving your resume or occupational profile in an online database or posting employment-related information in social media where it can be viewed by employers seeking prospective candidates for their open jobs. In effect, you put your work record into permanent circulation. Your credentials are visible 24 hours a day, 7 days a week, 365 days a year, and that visibility, in turn, continuously expands the number of people who know you.

This visibility can be helpful in two ways. If you're actively looking for a new or better job, it can put your work qualifications in front of employers and recruiters with unadvertised as well as advertised openings to fill. In other words, displaying your resume, profile or employment-related information online is yet another way to crack into the hidden job market.

On the other hand, if you're not looking for a job, displaying your work qualifications online is yet another way to increase the number of people who know you. That exposure helps ensure that you won't be overlooked when you are ready to move. In the past, some employers frowned on such self-promotion. Today, it's an accepted form of career self-management.

Whatever its format, your work record and credentials can now be stored on at least two kinds of sites:

- social media sites, also known as social networking sites;

  and

- employment Web-sites, also known as job boards or career portals.

Today, there are over 200 social networking sites. As their name indicates, some are intended for social interaction, but others have a decidedly professional or work-related purpose. The latter includes LinkedIn.com, Google +, and BranchOut.com, the professional area on Facebook.com. The former encompasses Facebook.com, Twitter.com and Bebo.com.

Whatever their stated purpose, however, the work-related information you post is the core content of such sites and publicly accessible by some or all of their visitors. Therefore, it's very important that you adhere to a number of guidelines when posting information about yourself and your career:

- First, keep the information current and complete;

- Second, only post information that is true and accurate;

  and

- Third, never post information (including pictures or commentary) that is defamatory or unprofessional.

Job boards, in contrast, are much more prevalent and typically store resumes and profiles in a separate, searchable database. There are now over 100,000 job boards in operation in the United States alone, and more are opening their virtual doors every day. Not all of them offer a resume or profile database, but the vast majority of those that do will permit you to archive that document at no charge for a fixed period of time (e.g., six months, a year) or even indefinitely.

Regardless of the time limit a site might impose, however, you should adhere to the same guidelines as those listed above for social networking sites when posting work-related information on a job board. An out-of-date, inaccurate or unflattering record that's visible 24/7 can be just as debilitating to your networking—and may actually be more—as not having a record online at all.

Job boards generally fall into one of two categories:

- General purpose sites: These job boards provide employment opportunities in almost all professions, crafts and trades, at almost all skill and salary levels, in almost all industries, and in most locations nationwide. They include Monster.com, Indeed.com, CareerBuilder.com, NationJob Network, SimplyHired.com, and Jobing.com.

- Niche or specialty sites: These job boards focus on employment opportunities in a specific career field, industry, location, individual affinity or some combination of those factors. They include FlexJobs.com, CoolWorks.com, VetJobs.com, CollegeRecruiter.com, JobsinLogistics. com, and the Web-site of the newspaper in your local area.

How do you know which of these sites to use when archiving your resume or profile online? There are two important factors to consider when making a selection:

Unfortunately, some will sell the contact information on your resume to marketing companies that will then pester you with product and service promotions. Others will charge you a fee for a service or product (e.g., a review of your resume, a marketing plan) and never deliver it as promised. To avoid such situations, use sites that have joined the International Association of Employment Web Sites (www.EmploymentWebSites.org). This organization is the trade association of the global online employment services industry, and its members have committed their organizations to adhering to a publicly posted Code of Ethics in their business operations.

There is no one-stop shop for career success online. The only way to ensure that your resume or profile will actually network effectively for you, therefore, is to archive it in the database at more than one site. The optimum number of sites is five, selected according to the following formula:

$$3N + 2GP = 1GJ$$

where

N = niche or specialty sites.

GP = general purpose sites.

GJ = the great job you want to find.

Among the three niche sites, pick one that specializes in your career field, one that specializes in the industry in which you have experience, and one that specializes in the location where you live or want to. If one of these factors is not important to you (e.g., you are willing to relocate), double up and archive your resume or profile at two sites in one of the remaining niche categories.

For the two general purpose sites, pick those that consistently post the kinds of jobs you want (and can realistically attain), at the salary level commensurate with your expertise and experience, and with the caliber of employer for which you would be willing to work.

Finally, archiving your work history online is certainly your right, but doing so can cause uncomfortable situations and even serious problems unless you take certain precautions. Why is that? Because, once your resume or profile is stored on a social networking site or in an open database online, it becomes a public document. It can and likely will be copied and copied again by software programs operated by other sites and by recruiters. Therefore, even if you remove your resume or profile from the database where it was originally archived, other copies are almost certain to be out there somewhere on the World Wide Web waiting to be found.

That reality can spell trouble when you're happily employed and your boss or one of your employer's recruiters goes online and finds your resume or profile. Although you may have archived that document online during a job search years before, they may leap to the conclusion that you are unhappy or looking for a better job elsewhere.

While posting your resume online is certainly your right and will strengthen your networking, your employer may decide that you are no longer loyal to the organization. That change in your standing can cause you to lose a plum assignment or a promotion you would otherwise have received. According to some reports, the appearance of an employee's resume online has even led to their termination as organizations try to insulate themselves from the potential loss of trade secrets and/ or industrial sabotage.

How can you protect yourself from such situations?

- First always date your resume and, if possible, any profile that you archive online. Place the date directly beneath your name where it can't be missed. That way, it will be immediately clear to anyone who finds the record in the future that it is the artifact of an earlier submission.

- Second, only archive your record on those social networking sites and job boards that offer a privacy or confidentiality feature. This feature may enable you to limit who can see some or all of the information you've posted about yourself. Alternatively, it may remove your name and contact information from public view, but provide a mechanism for you to release it selectively, to employers in which you're interested.

Posting your resume or profile online can also become a serious problem when it facilitates identity theft. Stolen personal information can, of course, have serious financial consequences, including lost savings and degraded credit. The harm that's done is further exacerbated by the extraordinary investment of time and effort typically required to repair the damage. There have been incidents involving identify theft that can be traced back to a resume or profile that was archived online. It's important, therefore, to guard against such threats, however unlikely they may be. To do that:

- Never provide your social security number or any other sensitive personal information to anyone who says they are an employer and contacts you via e-mail or telephone. Such information is necessary to verify your work eligibility, but legitimate employers will always ask for it in a face-to-face interview or meeting.

- Remove your home address and telephone number from your resume or profile and replace them with a cell phone number and e-mail address. Your identity cannot be easily appropriated without your home address and, often, your telephone number, so thieves will have to search elsewhere online for that information. While it is probably available on the Internet, the additional effort that's required will likely induce them to look elsewhere for an easier target.

- Always check with the site involved before uploading a tool bar or other "job search aid," even when they are offered via a message from what appears to be a legitimate job board. Unfortunately, identity thieves have learned how to imitate the look and feel of job board communications and use such deceptive messages to install malicious "spyware" on your computer. These programs track your key strokes when you do electronic banking or use your credit card online and steal that information without your even realizing it (until your bank account is drained).

Online Research

The online research associated with e-networking helps you in two ways. It speeds you to success by:

- removing at least some of the uncertainty involved in interacting with individuals whom you meet online and don't yet know well;

  and

- enabling you to find and connect with individuals who have the potential to be helpful to your career but with whom you have lost contact.

Removing Some of the Uncertainty

As we all know, contacts that occur online can be dangerous. Indeed, it's naïve to assume that everyone you meet on the Internet will have your best interests at heart. The people you connect with in cyberspace may or may not be who they say they are; they may or may not have the information or contacts they say they do; and they may or may not be trying to help you. They are strangers, and as your mother taught you very early on, you should be very careful when interacting with them … until you know them better.

That's what online research can do for you. It can help you learn more about the background and current role of the individuals you meet while networking online. That research can help you assess their credibility, reliability and the probability of their actually being able to assist you. Think of it as a reference check you conduct before you invest a lot of time and effort in building a relationship with someone.

You can also use online research during an active job search. It is an effective tool for acquiring information about an employer's representatives. Because you've submitted a resume or application, they know a great deal about you, yet you know absolutely nothing about them. That imbalance makes it difficult to uncover any connections you may have with those individuals—you might, for example, share an alma mater or have previously worked for the same employer—connections that could help your candidacy.

To avoid such disconnects, use the Internet to research the background and current role of:

- Individuals you meet in the course of your networking online—to confirm what they have told you about themselves and/or acquire information that could help you begin and develop a professional relationship with them;

- Recruiters who contact you about open positions with their organizations—to uncover interests, experiences and/or traits you have in common as those connections may encourage them to assess your credentials more favorably;

and

- Hiring managers who interview you for a job in their work unit—to uncover interests, experiences and/or traits you have in common as such associations might enhance their assessment of your potential contribution to their team and its work.

How do you conduct online research in support of your e-networking? Use browsers, search engines, online databases and business networks to acquire information posted online in the public domain. This kind of investigation is not snooping, playing Big Brother or Big Sister, or, in any way, intruding into the personal lives of others. Instead, it uses publicly accessible technology to help you acquire public information about those with whom you are networking. As such, it simply advances the informal information gathering we have always done over the backyard fence or around the water cooler when we meet someone for the first time.

Some of these technology-based tools are free, while others will charge you a fee to use them. The browsers and search engines include:

- Ask (www.ask.com)

- Bing (www.bing.com)

- GigaBlast (www.gigablast.com)

- Google (www.google.com)

- Yahoo! (www.yahoo.com).

Use these tools to search the Internet at large for information about specific individuals that appears in public documents that are accessible online. Simply enter their name in the keyword or search criteria field on the site's home page and explore the search results it produces.

It's unsafe, however, to rely on any single document in your research. There is a lot of inaccurate information and even some disinformation posted on the Internet—although probably no more than what is typically found over those backyard fences and around those office water coolers—so it's best to adopt the journalist's rule: don't rely on anything as fact unless you can confirm it with multiple sources.

The online databases and business networks include:

- JASEzone (www.jasezone.com)

- LinkedIn (www.linkedin.com)

- Yammer (www.yammer.com)

- Ziggs (www.ziggs.com)

- ZoomInfo (www.zoominfo.com).

Use these tools to search for information about individuals that has been compiled at a specific location for you. In some cases, this information will be descriptive, providing data or details about an individual, and in other cases, it will be subjective, amounting to little more than opinion, speculation or even gossip. In both cases, therefore, evaluate the credibility and reliability of the source of the information before giving it any credence in your effort to get to know a stranger.

Enabling You to Reconnect With Former Acquaintances

As noted previously, people you've known in the past can be excellent resources for uncovering opportunities that are just right for you in the future. The key to networking with them, of course, is accurate, up-to-date contact information. Online databases and search engines can help you uncover such information quickly.

These tools include:

- Google.com—a search engine that can uncover documents which include residential and business addresses, phone numbers and email addresses;

- The New Ultimates (www.newultimates.com)—a meta-directory of seven different directories, each providing access to a different kind of contact information (e.g., e-mail addresses, telephone numbers, postal addresses);

- WhitePages.com—a directory of telephone numbers for individuals and businesses;

  and

- Yahoo! People Search—http://people.yahoo.com, a directory of phone numbers and postal and email addresses.

In most cases, all you need to use these tools effectively is the name of the person you're trying to reach and the name of the city where you think they currently work or reside. If you're no longer sure of their address, use their last known location. Many of the directories store previous as well as current addresses, so it's often possible to find an individual even with out-of-date information.

Since you've not recently been in touch with these former colleagues and friends, it's best to approach them with care. If possible, avoid the filters and inaccuracy of office telephone systems and receptionists and reconnect with them when they're at home. E-mail is preferable, but the telephone is acceptable if you time your call to avoid being intrusive.

Begin with a succinct, but detailed "memory jogger" to establish your relationship. For example, Hey Jim, this is Sam Edwards. We worked together in the Accounting Department at Busch's a couple of years ago. Then, ask if there would be a convenient time for you to get reacquainted. Don't put them on the spot, but do try to set a specific time and date for a follow-up phone call or meeting.

Building a strong career circulatory system means using traditional and technology-based networking to make yourself ever-better known to an ever-expanding network of personal and professional contacts. For an athlete, a healthy circulatory system increases their red blood cell count and enhances the flow of oxygen to their body. Those developments give them more strength and greater endurance.

For people in the 21st Century workplace, a strong career circulatory system increases the number of people "who they know" and "who know them." These contacts give them the ability to upgrade their performance on-the-job and to be considered for the best employment opportunities, including those in the hidden job market. Those advantages, in turn, put them within reach of earning a bigger paycheck and greater satisfaction from their work.

Exercise Strides for Career Circulatory System Fitness

Stride 1: While you are attending the local and/or national conferences, seminars and other events sponsored by your professional or trade association (see Exercise I), work on meeting and building a relationship with both people you know and those you don't.

Repetitions: At each event, practice the 2:1 Rule: introduce yourself to at least 2 people whom you've not met before and engage in at least 1 extended conversation with someone you already know.

Use these conversations to:

• Look for interests, experiences or aspects of your background (e.g., college(s) from which you were graduated, employer(s) for which you've worked, place(s) where you've lived) that you have in common;

• Share your knowledge, expertise and experience, not to promote yourself, but to help those with whom you are interacting;

and

• Seek assistance (should you need it), but only from those whom you have previously met and with whom you have already developed a relationship.

Where will you perform this stride in your work?

Whenever you are online with the discussion forum offered by your favorite LinkedIn group or employment Web-site (see Exercise I), look for ways to interact with and get to know more of the other participants. Respond to their questions, refer to their earlier posts and/or engage them in a dialogue, so that they are more familiar with you and more comfortable with your understanding of the field in which you both work.

If you have the time and inclination, start your own blog and contribute to it regularly. Respond to others who read and comment on the blog; show them the courtesy and respect they're due and, wherever possible, establish an on-going dialogue with them.

Repetitions: Reach out to and interact with at least 1 person during every online session. (As indicated in Exercise I, participate in these sessions 2-times per week.)

Use the time you invest online to:

- Make meaningful contributions consistently to specific individuals online;

- Establish yourself as a unique person with a well defined (and positive) persona;

  and

- Enhance your occupational stature through the quality of your posts and the commitment you show to supporting your peers.

Where will you perform this stride in your work?

Stride 3: Using whatever medium is most comfortable and effective for you (e.g., software, Rolodex or an old fashioned address book), set up an archive or database of professional contacts with whom you have established a relationship and keep it current.

Repetitions: Add the names of at least 5 new contacts per quarter to your database. Use Strides 1-2 to identify appropriate colleagues, coworkers and peers.

Once established, this archive/database will:

- Provide a visible way for you to measure your progress in building a strong circulatory system;

- Help you keep track of the movement of your contacts as they pursue their own careers; and

- Make it simple and easy for you to keep your records up-to-date for each and every person in your expanding circle of occupational and other connections.

Where will you perform this stride in your work?

Stride 4: Interact with the individuals in your archive/database on a regular basis. You can connect with them using Strides 1-2 or with a telephone call, an e-mail message or even a hand-written note delivered the old fashioned way by postal mail.

Repetitions: Network with at least 10% of those in your database at least once a month, thereby ensuring that you will interact with at least 100% of your contacts each year.

These interactions will help you build familiarity and trust by:

- Signaling your commitment to getting to know your colleagues and peers better;

- Deepening and enriching the relationships you have with others (e.g., by remembering their birthday, congratulating them on a recent accomplishment or simply by being in touch);

  and

- Making yourself available to others and, thus, in a position to help them whenever they need it (just as you hope they will help you).

Where will you perform this stride in your work?

Other Strides

The preceding exercise strides are the minimum essential for building a strong circulatory system for your career. If you are interested and able, you can supplement them with the following additional activities:

- Build a relationship with one or more executive recruiters who specialize in your field.

- Chair an educational event or conference and/or run for office in your professional society.

- Get to know the Executive Director of your trade association or your undergraduate or graduate school's alumni association.

- Attend a reunion of your high school, college or graduate school alumni organization and reconnect with former classmates and friends. If one is available, add your name and contact information to the alumni directory it maintains.

- Further hone your networking skills by reading a book or attending a training course on the subject.

What additional acitivies will you add to your Career Fitness strides?

My Exercise Record

Use the following worksheet to:

- Plan the time you are going to devote to each stride in the exercise and to set up a schedule for that activity in the upcoming months.

- Record your plan for and actual repetitions of each stride. Make sure your entries are accurate and up-to-date.

- Monitor your commitment to the work-in and to this exercise, in particular. Make corrective adjustments, as necessary.

The record is organized as an annual progression of monthly activity. Not every stride in every exercise is performed on a monthly basis, but the planning for and monitoring of your performance is. That continuous preparation and review optimizes the impact of your activity and ensures that you derive the maximum benefit from your effort.

Plan / Actual	Step 1	Step 2	Step 3	Step 4
Month				
Month				
Month				
Month				
Month				
Month				
Month				
Month				
Month				
Month				
Month				
Month				

III. Develop All of Your Career's Muscle Groups

Exercise Strategy

The scope or breadth of your expertise is the musculature of your career. The greater the diversity of your occupational skills and knowledge, the greater the likelihood your career will both support you in your current work and propel you forward toward ever more interesting and challenging employment opportunities. Said another way, the more multidimensional your capabilities, the stronger you are as an employee and as a candidate for a new or better job.

One-dimensional people can fill a single position well, as long as they are at the top of their game. Historically, they have been valued employees because they could be counted on to perform admirably in their assigned job. They were competent in their field and delivered their skill as required by their position description. In the 20th Century, their employers expected and needed no more.

The 21st Century, however, has dramatically altered the nature of the marketplace, pressuring employers with new and vastly more complex forces. They are now confronted with a seemingly unending stream of stronger competitors in global and domestic markets, higher shareholder expectations, more capable workers in other countries, rapid technological obsolescence and development, broad process innovations and re-engineering, and more aggressive regulation by federal and pan-regional governments. This conglomeration of pressures has produced a business environment that is faster-paced, more demanding of rapid innovation, and less forgiving of strategic and tactical errors than ever before.

Employers must adjust to these new dynamics or fall behind and eventually fall apart. They cannot wait them out. They cannot hold on until the old way of doing things returns. It never will.

These changes are not aberrations or short-term phenomena. They are permanent and pervasive; they affect local as well as multinational employers, small as well as large enterprises, service as well as manufacturing organizations. As a consequence, they have also changed the world of work, creating a workplace unlike any other in history. It is unprecedented, unfamiliar and unnerving, and it is here to stay.

This new workplace continuously rearranges:

- the number of jobs required—what work must be done;

- the nature of the required jobs—how the work must be done;

- the kinds of talent capable of performing the required jobs—who will do the work;

- the location of the required jobs—where the work will be done;

  and

- the pace at which the required jobs must be performed—when the work will be done.

Most of us have probably already had some experience with these changes, but we are loathe to admit that they now define the reality of our workplace. And yet, they do. They alter both the substance of our work and the baseline requirements for a meaningful and successful career.

Jobs that are available today can evaporate, be significantly redefined, moved or combined with other jobs tomorrow. As those shifts occur—as the new reality of the workplace continuously evolves—the skills and knowledge required to obtain employment morph, as well. For that reason, expertise in a single skill—no matter how well developed or critical to an employer's current success—is no longer sufficient for career security.

Uni-dimensional capability leaves you without a fall-back—a way of adjusting to the rapidly evolving climate change in business. What worked in the 20th Century—a highly focused specialization of capability—doesn't work in the 21st Century. It denies you the resilience and capacity necessary to adapt. To put it bluntly, it makes you a dinosaur.

What must you do to survive and prosper in this redefined and substantially more complex workplace? Achieve multidimensionality.

Multidimensional workers can cope with ever-changing circumstances because they can adapt to the new requirements for career success as they emerge. They have multiple capabilities—two or more skills or areas of knowledge. They see themselves and encourage employers to view them as several different workers-in-one. As employees, therefore, they offer a broader spectrum of potential contributions.

Multidimensional workers:

- are expert in their primary field (see Exercise I);

    and

- acquire "switch expertise" which enables them to use all or part of another area of expertise to expand the kinds of work they can do in the workplace;

    and/or

- acquire "applications expertise" which enables them to use their primary expertise more effectively and/or in a variety of workplace situations.

This diversity of capability empowers multidimensional employees to work in more than one set of conditions and/or in more than one job. They are the triple threat who can compete in multiple events on a track team, the versatile performer who is equally adept at the hill climbs and the straight-away sprints in cross country.

They can fill in when coworkers are sick or away on maternity or family leave or on vacation. They can move to another position and take on new responsibilities when an employee departs or is terminated. They can help out when the pace of activity surges in other parts of the organization, and they can switch to a new assignment when marketplace demands alter what their employer needs.

From an employer's perspective, a multidimensional worker is "the complete package." These individuals bring multiple talents to their employers and consistently apply those talents in different roles and situations. They aren't overachievers; they are ultra-achievers. They contribute broadly, as needed by their employer. Their strength isn't specialized knowledge; it is diversified capability.

Organizations will compete to hire multidimensional workers, and they will pay dearly to hang on to them. Why? Because they provide greater value in the workplace. They:

- perform their assigned job superbly;

- help raise the performance of coworkers in their assigned jobs;

- adjust to new requirements in their current job and accomplish them effectively;

    and

- tolerate reassignment to new jobs and perform them superbly, as well.

Such employees are the superstars of the 21st Century workplace. Their multifaceted excellence fuels the success of their employers. Indeed, those organizations will struggle to survive let alone prosper without them. This multidimensionality, therefore, acts as the growth hormone of career security. It infuses workers with versatility, ensuring that they can deliver peak performance in a broad array of roles and situations.

How do you build multidimensionality?

First, you have to understand and accept its importance in the 21st Century workplace. Then, you must determine which additional dimensions of capability are likely to serve you best in that environment.

While requirements are almost always evolving, there are certain foundation areas that are unlikely to diminish in importance. Indeed, many of these core components of expertise are actually projected to become even more essential to organizational success over the next five years. Identified in a study conducted by The Conference Board and the Society for Human Resource Management, they are:

- Critical thinking / problem solving skills;

- Information technology application skills;

- Teamwork / collaboration skills;

- Leadership skills;

- Oral communication skills;

  and

- Written communication skills.

It would be difficult to argue about the importance of any of these factors, but without any workplace context, it's impossible to know what to do with them. To determine how best to employ such capabilities in your career, therefore, you must recognize the limitations everyday living imposes on you—that means setting priorities—and provide a framework for their application on-the-job—that means organizing these skills into two categories:

- Functional

  and

- Performance.

Functional skills enable you to accomplish specific tasks. They determine what work you can do. They are the building blocks of your primary and switch expertise. Performance skills, in contrast, enable you to improve the way such tasks are accomplished (e.g., the caliber of the contribution your work makes to an employer, the degree of influence your work has on the organization and your coworkers). They determine how well you can do your work. Performance skills are the building blocks of your primary and applications expertise.

Functional Skills

The baseline for your development of functional skills is the currency and depth of your knowledge and experience in your profession, craft or trade. As detailed in Exercise I, you must achieve and sustain a state-of-the-art capability in your primary field of work and deliver it on-the-job in order to maintain a healthy career.

That degree of expertise, however, is only your starting point. You should also augment your workplace capacity with skills that enable you to perform:

- in a greater variety of circumstances and situations;

  and

- with a greater variety and number of coworkers and customers.

These skills "plus-up" your ability to function and contribute on-the-job and/or beyond-the-job. They add to what you can do within your current job and within your current employer.

While there are many functional skills from which to choose, two are particularly important in the 21st Century workplace. They are illustrated in the examples below.

EXAMPLE #1: You are employed as an accountant and are already an expert in the principles and skills of accounting.

If you then acquire an additional skill in using project management software, you have extended your capacity to contribute to your employer because now you can work effectively in a number of functional areas within the enterprise. These might include the Finance Department, where your contribution would draw on your accounting expertise or in a line division or on special project team, where your work could encompass the planning and coordination of operations and the monitoring of their financial status.

EXAMPLE #2: You are employed as a sales clerk and are skilled in all aspects of customer service and retail selling.

If your native language is English and you acquire the ability to speak Spanish, you have extended your capacity to contribute to your employer because you can now effectively function in a number of different retail environments. These might include its stores in English-speaking, Spanish-speaking or mixed language neighborhoods as well as in stores where neighborhoods are changing from one predominant language to another. In addition, you can train and/or assist your coworkers who are limited in their ability to serve and sell to customers because they speak only one language.

The first example describes the acquisition of technological literacy; the second demonstrates the extension of one's communication literacy. More than any others, these two competencies can plus-up your functional capacity and reinforce your contribution to an employer.

Should you acquire other functional skills during your career? Of course. Career Fitness, however, focuses first on developing and refining these two capabilities (plus two performance skills described later) as they are likely to have the greatest beneficial impact on your perceived (and actual) value as a job seeker or employee.

Technological Literacy

Advanced technology is the key enabler of functional diversity in all organizations today. Regardless of an employer's industry, location, products or services, the availability and appropriate application of state-of-the-art hardware and software enable it to streamline processes and procedures, optimize operations and improve results. Whether it's the use of robotics on an assembly line or the installation of a customer relationship management system in a bank, the technology empowers the organization's employees to function more efficiently and effectively. As a result, the organization achieves higher quality output, lower costs, stronger productivity, and better customer service.

Despite all of its power, however, advanced technology is simply a lot of expensive silicon chips and software code, unless it can be effectively used on-the-job by an organization's employees. Technology is potential—nothing more, but nothing less. Technology used by people realizes that potential, at least in part, while technology used competently by people enables them to achieve superior results.

Although not every employer understands that axiom, the most successful organizations do. They recognize the value of employees and employment candidates who can leverage technology to extend their own functional prowess as well as the performance of others around them. In most cases, this capacity does not involve programming in computer languages or the administration of complex information systems. For the majority of us, it is, instead, the ability to accommodate technology as a coworker and, in collaboration with it, to produce a competitive advantage for our employers.

Technological literacy can include, but is not limited to any of the following:

- The ability to use advanced hardware and software systems in the office and/or on the plant floor (e.g., computers, manufacturing systems);

- The ability to troubleshoot and/or identify and fix problems with such systems;

- The ability to use business operations software (e.g., database management, enterprise resource planning) in designing, implementing and monitoring local and/or dispersed activities;

- The ability to use communication technology and/or the Internet to acquire and/or distribute operations-related information;

  and

- The ability to communicate effectively with hardware and software developers when describing technology-related problems, requirements and opportunities.

If you are technologically literate, therefore, you strengthen your career security in two ways:

- Because you can help an organization maximize its return on investment in advanced technology, you are much less likely to be the target of a restructuring or downsizing program. In a very real sense, the organization needs you in order to achieve its own success, and that need translates into value in the labor market. It gives you security, even in an ever-changing and, therefore, insecure business environment.

- Your ability to use advanced technology also gives you a stronger negotiating position when discussing a starting salary or a raise. In other words, you can use the market demand for your skills the same way an employer does for its products or services: the greater the demand, the higher the price you can (and should) charge. Such behavior isn't inappropriate or indulgent; it is, as company executives are fond of saying, simply the market behaving rationally.

Communication Literacy

The 21st Century workplace is dependent upon the acquisition and assimilation of information. Information itself, however, has little or no value—indeed, it can actually be harmful—if it is not clearly and accurately communicated.

The effective transfer of information from one party to another is the only way that information can be used for:

- Strategy formulation and execution;

- Research and development;

- Service and product design, development and delivery;

- Sales planning and closing;

- Customer service and support;

- Decision-making;

- Problem-solving;

  and

- Management and leadership.

Virtually every activity in today's organizations—from Finance to Strategic Planning, from Marketing to Human Resource Management—depends upon the communication literacy of its workforce.

What happens when communication literacy is lacking? A brilliant research scientist cannot describe his breakthrough to his boss, and the budget for his program is cut as a result. A customer cannot get the service they want and leaves the store empty-handed. Two otherwise successful business people fail to negotiate a contract that would be good for both of their employers.

Communication literacy is thus central to organizational success, and its importance is only increasing even as its definition is becoming more complex. The American workplace is growing ever more diverse, the American education system is graduating ever fewer students competent in English, and U.S. companies are pushing ever further into the global marketplace. As a consequence, the ability to speak, write and comprehend English and one or more additional languages—a multilingual expertise—is fast becoming a precious organizational asset. Those who have it offer a broadly utilitarian capacity to employers.

For example, those who can speak:

- Spanish as well as English can help an organization reach Hispanic consumers, the fastest growing demographic group in the United States;

- Chinese as well as English can help an organization reach the consumers of China, the fastest growing market in the world;

- German as well as English can help an organization negotiate a joint venture that will bring new products or services into the U.S. market;

  and/or

- Russian as well as English can help an organization negotiate contracts for the oil, gas and other natural resources required for the manufacture of products destined for both the U.S. and world markets.

In short, communication literacy powers an individual's functional diversity that, in turn, enables and multiplies organizational success in both domestic and world markets. It is a capability every employer needs and struggles mightily to find.

According to a 2004 poll of 120 major U.S. companies by the College Board, correcting workers' deficient communication skills now costs employers $3.1 billion annually. A 2006 study by the Conference Board determined that such remediation is undertaken because 81% of employers find their new hires lack even basic English composition skills.

They are unable to write memos; compose business letters; or author, contribute to or edit technical reports. Further, researcher and author Graciela Kenig has found that this English language deficit is compounded by a growing need for employees who can also speak a second language competently, especially in such industries as healthcare, financial services, sales and marketing, social services and public services.

If you develop communication literacy, therefore, you strengthen your career security in several ways:

- First, you are able to articulate your knowledge and ideas with precision and impact so that they can be understood, acted upon, and appreciated by your boss, your coworkers, and your employer's customers and business partners. However, since the workplace is a multimedia environment, you gain this advantage only if you are competent in both written and oral communications.

- Second, you can work for a greater variety of employers in a greater range of geographic locations and work situations. That capacity, in turn, increases the number of employment options for which you are qualified, and those options give you greater control over what work you do and where and how you do it.

- Third, the scarcity of multilingual competency among workers in many regions of the U.S. will make you a more valuable employee or employment prospect. As with technological literacy, that value will increase the demand for your services in the labor market, and that escalating demand, in turn, will raise the level of your compensation.

Complementary Areas of Expertise

In addition to technological and communication literacy, there are other, complementary areas of expertise that can enhance your functional capacity. These capabilities enable you to accept additional responsibilities with your employer. Using technology effectively and communicating clearly extend what you can do within your assigned function; the acquisition of complementary expertise extends the number of functions to which you can be assigned.

To determine which complementary areas of expertise you should acquire, explore your current place of work. Identify critical functions that would undermine organizational performance if they could not be accomplished. Focus on those tasks or activities that interact or intersect with your own job:

- If you work as a member of a team, unit, department or other group, learn how to perform one or more functions that are normally the role of one or more other members of the group.

- If you work alone, learn some of the functions of others in the organization who produce whatever you need (e.g., information, material) to do your job or who use whatever you produce (e.g. information, materiel) to do theirs.

Once you've selected a specific function, learn the skills involved by cross-training with your coworkers on-the-job. Acquire the expertise necessary to "pinch hit" for those employees when they're not available. This capability, however, should be limited to that required to execute a key, but clearly delineated subset of their tasks, not the entirety of their job.

Your goal is to support, not replace them. You're positioning yourself to help them in the event of a sudden spike in their workload or to provide a partial substitute for them in the event of an unusual or unexpected situation on-the-job—an illness, an emergency at home, even a crisis in their unit when they're away on a business trip.

Performance Skills

Multidimensionality can also be developed through the acquisition of skills that strengthen the way you perform your work. Such skills give you the capacity to apply your expertise to its maximum benefit in an organization. In other words, performance skills are enabling competencies.

They promote your ability to achieve a more focused and directed impact in the workplace. They help you improve your effectiveness on-the-job, regardless of the position you hold or the employer for which you work. As a consequence, performance skills upgrade the caliber of your work—the contribution you can make to an organization—and, thus, your value to it.

There are two kinds of performance skills that are especially important to achieving career health in the 21st Century. As noted with functional skills, Career Fitness focuses on your acquisition of these capabilities first as they can more immediately and significantly enhance your career than can other enabling competencies. These skills are:

- Business literacy;

  and

- Leadership.

Business Literacy

Every organization creates a track record of its operations and their outcome. It may be successful, it may be failing, or it may be bumping along somewhere in between. Its performance may be stable or it may be moving in a new direction, and that shift may be for the better or for the worse. It may be building a strong foundation for the future or it may be frittering away whatever advantage it has achieved in the past.

The only way to know for sure, at least in the business world, is to examine the record. The language of employers is numbers, however, so the only way to understand the record is to know how to read financial statements. Especially in for-profit enterprises, if you understand the data provided on the balance sheet and income statement of your employer, you have an unvarnished and accurate picture of its health and future prospects.

The ability to parse and interpret these data is business literacy, a subset of professionalism in every field of work. It, too, enhances your career security because the knowledge it provides helps you optimize your performance on-the-job and avoid unexpected changes or developments for which you are, as a result, unprepared.

Business literacy clearly depends on data, however, and an employer's records are not always available. If you work for a public company—one that sells shares of its ownership to individuals and institutions in the public domain—you can obtain these data. Such companies must report key financial metrics to their owners, the U.S. government and the public at large.

To acquire these records:

- call or write the Investor Relations department of the company and request its Annual Statement or Report;

  and/or

- access the EDGAR database of the U.S. Securities and Exchange Commission, which is open to the public at the agency's Web-site (www.sec.gov) and review the company's 10-K (annual) and 10-Q (quarterly) filings.

If you work for a private company, on the other hand, the record is likely to be more difficult to obtain. A private company is not required to release financial statements to the public, and most of these organizations seldom do. It may be possible to gain some perspective on your employer's performance, however, by requesting the voluntary release of a partial record. Ask the owner or appropriate executive to provide a subset of the company's financial data that will provide at least an indication of the organization's status, without intruding on its owner's right to privacy.

These data might include:

- quarterly revenue;

- the trend in revenue year-to-date (e.g., percentage increase or decrease from the beginning of the year);

- quarterly sales;

- the trend in sales year-to-date;

- the trend in expenses year-to-date;

  or

- the percentage change in revenue, sales and/or expenses from the prior year to the current one.

How do you acquire the skills of understanding and evaluating the financial records of employers?

There are usually courses available at community colleges and in the continuing education programs at four-year colleges and universities. In addition, you may be able to get some instruction from a friend who is a certified public accountant or even teach yourself by reading any of numerous primers that are available in bookstores.

Being business literate doesn't mean you have the expertise of a Chief Financial Officer or a stock market analyst. Rather, it indicates that you are able to comprehend your employer's business model—the fundamental dynamics of how it generates revenue and controls expenses in order to produce a profit—and to determine the direction of your employer's financial health—up, down, or sideways. That insight, in turn, positions you to maximize the impact of your work in the organization and to minimize the risk to you of bolt-out-of-the-blue changes in corporate policy, strategy or status.

Business literacy, in essence, is the skill of knowing what to look for in the financial records of an employer. That competency confers two important advantages:

- First, having a finite measure of an organization's financial performance enables you to assess the effectiveness of its leadership and strategy. Just as employers want to hire talented workers, you should try, whenever possible, to work for talented organizations—those with leaders who have the vision and operational acumen to succeed.

- Second, an understanding of how a for-profit company makes its money enables you to determine how your job fits in and contributes to the overall mission of the organization. You can make the connection between what you do and what the organization needs from you in order to accomplish its mission.

Even more important, you can trace the impact of your work on the organization's performance. While all of us can be motivated by the intrinsic satisfaction that comes from doing a job well, most of us also want to know that our work is useful and helpful to the organization that employs us. We want to know how to make a difference and the outcome when we do.

Leadership

In survey after survey, Chief Executive Officers in large and small U.S. businesses have consistently cited leadership as a skill that is central to organizational success, yet especially difficult to find among employees. Workers who see themselves as leaders and act on that vision—regardless of their title in the organization—provide their employers with several important advantages. They:

- bring their best work to the job each and every day;

- see challenges as opportunities to improve their work, not as an excuse for sub-par performance;

  and

- set an example that upgrades the performance of their coworkers and reinforces their morale.

Leadership is very different from management. Managers derive their authority from where they sit on the organization chart; leaders gain their authority from where they stand on principles. Managers focus on "know how" and doing things right. They rely on numerical analyses and strive to optimize organizational processes and practices.

Leaders, in contrast, value data and analysis, but focus on "know why" and doing the right things. They rely on human character and strive to optimize the experience of those who are touched by an organization's processes and practices (e.g., coworkers, customers).

Recent studies seem to indicate that while employers have a sufficient supply of managers, they are facing a severe shortage of leaders. Senior executives know the importance of leadership—after all, that's what they provide in the organization—but they look around their offices and facilities and don't see an abundance of leaders. The organization may have thousands of employees, but CEOs recognize the right stuff in far too few of them.

Interestingly, most executives believe this scarcity is caused by the exceptional nature of the ability to lead. It is, in their view, an aptitude—a characteristic that you either have or you don't—while management is a skill that anyone can learn—witness the rapid growth and vibrant health of graduate MBA programs. These executives see leadership as a salutary, but extremely rate alignment of genes and leaders, therefore, as candidates for the endangered species list.

Organizational research, however, reveals that exactly the opposite is true. It convincingly demonstrates that:

- All organizations have two types of leaders: formal leaders who hold titular leadership positions, and informal leaders who can (and do) occupy staff and other non-supervisory positions. Formal leaders rely on the authority of their position to impose their will on the organization; informal leaders leverage the caliber of their own work and their character to influence the actions of others, to model superior standards for their coworkers, and to nurture the pride and esprit of everyone in the organization.

- The quintessential characteristic of a leader—to view their role more broadly than self-interest, to use the best they can be to the benefit of those around them as well as themselves—is an innate attribute of the human species. It is an element of our spiritual genome. In effect, we all have the DNA to become a leader, to infuse our approach to employment with a commitment to serving others, to imbue the purpose of our work with a more inclusive, more impactful vision.

Leadership, therefore, is a fundamental aspect of our Natural; it is a potential that's resident in all of us. Whether we realize our potential, therefore whether we exercise that ability to lead through our best work is a matter of choice. We make the decision to be (or not) this part of who we are.

You can't simply declare yourself a leader, of course. As with every other aspect of your Natural, the realization of your leadership potential can only be achieved with practice. Regardless of your experience as a leader—whether you are already playing such a role in your field or have just begun to probe how best to do it in your work—you must continuously stretch your understanding of leadership principles and practices.

In other words, leadership may be an inherent human trait, but its effective expression is an art achieved through rigorous personal development. It must be continuously honed and exercised to achieve and sustain its full potency. For that reason, successful leaders are always students, not of case studies and theories, but of human behavior and values.

The research makes clear that, despite conventional perception, no shortage of leadership talent actually exists today. Quite the contrary, all organizations have an unlimited and largely overlooked supply of leaders. It resides as potential in every one of their employees. The decision to realize that potential, however, is an individual one and can have unintended consequences. It may, for example, surprise or alarm some of your coworkers and even threaten others.

Nonetheless, for good employers, the development and expression of your natural leadership talent will be viewed as a "found asset"—a positive discovery that dramatically enhances the perception of your performance and the assessment of your value as an employee. If institutional leaders are hard to find, you are an even more rare phenomenon: an employee who leads their coworkers by example.

This revised view of your contribution to the organization, in turn, gives you several career invigorating benefits:

- Because you can be consistently relied on to do your best work and to upgrade the work of others, your employer will give you its most important and interesting assignments;

- Because you deliver a premium return on every dollar your employer invests in you, it is likely to pay you at the top of the scale for your field and to spend more on your training and development, strengthening even further your capabilities and position in the workplace;

- Because you see it as a part of your job to empower and help others to do their best work, you will enjoy the respect and the loyalty of your peers;

  and

- For all of these reasons, you will have countless employers knocking on your door all of the time to present new opportunities and more interesting and rewarding challenges.

Finally, there's an old saying in the workplace that employers want workers who can pull their own weight. In the past, that phrase described employees who could and would do the work they were assigned with a minimum of direction and assistance. They were valued because they got the job done.

Today, that phrase has been reformulated. To be a valued employee in the 21st Century workplace, you must be able and willing to pull more than your own weight. You must have the strength to expand both the variety of roles you can play in an organization and the variety of situations in which you can play them. In essence, you are valued because you have the scope or breadth of expertise to get lots of jobs done and do all of them effectively and efficiently.

The following exercise steps will help you build the career musculature to perform at that level.

Exercise Steps for Career Musculature Fitness

Stride 1: Enroll in a training or academic program that will build your functional capacity or performance expertise.

You can either volunteer for a training program provided by your employer or take a course offered by a commercial vendor or academic institution. Before beginning, make sure you're operating at the top of your game in your own career field and that you're making a meaningful contribution in your own job.

It's also very important not to overdo your commitment to learning. While this set of activities is entitled Develop All of Your Muscle Groups, it does not end with skill acquisition. Employers do not value serial course-takers; they value people who get work done.

Build time into your work-in for practicing on-the-job what you've learned in-the-classroom. Seek out assignments that will let you flex your new occupational muscles. If your employer can't provide them, take the initiative to for opportunities in your professional association or in volunteer organizations.

Repetitions: Take a minimum of 1, but no more than 2 skill-building courses every two years.

Embarking on a continuous curriculum of developmental activities will:

- Give you the tools to define a larger role for yourself at work and to execute that role effectively;

- Reinforce your confidence in your ability to adapt to changing conditions and requirements in the workplace;

  and

- Enhance your standing with your employer and your peers as they become aware of your commitment to supporting their success as well as your own.

Where will you perform this stride in your work?

Stride 2: Improve your peripheral vision by using your breaks at work as instructional opportunities.

You can learn a lot about other parts of the organization for which you work by simply walking around. Make sure, of course, that these excursions do not interfere with your daily on-the-job responsibilities or interrupt the work of others. If your facility is too small for such an exploration or your employer is a virtual organization with a widely distributed workforce, meet up with your coworkers in other venues (online and off). These might include employer-supported special interest groups, ad hoc committees and task forces, and volunteer activities.

Repetitions: Take 1 such perspective-widening walk around the organization (or participate in 1 meeting) each month.

This process of "learning by observing" will:

- Strengthen your circulatory system (see Exercise II), providing an opportunity for you to meet more of your colleagues at work;

- Make you smarter about how and where work gets done in your employer, helping you to understand your own role in the organization better and determine how and where you could potentially enlarge that role;

  and

- Help you to select the functional or performance skills that will best prepare you to expand the scope of your contribution in the workplace.

Where will you perform this stride in your work?

Work Strong

Stride 3: Join a local self-improvement group that will help you enhance your capabilities at work.

Such groups exist in most communities and in a growing number of workplaces. Many employers now support onsite meetings of such organizations as Toastmasters, where you can hone your verbal communication skills, or a PowerPoint or Apple User's Group, where you can enhance your technological literacy.

The location of a group's meetings, however, is less important than the caliber of the insight it makes accessible to you. Select a group that will connect you with others who can consistently expose you to new information and knowledge and, in the process, expand your skill set.

Repetitions: While your opportunity for participation will be determined by the group's meeting schedule, try to find one that gets together for at least 2 hours each month (in 1 or more meetings) and then attend regularly.

Use these interactions to:

- Connect with others who have different work skills that are complimentary to yours;

- Acquire additional knowledge and skills that will extend your ability to contribute in the workplace;

  and

- Enhance your stature through the assistance and support you are able to provide to your coworkers.

Where will you perform this stride in your work?

Stride 4: Make yourself an apprentice. Seek out an expert and solicit their assistance in acquiring a specific functional or performance skill.

This individual is not your mentor; rather, they act as a special coach who imparts knowledge to you about a discrete subject or task. They are, in essence, a guide to practical workplace expertise.

You will, of necessity, apprentice with a number of different experts throughout your career. The key to this stride, therefore, is to ensure that you are always interacting with one and that those interactions are useful. Be realistic, however, about the expert with whom you seek to work:

- Don't aim too high—for example, it's probably not appropriate to ask your employer's Chief Financial Officer (CFO) to teach you how to read an income statement.

- Don't overlook aiming low—those who are situated beneath you on the organization chart may well have the expertise you seek.

- Don't only aim where you work—there are experts with knowledge that can be helpful to you but are not collocated with you or working for your employer.

Repetitions: Interact with an expert at least 1 time every 2 months.

These apprenticeships will help you:

- Gain an appreciation for the mastery and wisdom of those working around you;

- Acquire new skills from someone who has tested and refined them in real world applications; and

- Position you among your peers as a person who has both the humility to recognize what you don't know and the determination to expand what you do know.

Where will you perform this stride in your work?

Other Strides

The preceding exercise strides are the minimum essential for building a robust musculature system for you career. If you are interested and able, you can supplement them with the following additional activities:

- Hone your leadership skills by seeking office in the local or regional chapter of your professional association or trade association.

- Find a coworker who speaks another language and sit next to them at lunch. Ask them to teach you some basic phrases over your soup and salad.

- Tune out the in-flight movie on business trips and tune-in to a self-instructional program that you've downloaded on your personal computer or PDA.

What additional acitivies will you add to your Career Fitness strides?

My Exercise Record

Use the following worksheet to:

- Plan the time you are going to devote to each stride in the exercise and to set up a schedule for that activity in the upcoming months.

- Record your plan for and actual repetitions of each stride. Make sure your entries are accurate and up-to-date.

- Monitor your commitment to the work-in and to this exercise, in particular. Make corrective adjustments, as necessary.

The record is organized as an annual progression of monthly activity. Not every stride in every exercise is performed on a monthly basis, but the planning for and monitoring of your performance is. That continuous preparation and review optimizes the impact of your activity and ensures that you derive the maximum benefit from your effort.

Plan / Actual	Step 1	Step 2	Step 3	Step 4
Month				
Month				
Month				
Month				
Month				
Month				
Month				
Month				
Month				
Month				
Month				
Month				

IV. Increase Your Career's Flexibility & Range of Motion

Exercise Strategy

In addition to a well developed musculature, the health of your career is also dependent upon the flexibility and range of motion you can apply to your work. These qualities enable you to assume alternative positions in the workplace and thereby adjust your career to the shifting situational reality of the 21st Century workplace.

Such adjustments are critical because the ever morphing context for your work makes it all but inevitable that you will experience one or both of two kinds of course changes in employment:

- Externally-directed transitions;

    and/or

- Self-directed transitions.

These transitions are not changes in jobs (for which you need musculature); they are changes of jobs. And, changes of jobs are uncomfortable. Indeed, more often than not, they feel like a cramp in our work and career. While self-directed transitions are usually a healthy experience, however, externally-directed transitions may or may not be. They can be hard on us for several reasons:

- **Embarrassment: Externally-directed transitions can leave us feeling ashamed.**
  Whether they're called layoffs, reductions in force, downsizing or any other term of workplace art, these changes can and often do catch us by surprise. Everything is going along fine in our job, when one day—like a bolt-out-of-the-blue—we're told by our employer that we're no longer needed. Whether it's true or not, that judgment comes across as a critique of our work and a devaluation of our worth as an employee. Others are retained on-the-job, and we aren't. Even though we know there are a host of other possible reasons for the loss of our job—the state of the economy, shifts in the marketplace and the introduction of new technology, to name just a few—termination often seems to brand us as a substandard performer and that scarlet letter leaves us feeling embarrassed in front of our peers, family and friends.

- **Anxiety: Externally-directed transitions can leave us feeling unsettled and uncertain.**
  These changes force us outside our comfort zone. They push us away from what we are familiar with, what we have learned to count on, what we understand. They make us do the one thing we humans most hate to do: change. We go from the familiar—our current employer, our current commute, our current boss, even the field or industry in which we've worked—to the unfamiliar. Inevitably, such a transition alters the conditions for our success. We must measure up to different requirements and responsibilities on-the-job; we must perform according to redefined expectations and standards. We are confronted with an entirely new challenge, and that unknown reality introduces doubt. It raises the disconcerting possibility of personal failure. The certainty we gained from what we knew in the past is replaced by the anxiety we feel about what we don't know of the future.

- **Helplessness: Externally-directed transitions can leave us feeling out-of-control.**
  These changes undermine our confidence in ourselves and in our ability to determine our future. All of a sudden, what we believed we could do, what we thought we knew how to do is called into question. Our goals and expectations are replaced by doubts and questions. Everything we had counted on—our certainty about the direction and content of our career— no longer seems realistic or even possible. We are pushed and shoved around by forces that appear to be unpredictable and indifferent to our wellbeing. All we are able to do is play catch-up. Over and over again, we are forced to react to what happens to us, rather than determine where we want our career to go. As a consequence, we feel powerless to set goals

with any meaning, find employment with any security or engage in work with any prospect of enduring fulfillment.

These emotions are neither abnormal nor inappropriate. Transitions that are imposed on us and thus disrupt the course of our career are a shock to our hearts, our minds and our spirits. Unfortunately, however, these feelings can also cause our careers to lock up.

When we let embarrassment, anxiety and helplessness replace the energy and excitement of reaching for the best we can be, we lose the confidence and energy we need to take the initiative. In effect, we allow ourselves to be "psyched out" by the situation. Our ability to recover is reduced, and the length of our transition is extended.

The key to Career Fitness, therefore, is to acknowledge the emotions that are caused by externally-directed transitions—to give them their due—but also to move beyond them. We must empower ourselves to take charge of the transitions in our career and guide them to outcomes that benefit us. To do that:

- We must understand that transitions are now not only inevitable but also useful to us and therefore plan for them appropriately. We must position ourselves to be in charge of these transformations, rather than their victim.

- We must see ourselves as a work-in-progress, rather than a finished product. We must accept a new paradigm in which there is absolutely no shame and considerable merit in:

  o learning new skills for our current job;

  o acquiring additional expertise for a new or different job;

     and

  o re-educating ourselves in preparation for a new career.

How do we accomplish this shift in perspective? First, we have to recognize the dynamics involved in the two kinds of course changes we face in the 21st Century workplace. Then, we must acquire the skills necessary to minimize the negative effects of transitions we don't initiate and maximize the positive effects of those we do.

Employer-Directed Transitions

Today, the marketplace is being buffeted by the almost continuous introduction of new technology, new competitors, new products and services, new laws and regulations, and new ideas. These agents of change, in turn, have caused a pandemic of reactions—far-reaching revisions to assumptions, beliefs, strategy, practices, processes, even values—among employers. Such second order changes are neither trivial nor temporary. They are pervasive and powerful. They are also likely to increase in frequency and intensity as the 21st Century unfolds.

Employers, of course, must adjust to accommodate this new reality, and when they do, they force us to make adjustments, as well. To implement the second order changes—their responses to the shifting conditions they face in the global and domestic economies—and to ensure those changes have the desired impact on their workplace, organizations are imposing extraordinary new expectations on their employees.

For example:

- A person employed in the manufacturing field must both acquire the know-how necessary to work with computer-controlled tools and statistical process control techniques on the assembly line and be able to build better products than their employer's competitors anywhere around the world;

- A recruiter will be expected both to know how to use advanced human resource information systems and Internet-based candidate sourcing methods and be able to attract the best talent in the right demographic groups for their employer;

- A salesperson must both be expert in the use of customer relationship management systems and an array of differing individual privacy laws around the world and be able to outsell their employer's competitors in a global marketplace that operates 24 hours a day, 7 days a week;

- An operations professional will be expected to have the skills and knowledge both to use enterprise resource planning tools and the best practices to streamline information flows and activities and be able to achieve greater workforce productivity and responsiveness than their employer's domestic and international competitors;

  and

- A logistics person must both be competent in using routing and scheduling software and the latest process optimization theory to allocate and deploy organizational assets effectively and be able to give their employer better on-time performance than its competitors in the marketplace.

These expectations can and often do impose a fundamental re-conceptualization of the way we work. In 20th Century terms, such adjustments change the "requirements" and "responsibilities" of our jobs. In 21st Century terms, they alter the way we use our Natural to achieve an optimal experience on-the-job.

In effect, the definition of what it means to be qualified is now different. Whether we're looking for a new job (and thus to be a "qualified applicant") or to succeed at the one we already have (and thus to be a "qualified performer"), we must have the flexibility and range of motion to lean this new definition and apply it in our careers. We have to knead out the shock, distaste and discomfort of imposed changes and exercise the nimbleness and capacity necessary to put the altered conditions in the workplace to work for us.

What are these altered conditions? They are a crazy quilt of revisions that can influence:

- the priorities of your current job;

- the tasks you perform—the work you do—in that job;

- the tools you use to do your work;

- the pace at which you work;

- the people with whom you work;

- the location of your work;

- the schedule of your work,

  and/or

- the boss who supervises your work.

Some of these employed-directed changes are benign; they require that you adjust by taking a training program or altering your commute or learning the preferences of a new supervisor. They may be inconvenient and even unsettling, but they are not normally disruptive or harmful to your career. If properly addressed in a timely fashion, they do not warrant or demand a career altering response on your part. They are not unimportant, for they affect the substance of your work experience, but they are not so significant a revision to the historical norm that they force a reorientation in your employment or an adjustment in your path across the career jungle gym.

Other of these externally-directed changes, however, are not so benign. They can cause your job to be offshored or eliminated. They can roll your work into that of another position and leave you redundant and unemployed. Or, they can so change the requirements and responsibilities of the job that you no longer want to do it. These more destabilizing revisions sap the momentum out of your career and leave it weak and vulnerable.

You cannot survive by simply making a minor correction to what you do and how you do it. Your only career-saving option is a transition—you have to step out of your previous employment state and enter a new one.

You must move:

- from one job to another within your current employer;

- from one organizational unit to another within your current employer;

- from your current employer to a new employer in the same geographic location;

- from your current employer to a new employer in a different geographic location;

- from a job in your current industry to a similar job in a new industry;

    or

- from one career field to an entirely new career field.

These transitions are not voluntary in any respect. You do not decide if they will happen; you do not determine when they will happen; and you do not control how you (and others) will learn about them. They are externally initiated, not to inflict harm on you or your career, but to serve the wellbeing of others.

Employers embark on such changes to preserve and, where possible, enhance the success of their owners. For private companies, that may mean just a handful of individuals, but for public companies, it can mean thousands, sometimes hundreds of thousands of people. Ironically, with over half the U.S. population now invested in the stock market—either directly or through 401(k) and other retirement funds—at least some of those owners are the very same employees who are affected by externally-directed transitions.

While all organizations make such changes, therefore, good employers carefully manage their impact on workers, while abusive employers do not. The difference is obvious. The more arbitrary, secretive and heavy-handed an employer's actions, the less control you have. This lack of control makes it extraordinarily difficult to implement your transition successfully. It cripples your ability to prepare appropriately, and that lack of preparation, in turn, forces you into a reactive mode that sub-optimizes the outcome you are likely to achieve.

You must, for example, take the first open job that comes along because you didn't know—until it was too late—that your employer was going to make your old job redundant. You don't have the time to plan and implement a well conceived transition. Or, you must accept a position with lower pay than you were previously earning because you can't sell your home and relocate to a better job market. Your employer's decision to abandon its facility in your town has so depressed the price of real estate that you're stuck.

The antidote to such harmful transitions is "proaction." Proaction is the integration of knowledge and preparation. Knowledge provides the lead time—pro—and preparation gives you the capacity—action—to stay one step ahead of disruptive changes. You make it part of your job to evaluate continually the conditions of your employment and to make your own adjustments, as necessary, to preserve your wellbeing. In essence, proaction is the way you implement self-directed transitions.

Self-Directed Transitions

Left to our own devices, most of us would avoid making significant or frequent changes in our lives. In the 21st Century workplace, however, mid-course recalibrations to your career will be both necessary and ongoing. They are the inevitable byproduct of your growth into more expansive dimensions of your Natural and your journey across the career jungle gym.

With your career focused on being the best you can be and no longer bound by a static concept of work, you have to plot your own course through the wide array of alternative positions and employers in the workplace and pursue your Happiness by staying on course without deviation or let-up.

Only you can decide the direction and steps that will best serve you and your career, at any point in time. But, how do you make those decisions? How do you decide when to embark on a transition? If you have a job, for example, how do you determine whether it's the right time to:

- Seek additional responsibilities in your current job;

- seek a different position within your current employer's organization;

- move on to another job with a different employer;

  or

- stay right where you are.

Similarly, if you're in the job market and actively searching for a position, how do you decide:

- which openings to pursue;

- which employers are likely to offer the best opportunities for you;

  and

- whether your best prospects for employment dictate that you shift to a new career field, industry or location.

All of these options are viable and potentially appropriate courses of action for each and every one of us. The best course for you is unique to who you are at any given moment in the workplace and who you hope to become. There is no generic solution. There is no one-size-fits-all plan. That kind of lock-step behavior went out with the career ladder.

For you, the optimal way forward at any moment in time depends on the health of:

- your career—your individual work history;

- your job—your current employment situation (i.e., your fit with your boss and coworkers);

- your current employer (i.e., its current financial status and future prospects);

- the economy in the area where you live;

- your profession, craft or trade;

- the industry in which you work;

  as well as

- your family situation and responsibilities.

The one option you don't have in considering what to do next is to jog in place. Happy-go-lucky hanging around and hanging-on went out with carbon paper. You can't stay where you are forever and expect to survive, let alone prosper in a world that is constantly changing about you. The key is motion—not motion for the sake of movement—but motion that produces progress toward your Achievement, Advancement and Development goals, toward reaching for and realizing the best you can be.

Externally-directed transitions can be overwhelming—you lose control of your career. Self-directed transitions, in contrast, are liberating. You determine which course to take and when to take it. And, you make those decisions based on your assessment of each option's potential to:

- advance the maturation and expression of your Natural;

- leverage the talent you've developed in the past so that you can perform at your peak in the present;

- maximize the satisfaction and the paycheck you bring home from your current job;

  and

- position you for even greater success in the future.

Self-directed transitions are a Copernican shift in what constitutes the center of the American workplace. They change its base dynamic. They replace its historical bias for reacting to employment changes that happen to you with a new commitment to initiating changes that serve you and your interests, your opportunity and, ultimately, your prosperity.

They transform you from an organizational resource that is managed to maximize its contribution and minimize its cost to a self-defined person of talent whose career is managed to optimize the contribution you make to your employer and the happiness you create for yourself. In the surplus labor market of the 20th Century, self-directed transitions were beyond the reach of all but a select few—professional athletes and entertainment and media stars. In the shortage labor market of the 21st Century, they are not only accessible to you and everyone else, they are your birthright to claim.

Self-directed transitions, however, are also a personal responsibility. By definition, they cannot occur unless you cause them to happen, and they cannot proceed satisfactorily unless you shape and guide them to serve your best interests. You must become the master of your career transitions rather than their victim because when you do, you gain two potent benefits:

- *Freedom from the instability of externally initiated change.* While the unpredictability of today's economy can play a role, these changes are typically caused by a vacuum at the center of your career. That vacuum occurs when you abdicate your responsibility for managing your own transitions or when you fail to learn how to do so effectively. To put it another way, you gain the right to control your career by claiming it, by holding on to it, by making it your own.

- *The opportunity to pursue Happiness through your work.* You select organizations and jobs that position you to excel at work, grow in your occupational field, and prepare for future transitions. In effect, you give yourself the opportunity to express and experience your Natural and to do so in an endeavor you find engaging and meaningful. You make the one-third of the day you spend at work as rewarding as the rest of your day.

Exercising Control of Your Transitions

While transitions can be unsettling—they do involve change, of course—it is possible to transform them into healthy events in your career. The key to achieving that end is focus. You must discipline yourself to remain perpetually committed to:

- the next bars you are striving to reach on your career jungle gym—your Achievement, Advancement and Development goals;

    and

- the end state you are seeking to realize—to be the best you can be in work that enables you to explore more of your Natural.

That focus is achieved by re-imagining your transitions as actions you take to better yourself.

- The transitions you initiate within your current employer should no longer be viewed as positioning yourself for promotion—that may happen, of course, given the value of your contribution—but instead, as stepping up your own game. Whether they enable you to acquire new skills, new responsibilities, new challenges or new perspectives, the goal is always to advance the fullest possible realization of your talent.

- The transitions you initiate to move to other employers should no longer be viewed as an exercise in increasing your income, improving your benefits or shortening your commute. While those factors are not unimportant, your decision to move should always be driven by your quest for work that will support the development and expression of your Natural. Hence, don't change jobs—a shift in the requirements and responsibilities of your employment—but do change career advancement opportunities—an expansion of the challenges and discoveries of your work.

With this re-imagination of transitions, these career adjustments become the way stations on your journey to the fullest expression of what you do best and most like to do. You, of course, want to control when, where and how you reach those stations, but ultimately, your success depends upon the vista of possibilities you recognize—the kinds of opportunities you are willing to acknowledge and consider in your career. The more encompassing that vista—the greater the range and diversity of transitions that are acceptable to you—the more likely you are to achieve an outcome that will be positive for you.

The surest path to career health, therefore, is to expand as much as possible the dimensions of what you can and will do in the workplace. And, to achieve such an expansive perspective, you must develop your flexibility and range of motion. In essence, you must extend your comfort zone with regard to both the content and conditions of your work.

On the career jungle gym, you can reach career victories by moving forward, sideways, laterally, or even backwards. The direction is irrelevant, because the outcome is not based on where you sit in an organization, but rather on where you stand in your career—in your journey to personal growth and accomplishment. Said another way, the only limitations on the development and expression of your Natural are those you set.

What does flexibility and range of motion do for you? They loosen your self-imposed limits. They enable you to get comfortable with the widest possible array of work opportunities, including those you might otherwise never even have contemplated.

This capacity to think "outside of the foul lines" in your career gives you permission to consider:

- taking a salary cut or a sabbatical to go back to school;

- accepting a lateral assignment in order to learn a new skill or gain the perspective of a new experience;

- going to work for a start-up company that offers less pay but more interesting and rewarding employment;

- relocating to a new city or state in order to take a new or better job;

- moving into a new industry that offers you more growth opportunity;

- embarking on a new career field that offers more fulfilling and/or rewarding work;

- going into business on your own, either by starting your own company or buying a franchise; and

- shifting from one segment of the economy into another—from for-profit businesses, for example, to the government or not-for-profit organizations.

The foundation for this more fulsome perspective is knowledge. You must eliminate surprises and maximize choices.

To Eliminate Surprises

"Business intelligence" is a term used to describe information about the status, capabilities and likely plans of potential influencers in an organization's marketplace. The better that organization's business intelligence, the more precise its situational awareness will be and, therefore, the lower its risk of having to deal with an unexpected (and potentially harmful) situation.

The same is true with "career intelligence." The better your information about potential influencers in the workplace, the better able you are to eliminate surprises (and the harm they can potentially do to you). These influencers include:

- *Your current employer.* The more you know about its financial situation and competitive position in the marketplace, the less likely you are to be surprised by a transition involving a layoff or downsizing.

- *Your current work unit.* The more you know about the perception of its role in the organization and its contribution to your employer's bottom line success, the less likely you are to be surprised by a transition involving a reorganization or a decision to discontinue operations.

- *Your current boss.* The more you know about their stature in the organization and their position in its power structure, the less likely you are to be surprised by a transition involving a new boss with different priorities and goals.

- *Your current industry.* The more you know about its present status and future prospects in the global economy, the less likely you are to be surprised by a transition involving permanently reduced employment prospects.

- *Your current hometown.* The more you know about its reputation as a place to do business and the incentives it offers commercial enterprises, the less likely you are to be surprised by a transition involving the relocation of your employer out of the area.

- *Your current career field.* The more you know about the trends and developments that affect its contribution in the workplace, the less likely you are to be surprised by a transition imposed on you by declining or even nonexistent employment opportunities.

To Maximize Your Choices

One of the cardinal rules of effective career self-management is as simple as it is profound: *never sell yourself short.* Don't overlook, eliminate or assume you are incapable of reaching new and more expansive dimensions to the best you can be. How can you avoid such self-defeating behavior? Acquire as much "career intelligence" as possible about:

- The latest developments and emerging trends in your career field;

- The prevailing dynamics and potential structural changes in your industry;

- Other industries and segments of the economy that provide work in your career field;

- Other career fields that provide employment opportunities in your Natural;

- Other organizations in your hometown that offer employment opportunities in your field of work;

- Other organizations in your hometown that offer employment opportunities in the industry in which you have experience;

- Other organizations in other locations that offer employment opportunities in your field of work;

- Other organizations in other locations that offer employment opportunities in the industry in which you have experience;

  and

- The successes and failures of others who have previously worked in your career field or work in it now.

The more you know about potentially destabilizing situations (i.e., surprises) and potentially beneficial opportunities (i.e., choices), the more effective you can be in accommodating and/or leveraging them in your career. That insight gives you the lead time necessary to prepare for and even avoid hazardous, externally imposed transitions. That knowledge also gives you the lead time to select and implement invigorating, self-directed transitions. It is, in a very real sense, the foundation of your career security.

The acquisition of "career intelligence," therefore, must be continuous. You can't sit back and wait for the insights to come to you; you have to find them on their own. You have to be proactive. You have to go out and collect the information you need by embarking on a disciplined and resilient "environmental scan."

This scan is only effective, however, if it is conducted by personal observation and research. It is, in essence, a commitment to paying attention to the ever-shifting reality of the 21st Century workplace, to assessing the implications of its changes for the course and content of your career.

Considering such options does not obligate you to embark on any specific one of them. It simply increases the size of your playing field and, thus, the richness of your occupational possibilities.

Think of it as a treaty with yourself to expand your frontiers in the land of opportunity. The more alternatives you evaluate and the more you know about each one, the greater the probability that you will find and select the best one to optimize the health of your career. In other words, the greater the degrees of freedom you have in your thinking, the more unbounded your prospects for success.

That information, however, only becomes helpful to you—it only increases your flexibility and range of motion—if you do something with it. You must transform the more fulsome perspective you gain into a more creative and self-fulfilling course for your career. You must act on the opportunity inherent in your more fulsome set of options. You must both recognize the freedom you have to act and you must exercise that freedom by acting.

That's true even when your personal circumstances impose constraints on your options. Life isn't always cooperative, and you may feel as if you have no choice but to move in a less-than-optimal direction from time-to-time. Such situations can be caused by a family priority—the desire to keep your children in a certain school, for example—or your financial status.

With well developed flexibility and range of motion, however, you set the limits. You make the decision, and you do so with full understanding of its rationale and implications. You determine the length of your detour and its timing, and you remain vigilant for other options that will enable you to get back on track. As a consequence, you are in control of what happens and thus able to manage its outcome and impact on the long term health of your career.

The transcendent feature of your career remains motion. Transitions are inevitable and unending in today's world of work; the only question is who will direct them. With well developed flexibility and range, transitions will no longer be painful changes imposed on you, but mile markers of progress on a career course you set. Hunkering down, hanging on, and standing still makes you an easy target for forces outside your control. Looking out, launching off, and moving on takes you beyond the reach of disruptive career surprises and within reach of the goals you've set and the dreams you cherish for your career.

Exercise Strides for Career Flexibility & Range of Motion

Stride 1: Hold your finger up and see which way the wind is blowing in your organization.

Use Exercise III, Stride 2—walking around your employer's facility—to gather intelligence about the perceptions of your work unit and boss within the larger organization and any rumors that may be circulating about their future prospects.

These views need always to be carefully vetted, of course, but research has shown that rumors are at least partially accurate over 50 percent of the time. Moreover, the goal of this exercise is not to gossip about what you learn, but rather to use that information to build a composite picture of what the future might look like for your team and its leader.

Repetitions: Perform this analysis 1 time each quarter, using the information you acquire when walking around your employer's facility.

This internal scouting will:

- Help you avoid externally-directed surprises that can negatively affect your employment;

- Give you additional lead time to prepare for changes in the conditions and/or expectations of your work;

    and

- Provide some of the information necessary (more is acquired in Stride 2 below) to plan and implement self-directed transitions successfully.

Where will you perform this stride in your work?

Stride 2: Use the Internet to research what's being predicted for your career field, industry, employer, and location.

To help sift through all of the published information that might address this topic, sign up for the free RSS feed from Google (www.google.com), Yahoo! (www.yahoo.com) or Bing (www.bing.com). These services enable you to specify the kind of information you want to see and will automatically and continuously send you only that information or notices indicating where it can be found online.

Assess the credibility of what you read by discussing it with friends and colleagues, a mentor if you have one, and/or your boss if they're willing.

Repetitions: Devote 2 hours each month to this research.

Your investigation will:

• Expand your awareness of external dynamics that could either create an opportunity for you or pose a challenge to your career security;

• Provide important background and insight as you set and refine your Achievement, Advancement and Development goals;

and

• Help you anticipate and prepare for the self-directed transitions necessary to ensure the continued health of your career.

Where will you perform this stride in your work?

The best athletes are able to focus their imagination on a desired end state—the physical achievement or victory they seek—and then mentally "see" themselves through the actions required to implement that vision. Use that same technique to imagine the next transition in your career.

Empower yourself to "see" a way past any constraints that may impede your progress or any reservations you may have about your own capability. Then, think through the strides you should take, the decisions you must make to transform this possibility—no matter how remote it may seem—into reality.

Repetitions: Devote 4 hours per month to thinking about the next transition in your career and how you will execute it successfully.

This preparation will:

- Diminish the uncertainty and anxiety that career changes can cause, even when they are self-directed;

- Improve the likelihood that your self-directed transitions will be well executed and successful;

  and

- Embed transitions in your career so that you "think outside the foul lines" when setting and striving to meet your goals.

Where will you perform this stride in your work?

Stride 4: If you have a spouse or life partner, talk to them about the possibility and importance of transitions in your career. If you don't have a spouse or life partner, talk to members of your family.

Surprises are as hard on those you care about as they are on you. Help them to understand what could happen and why; explain the downsides of externally-directed transitions and the upside of self-directed ones. Then, discuss the implications of the next transition you anticipate (see Stride 3) in your career. Explore its potential impact on them and/or your family, respecting and accommodating, as best you can, the misgivings they may have about the change.

The goal is to practice flexibility and range of motion with them so that they have a vision for your career that's identical to and aligned with yours.

Repetitions: Spend at least 4 hours per quarter discussing your next career transition with your spouse/life partner and/or family.

These conversations will:

- Deepen your spouse/life partner's and/or family's understanding of the challenges you face and the opportunities you have in today's workplace;

- Help diminish the stress and anxiety they are likely to feel when transitions occur in your career;

   and

- Add the insights and ideas of those who care about you to your assessment of and plans for changes in your career.

Where will you perform this stride in your work?

Other Strides

The preceding exercise strides are the minimum essential for increasing the flexibility and range of motion you bring to your work. If you are interested and able, you can supplement them with the following additional activities:

- Go to a Business Opportunity Expo where you can explore the options that are available to you in franchises, distributorships, and other forms of business ownership.

- Participate in a career fair for your field and/or industry and assess the benefits and risks of the available opportunities and how competitive you might be for those in which you are interested.

- Take some time on business trips to explore parts of the country where other firms in your industry are located.

- Establish a career transition fund which, like the savings account you set up for your kids' college education, would preserve your ability to make a career enhancing transition even if it diminishes your compensation. For example, you might tap the fund in order to be able to take a challenging position with a smaller employer or to spend some time in school to update your skills.

- If you're in an active job search and it's progressing slowly, consider going to work for a staffing company that's providing its clients with temporary or contract workers. Such a move can have at least three advantages:

(1) you start earning an income again right away;

(2) you will often be given training in the key skills their customers need, in effect adding to your career musculature;

and

(3) you get exposure to employers that might consider hiring you for a full-time position if you do well in your assignment. In fact, the American Staffing Association has found that 30 percent of all temporary workers are ultimately hired for a full time position by the organization where they were assigned to work.

What additional activities will you add to your Career Fitness strides?

My Exercise Record

Use the following worksheet to:

- Plan the time you are going to devote to each stride in the exercise and to set up a schedule for that activity in the upcoming months.

- Record your plan for and actual repetitions of each stride. Make sure your entries are accurate and up-to-date.

- Monitor your commitment to the work-in and to this exercise, in particular. Make corrective adjustments, as necessary.

The record is organized as an annual progression of monthly activity. Not every stride in every exercise is performed on a monthly basis, but the planning for and monitoring of your performance is. That continuous preparation and review optimizes the impact of your activity and ensures that you derive the maximum benefit from your effort.

Plan / Actual	Step 1	Step 2	Step 3	Step 4
Month				
Month				
Month				
Month				
Month				
Month				
Month				
Month				
Month				
Month				
Month				
Month				

V. Work With Winners

Exercise Strategy

Working with winners is the best way to tone your career, giving it the definition or shape that optimizes your prospects for success. There are two kinds of winners in today's world of work:

- Individuals who are recognized (by their peers and employers) for their consistent ability to deliver superior performance on-the-job;

  and

- Organizations that are recognized (by their customers and investors) for their consistent ability to deliver superior products and services in-the-marketplace.

In short, winners are all stars in their chosen field or mission. Over and over again, they produce extraordinary results that are valued by others. No less important, they provide an example and, often, even the support that can raise the performance of those around them. They are successful themselves, and they aid and abet the success of others.

One of the best ways to build a healthy career, therefore, is to associate with winners. If possible, work with or for them—and preferably both—all of the time. If that's not possible, then, at least, interact with them as frequently as you can.

Regardless of your seniority or level of experience, you can always upgrade your performance by working shoulder-to-shoulder with or learning from those who are highly regarded in your field. And, regardless of your individual accomplishment, you can always challenge yourself to do better by working for or interacting with the leading organizations in your industry. Both can position you for more frequent and significant career victories and accelerate the progress you make toward being the best you can be in your work.

For you to acquire those benefits, however, winners must also be willing to help you.

- Individual winners must accept you as a coworker or as colleague with whom they will share their knowledge and wisdom. They must recognize you as a peer or as a person they will, directly or indirectly, guide and support.

- Organizational winners must accept you as an employee and provide an environment in which you can succeed on-the-job and advance in your field. They must offer a culture and values with which you are comfortable and in which you can flourish.

To put it another way, there are many winners in the world of work, and the key to your success is to find those with whom you are most compatible and from whom you can learn the most.

Individual Winners

Whether you're an entry-level worker, a mid-career professional or a senior manager or executive, your success turns on a character trait that is seldom celebrated in today's workplace: humility. Humility is your acknowledgement that, in the modern economy, someone always has more or better information and experience than you and, as a result, their accumulated knowledge is more up-to-date, more accurate, more valuable (to employers) than yours.

The incessant, worldwide production of data, the relentless pace of technological advances, and the increasing complexity of domestic and international markets ensure that your personal expertise is always incomplete. Recognizing and accepting that fact isn't an admission of weakness, but rather, a predisposition for building strength. It sets you up to sculpt your own expertise—to add mass to and/or shape your occupational capacity—with the insights and wisdom of others in the workplace.

By working with individuals who are successful and willing to assist you, you position yourself for the continuous self-improvement that is the only pathway to enduring individual success. Your learning may be accomplished in your employment relationship, in a structured discussion or meeting at work or in casual conversation outside the office. It may involve working side-by-side on-the-job with an expert in your field or scheduling an occasional lunch together in the cafeteria. However and wherever it occurs, you extend your personal best by your willingness to admit you are incomplete—a work-in-progress—and by your determination to achieve greater completeness through the respectful acquisition of others' expertise and experience.

This challenge is nearly universal in the 21st Century workplace. It has, in many cases, upended the traditionally chronological sequencing of work relationships. Today, you can be under the age of thirty and find yourself hiring someone who is twenty years older and vastly more experienced than you. Similarly, you can be over the age of fifty and find that you are now reliant on people who are not only twenty years younger than you but also far more technologically adept and capable. In both kinds of situations, humility is the only balm that soothes the natural feelings of insecurity and trepidation that can arise.

Your humility predisposes you to seek two kinds of experiences. They are:

- **Working with a winner who is a coworker.**
  When you combine your own excellence with the extraordinary capabilities of your fellow employees, and then you adopt the highest standards in applying those capabilities on-the-job, you expand the possibilities you see in the workplace and the potential on which you can draw to realize them.

  As a career athlete—a person committed to the principles of Career Fitness—you have the preparation necessary to leverage the best of others to extend the best you can be. How does that dynamic work? Winners:

  o   are typically given the most challenging and important assignments by their employers;

  o   transform roadblocks and difficulties into opportunities for achieving higher levels of performance on-the-job;

      and

  o   model the behaviors and thought patterns of success so that they can be learned and emulated by others in the workplace.

  When you work with a winner who is a coworker, you share these attributes to your mutual benefit. Sure, you tap into their accumulated knowledge and wisdom. Absolutely, you draw on their skills and the tricks of the trade they've learned. But, the advantage that is gained has to be a two-way street. You must also add your excellence to theirs. You must reinforce their performance even as you upgrade theirs. That's why there are two n's in the word "winner." They represent the two Naturals—yours and the person with whom you're working—that are developed and expressed.

- **Working with a winner who is a personal guide.**
  As a work-in-progress, you are always a student of your profession, craft or trade. While some very small number of us are able to find our own way to personal excellence, most of us will have to ask for assistance from time-to-time. Your journey to self-mastery, therefore, is likely to benefit from the instruction of a guide—an individual who will lead you to greater understanding and capability in your field.

There are three kinds of workplace guides, each of which is particularly appropriate for a specific stage or situation in your career. You should work with:

o a mentor to acquire career guidance and support during the early and middle stages of your career;

o a counselor or coach to acquire advice and assistance regarding career questions and issues during the middle and advanced stages of your career;

and

o a tutor to gain the expertise required to address a specific shortcoming or challenge during all phases of your career (e.g., how to use a specific technology or how to solve an interpersonal problem at work).

Certainly, you can work with a mentor—a seasoned colleague in your field—during the later stages of your career, and a career counselor or coach—a trained career development professional—during the early stages of your career. For most of us, however, mentors are most helpful when you are building the foundation of your career, and counselors and coaches best serve you when you have some experience under your belt.

Whatever the timing, when you work with a winner who is a personal guide, you draw on the expertise and savvy of that person to your mutual benefit. As with coworkers, the advantage moves in two directions. You gain by learning from your guide, and they gain by the honor you accord them in recognizing their special talent. Here again, you are both winners.

While each of these work experiences is invigorating in and of itself, both are necessary to sustain a healthy career. You must be willing to seek out jobs where you will be able to learn from coworkers who are winners. You must also be aware of your own limitations and, when necessary, reach out to the appropriate guide at each stage in your career. In essence, humility means your acceptance of the imperfection of your Natural in its native state and your determination to address and reduce that imperfection—to better yourself at the activity that you most like to do and do best—from the first to the very last day of your career.

That outlook positions you for better and more rewarding performance on-the-job. This continuous association with others who are successful enables you to tone your career by:

- *Invigorating the environment in which you work.* As coworkers, winners are both extraordinary and all around you. They can be your peers, those for whom you work and those who work for you. Regardless of their position, winners are people who bring more than competence— even more than superior individual capability—to the workplace.

  They also arrive with an expectation of success and, equally as important, an instinctive understanding of how to achieve it. In other words, winners have both the self-confidence and the know-how to apply their competence on-the-job so that it yields consistently superior results. They are certain that their talent will create career victories.

  That unadorned self-confidence creates an aura of achievement that, like a rising tide, lifts the performance of everyone around them. They are able to expel the carbon dioxide of doubt—the fuel of mediocrity—and replace it with the pure oxygen of a justifiable belief in themselves—the fuel of extraordinary outcomes.

- *Sharing the secrets of championship caliber work.* As guides, winners offer the rare perspective and refined perception of a master craftsperson. They are not perfect—indeed, they often have their own limitations—but they are experts in and willing to reveal the true nature of select challenges and opportunities in today's workplace. Within that sphere of expertise, they know what works, what doesn't, and most importantly, what works best, and if you ask them, they will convey that knowledge and understanding to you.

Guides don't just share knowledge, however; they also draw on a track record that enables you to use that knowledge to enhance your own performance. They offer you wisdom. And, guides don't just share understanding; they also impart the maturity that enables you to use that understanding to reach for the best you can be. They offer you insight. As a consequence, the master craftspersons you select as your guides cannot earn career victories for you, but they can and do show you the way to achieve them on your own.

Your ability to acquire these benefits depends upon the level of your work with winners. That level is determined by the extent and nature of your workplace involvement with a coworker or guide. Not surprisingly, the more contact you have and the more substantive that contact, the greater the contribution to your career.

Your work with a coworker can occur at any of four escalating levels of involvement:

- Observation: your job in an organization is located near enough to a coworker's job that you can watch and learn from their performance;

- Casual interaction: your job in an organization puts you into occasional contact with a coworker and that unstructured interaction enables you to learn from them;

- Formal interaction: your job in an organization is actually linked to a coworker's job (e.g., you provide input to them or they provide input to you) and that structured interaction positions you to learn from them;

    and

- Tutelage: your job includes the specific assignment to learn from a coworker by placing yourself under their direction and/or setting up a formal program of instruction with them.

In most cases, you can achieve the first level of involvement on your own. All you have to do is identify the coworker who will teach you the most simply by observing them and make it your habit to watch what they do.

The other three levels, however, are largely determined by the employer for which you choose to work. Your evaluation of employment opportunities, therefore, should include the extent to which they will facilitate significant involvement with at least one coworker who is a superior performer. Any job that doesn't position you to work with one or more winners can harm the health of your career.

Your work with a guide, in contrast, offers two potential levels of involvement:

- Informal development—there is no set curriculum or program of instruction, so your learning unfolds as your job performance and/or career planning requires;

    and

- Formal instruction—there is a set curriculum which focuses your development on the achievement of specific learning objectives.

Clearly, these levels of involvement can occur only with the explicit approval of the guide. They must agree to participate in your education and to invest the time and effort required to fulfill that commitment. Your selection of a guide, therefore, must take those factors into account as well as the individual's ability to provide the knowledge you seek. The only guide who is truly beneficial to you is the one who is both willing and able to teach you.

Mentors, of course, provide their support on a pro bono basis. Career counselors and coaches, on the other hand, are employed as guides so, as noted earlier, they will normally charge you a fee for their services. When you pay this fee, however, you are actually spending money on yourself. You are financing the development of your Natural. You are making a contribution to your future that is as appropriate and important as the contribution you make to a 401(k) or other "retirement" fund. As long as you invest wisely, therefore, the fee you pay to work with a career counselor or coach is a positive and helpful stimulant to your career.

Moreover, while mentors are free, they do expect a quid pro quo for their assistance with your career. Working with a mentor effectively establishes a contractual relationship between you and them. To hold up their end of the deal, they must devote the time and effort necessary to support and assist you. To hold up your end of the deal, you must devote the time and effort to listen, learn and, ultimately, apply the insights of your mentor. You aren't required, of course, to do so in a rote fashion or by slavish imitation, but you are expected to put the wisdom you've been given to work in your career.

That's the Golden Rule of Working With Winners. It applies to mentors, to be sure, but also to every winner with whom you work. In such situations, you must pay attention and pay it forward. In other words, you should devote the same level of commitment and energy to the relationship that you expect of the other person. You should work at it as hard or harder as you would like them to work at it.

Just as you are asking them to share their knowledge and insights with you, you should commit to using that gift, as appropriate, to enhance the caliber and outcome of your work. It's not a matter of paying them back, but rather of paying them the respect of opening yourself up to their making a difference in moving your career forward. Your relationship with one another, therefore, is best seen as a partnership—a win-win arrangement that rewards you both.

Given this contractual basis, these relationships should not be dependent on friendship. A winner may become a friend, but the interaction, itself, is a work-related experience. It focuses on workplace performance, not social compatibility. Its purpose is to advance the health of your career. And, that goal can only be achieved if the person with whom you're working is a winner—a success in their field and career. That is the sole criterion for your entering into a relationship with them as a part of your Career Fitness Work-in.

While it would be nice if that relationship evolved into (or even begins in) friendship, that development is secondary—at least so far as this exercise is concerned—to your acquisition of career-enhancing knowledge and insight. You must be able to interact comfortably, but only to the extent necessary to serve that purpose.

For the same reason, you should also continuously assess the status of the coworker or guide with whom you've established a partnership. In today's rapidly evolving workplace, winners are no less susceptible than anyone else to falling out-of-step or, worse, falling behind. That does not make them losers or failures, but it does change your relationship.

The 21st Century workplace is an unforgiving (as well as opportunistic) environment that challenges everyone. Should a set-back happen to the winner with whom you're working, remember who and where you are. Career Fitness has transformed you from a reactive employee who must minimize the damage of unplanned career changes to an independent 21st Century champion who sets their own course across the career jungle gym. Don't step on those who drop off the pace as you were forced to do in the 20th Century. Instead, step up and be the best you can be in supporting and assisting them. Be the winner who works with them just as they were the winner who worked with you.

Providing such support, however, must be carefully managed. It's not your responsibility to carry a coworker through their challenge. It's not your job to get them back on track. Indeed, doing so would be a disservice to them. It is their responsibility to right their own course. They must reassert their role as the champion in their career. You should help them, to be sure, but you must also give them the space to reset their self-confidence, to reclaim their sure sense of their own ability to succeed. Do support them as best you can, but don't so concentrate on their situation that you deny them that career victory or neglect your own career.

Indeed, as difficult as it may be to accept, you must move on and establish a relationship with a new developmental partner. You must find another winner with whom to work and do so without delay. Your primary responsibility is to the fitness of your career. It is up to you to keep it moving forward. It is your job as your career captain to sustain your progress in your pursuit of Happiness at work. And to do that, you must reposition yourself to be touched, once again, by the halo of success that only winners can provide.

Establishing these relationships is not a trivial feat. Finding the right winner for you at any specific time in your career involves clearing two imposing hurdles. Not only must you identify someone with whom you want to work, but you must also find someone who is willing to work with you. This is especially true for coworkers. The fact that you and the individual both work for the same employer or, even, that you are both members of the same work team does not mean that you will be compatible with one another or that the individual will be amenable to helping you advance your career.

The sharing of hard-earned knowledge and insight is a qualitatively different experience from that which occurs among most individuals during a normal work day. When you work with a winner who is your guide or mentor, you are repositioning yourself in the workplace. Regardless of where you actually stand or sit on-the-job, you move to a station that is figuratively side-by-side with them. You place yourself where you can see and hear the expression of their Natural.

The experience is intensely personal and an extraordinarily generous act of engagement on their part. Your partner, in effect, permits you to access the source of their own happiness. They give you permission to tap into the best they can be in order to enhance the best you can be. Their openness is a special gift that you may seek or request, but must never expect or take for granted.

Organizational Winners

Individual winners are easy to spot. They are notable for what they do and how they do it. They stand out because they stand for excellence in the workplace.

Organizations can be equally as successful, of course, but they are harder to identify. There is no general consensus on what constitutes an organizational winner. According to media pundits, academic researchers and workers generally, the definition can encompass any of a wide range of characteristics. These include:

- Compensation: an organizational winner pays more than its competitors across town;

- Benefits: an organizational winner offers "family friendly" benefits such as on-site day care, flexible work schedules, and subsidized fitness club memberships;

- Convenience: an organizational winner is easy to get to with a hassle-free commute;

- Stability: an organizational winner employs a large number of people in the local area and/or has been around for a long time;

    and/or

- Leadership: an organizational winner has a CEO who is highly regarded for their character and vision and for the results they achieve.

To be sure, exemplary employers may have such characteristics, but these traits are not what make them winners. Rather, organizational winners are those employers that support and promote the health of their employees' careers. They accomplish their organizational mission—whether that is making a profit, paying quarterly dividends, increasing shareholder value or serving a social, professional or philanthropic mission—and do so without abusing the people who work for them. Organizational winners are, in short, "pro athletes." No other definition makes sense in the 21st Century workplace.

Organizational winners strive to achieve superior financial and operational results while respecting your career and life goals. Working for such an employer enables you to be a part of its success and surrounds you with an environment or culture that encourages and promotes your success. When compared to other employers, organizational winners give you more opportunity to grow on-the-job and are more supportive of your development in your profession, craft or trade. It's like making a dive from a spring board, rather than from the side of the pool. They give you more lift and momentum and, therefore, a greater arc of possibilities for your success.

An organizational winner can be large or small, a start-up or a well established company, a local or regional employer or a multinational one. What sets the winners apart from all of the others is their ability to create and sustain a value system that supports career athletes. They believe in and operate according to a set of principles that are founded on one enduring credo: their success can and will be achieved not by breaking down their employees, but by building them up. Not by making them losers, but by helping them become champions.

Ironically, that approach is easily recognized from a number of different vantage points in the American culture. In the for-profit sector, they are organizations that:

- business analysts and investors consider successful because of their rising bottom line and/or consistent payment of a dividend;

- consumers consider successful because of the extraordinary quality and/or innovation of their products and services;

- scholars and researchers consider successful because of their well designed and executed strategies, processes and practices;

- journalists and media representatives consider successful because of the openness of their leaders and the ability of those leaders to articulate a clear and compelling vision for their organizations;

  and

- working men and women generally, but especially their employees, consider successful because the policies and actions of the organization are always carefully shaped to treat every individual worker with dignity and respect.

In the not-for-profit sector, organizational winners have exactly the same attributes with two differences. They are not defined by business analysts and investors or by the consumers of their products and services, but by thought leaders in their field and the people or institutions they serve. Hence, they are organizations that:

- appropriate experts consider successful because of the sustained contribution they make to a specific community and/or mission;

- members or clients of the organization consider successful because of what they do for them and how they do it;

and also:

- scholars and researchers consider successful because of their well designed and executed strategies, processes and practices;

- journalists and media representatives consider successful because of the openness of their leaders and the ability of those leaders to articulate a clear and compelling vision for their organizations; and

- working men and women generally, but especially their employees, consider successful because the policies and actions of the organization are always carefully shaped to treat every individual worker with dignity and respect.

While all of these perspectives are clearly helpful in identifying an organizational winner, no single one is sufficient in and of itself. The positive views of the press, for example, or even those of business analysts won't ensure that an organization is, in fact, a peak performer. Unfortunately, business analysts can be duped or just wrong and business reputations can be carefully managed and burnished for public consumption. Therefore, the only sure way to identify an organizational winner is to adopt a multifaceted outlook—one that encompasses all of the perspectives. It alone provides insight into every aspect of business performance, and only an organization that excels in the totality of its performance is truly a winner.

This comprehensive outlook corrects our culture's current bias toward the first four perspectives. In today's perceived economic wisdom, every view is important except that of the working men and women who make an organization successful. It is their perspective, however, that points the way to those employers that will work as hard for you as you will be expected to work for them.

How does that happen?

These organizations provide a culture in which you are comfortable and a set of values with which you are compatible. If either or both of those environmental conditions are missing, you will not feel empowered or able to do your best work. In fact, the principal reason that people don't succeed when they are hired by an organization is not that they can't do the work, but that they don't feel as if they fit in. They aren't aligned with the organization, but instead, sense that they are out of place and out of step. They are an incompatible employee, and the resulting discomfort undermines their confidence, saps their ability to perform at their peak, and ultimately, harms the health of their career.

It's not enough, therefore, to work for organizational winners. You must find the specific organizational winners where you can contribute and grow. You must become a "smart consumer of employers." That involves taking two specific steps:

- **First, do your homework**
  Most employers provide recruiting literature and/or a career area on their Web-site that describes what it's like to work in their organization. In some cases, these descriptions are informative and accurate and in others, unfortunately, they are not. The only way to know for sure is to test the validity of their claims.

- **Second, "test drive" the employer**
  Evaluate the employment experience the organization actually provides to workers. No employer, of course, will permit you to perform such a test—the only exception being temp-to-perm staffing assignments (see Exercise IV) and intern programs for college students (see the Appendix entitled Rookies and Comeback Pros)—so you must use a surrogate. You must rely on a substitute experience that will give you a reasonable approximation of an organization's workplace reality.

Using a Surrogate

The best surrogate with which to evaluate an employer's culture and values is its recruiting process. You can get a good picture of the way an organization treats its employees by experiencing the way it treats its employment candidates. What happens to you on your way in the door reveals a lot about what's going on behind the door of an organization. It indicates what's important to the organization and gives you insight into the nature of its workplace environment. Fundamentally, your recruitment experience enables you to sample what your workday would be like within the organization.

There are several key questions you should try to answer as you pass through an organization's recruiting process:

- *Is the organization courteous and respectful in its interactions with you?*

  For example:

  o does it acknowledge the receipt of your resume or application or does it subject you to a submission experience that feels like your credentials have fallen into a big, black hole?

  o did it train its recruiters and hiring managers to prepare for and carefully execute their interviews with you or were they late for the session and/or unprepared for or inattentive during it?

- *Does the organization support you by providing ample information throughout the process?*

  For example:

  o does it give you feedback on your performance in interviews and on the results of background and reference checks or does it keep you in the dark about your status and what will happen next?

  o does it tell you when a position for which you have applied has been filled by another candidate or eliminated by the organization or does it lead you on and waste your time when you could be applying for opportunities with other employers?

- *Are the organization's employees friendly and collegial when interacting with you?*

  For example:

  o does the organization's receptionist greet you in a pleasant and polite fashion when you arrive for an interview or do they act as if you are an inconvenient and irritating intrusion on their day?

  o does the recruiter with whom you meet take the time to get to know you as a person or do they act as if you are just another check mark on a long, undifferentiated list of prospects they must move through the door?

- *Are the organization's employees engaged by and proud of their work?*

  For example:

  o does the organization encourage you to talk to employees during the recruiting process so you can gauge their commitment and satisfaction or are you segregated from the workforce and limited to staged interactions with carefully selected representatives? (If you are able to talk with employees, are they guarded or rehearsed in their responses to your questions—do they figuratively (or literally) look over their shoulder—or are they open and candid when describing their work and workday?)

o   does the organization feature employee testimonials and/or blogs in the career area on its Web-site so you can read about the day-to-day experiences of its workers or are its employees unheralded and absent from the site?

Organizational winners don't abuse employment candidates because they don't abuse their employees. They serve shareholders without bullying "jobholders." They do the right things in the workplace and do those things in the right way. They employ great talent and respect the talent they employ. They achieve their mission by helping you achieve yours—a healthy and rewarding career.

Ultimately, working with winners is an exercise in finding and interacting with people and organizations that will enable you to upgrade your performance by drawing on their own commitment to excellence. They provide you with the role models and wisdom and the environment and support you need to be the best you can be at each and every stage in your career.

Winners, in a sense, are the shoulders on which you stand to increase the number and magnitude of your career victories. They lift you up so you can avoid the roadblocks and dead ends that can complicate and disrupt your advancement. And, they hold you up so you can reach for and grab hold of the hidden opportunities that will enrich the happiness you can achieve in your work. When you work with winners, therefore, you are a winner too.

Exercise Strides for Working Out With Winners

Stride 1: Assess the caliber of those with whom you work.

Collect published information (in your local newspaper, in trade and business publications and on the Internet) and the views of credible industry analysts. Then, candidly evaluate your boss, your coworkers, other bosses in the organization for which you work, other employees in that organization and the organization, itself.

Form your own opinion regarding their status. Create a list of those you consider to be winners based on their current level of performance.

Repetitions: Perform this assessment 1 time each quarter, during your personal performance review (see Exercise I).

This evaluation of your current workplace will:

- Help raise your horizon—your level of awareness and understanding—beyond your day-to-day work requirements when directing your career;

- Enable you to determine if you're employed in an environment that is conducive to and supportive of your being the best you can be;

  and

- Identify those individuals in the organization who can advance your occupational development and multiply the opportunities you have for achieving career victories.

Where will you perform this stride in your work?

Stride 2: Conduct a "winners watch"—an environmental scan of your career field and industry to identify the individuals and organizations that are either recognized as leaders today or viewed as the up-and-coming leaders of tomorrow.

Tap friends and colleagues, published information and your own observations to build a list of those with whom you might like to work at some point in the future.

Repetitions: Conduct this environmental scan every 6 months, updating your list as necessary to reflect the shifting positions of individuals and organizations.

This research will:

- Help you understand the fullest possible dimensions of success in your field and industry;

- Uncover the alternative pathways to achieving that success in your career;

  and

- Enable you to spot, sometimes even before they are recognized by others, up and coming individual and organizational winners and lay the foundation for working with them.

Where will you perform this stride in your work?

Stride 3: Create a "career safety net" of potential employment opportunities and workplace contacts that could accelerate and multiply the success you achieve at work.

Use the lists you developed in Strides 1 and 2 and the networking techniques you apply in Exercise II to meet and develop a professional relationship with specific individual winners and with key employees of organizational winners. Build the widest possible circle of contacts consistent with your ability to get to know each of them well.

Repetitions: Devote at least 4 hours every 2 months to building this career safety net.

Your networking will:

- Help you enhance your personal visibility and stature with those individuals who can aid and abet the advancement of your career;

- Enable you to investigate those employers for which you might like to work and be recognized by the individuals who could help you to achieve that goal;

  and

- Acquire the necessary background on and understanding of specific individual and organizational winners to select the ones that best fit you at any given point in your career and compile a compelling case for your working with them.

Where will you perform this stride in your work?

Use the results of Stride 1 to make sure you're working with a winner in your current employment situation. If you are unable to secure such a position with a coworker, seek out a guide. If neither a guide nor a coworker is available, make sure the organization, itself, is a winner and that your work for it enables you to achieve significant growth on your own.

If such self-development isn't possible (and there continues to be no opportunity for you to work with an individual winner), use the results of Stride 2 to identify an alternative employer to which you can move. Make sure this transition is well planned but execute it as quickly as you can. It should position you to work with one or more individual winners within an organization that is, itself, a winner. If that isn't possible, always opt for a position that will enable you to work with at least one individual winner. In general, it's those coworkers and guides who will provide the most direct and enduring benefit to you.

Repetitions: Review your work situation every 6 months and confirm that you are working with and/or for winners. If you are, make sure you capitalize on the opportunity. If you aren't, make a change as soon as you can effectively do so.

These personal positioning efforts will:

*   Ensure that your employment always enables you to do your best work and continue your career advancement;

*   Help you determine the timing and direction of career transitions that will serve your best interests in the present and the future;

    and

*   Establish you in the workplace as someone who knows how to work with and for winners and is, therefore, a winner as well.

Where will you perform this stride in your work?

Other Strides

The preceding exercise strides are the minimum essential for you to tone your career by working with winners. If you are interested and able, you can supplement them with the following additional activities:

- Volunteer for a special assignment or to work on a project that will put you into contact with a winner who might not normally be accessible to you within your employer's structure or normal operations.

- Volunteer to serve on a special committee or task force for your professional or trade association where you will be able to meet and interact with the most successful individuals in your field.

- Reach out to a leader in your field and solicit their interest in coauthoring a paper for publication in a business or trade journal or in co-presenting at a professional or trade conference.

- If the leaders in your field write blogs, pick the person whose views seem most interesting to you and develop a relationship with them by contributing your thoughts and insights to their commentary.

What additional acitivies will you add to your Career Fitness strides?

My Exercise Record

Use the following worksheet to:

- Plan the time you are going to devote to each stride in the exercise and to set up a schedule for that activity in the upcoming months.

- Record your plan for and actual repetitions of each stride. Make sure your entries are accurate and up-to-date.

- Monitor your commitment to the work-in and to this exercise, in particular. Make corrective adjustments, as necessary.

The record is organized as an annual progression of monthly activity. Not every stride in every exercise is performed on a monthly basis, but the planning for and monitoring of your performance is. That continuous preparation and review optimizes the impact of your activity and ensures that you derive the maximum benefit from your effort.

Plan / Actual	Step 1	Step 2	Step 3	Step 4
Month				
Month				
Month				
Month				
Month				
Month				
Month				
Month				
Month				
Month				
Month				
Month				

VI. Pace Yourself

Exercise Strategy

You are unlikely to run the best time you will ever run in a marathon, the first time you enter one. You will almost certainly not play your best game of tennis, the first time you pick up a racket. And, you will probably not bowl a perfect game, the first time you visit a bowling alley.

The same is true with your career. You will not achieve the best you can be in your profession, craft or trade during your first year of work or even your first decade in the workplace. Indeed, the premise of Career Fitness is that you always can and must improve the capabilities and expression of your Natural.

That goal is too big and too significant to be achieved without constant practice. And, practice takes time and effort. Therefore, you must give yourself adequate time both to develop your Natural through its practical application on-the-job and to recuperate from the exertion of that activity off or away from the job.

Happily, practicing your Natural is unlike physical activity. Even when they involve physical tasks—in manufacturing, military service and professional sports—your personal bests in the world of work are not limited by age, but only by endurance. You may change how you use your Natural, but you can continue to push the boundaries of self-excellence for all of your working life.

To put it another way, there is no stop sign in your pursuit of Happiness ... if you give yourself adequate rest along the way. You can accomplish real and important career victories as long as you are willing to explore and extend the application of your personal talent and do so at a pace you can sustain and enjoy day-in and day-out.

In fact, career health is an aspect of the human experience that grows stronger and better with time. The longer you work at it, the fuller and richer its dimensions become. Precisely for that reason, there's no need to rush.

You won't lose anything by giving yourself the time necessary to practice at being the best you can be and to relax regularly so that your commitment to superior work can be regenerated. And, you won't gain anything by abusing yourself to achieve some goal that has only fleeting importance or by trying to prove your loyalty to an employer through the destruction of your own physical and mental health. The best way to build career fitness, in short, is to pace yourself.

In the 21st Century world of work, however, pacing is often hard to accomplish. While it would be easy to blame employers for this situation, the culprit is frequently ourselves. We labor too hard, too long and too fast for our own good. In effect, we allow ourselves to become addicted to work. We suffer from workaholism.

Workaholism

More and more Americans are working more and more hours than ever before. Some believe they must put in the extra time in order to hang onto their jobs, while others are convinced that spending a lot of time in the office or on the road is the key to career success.

- Sadly, those in the first group are often correct—some organizations have reduced the size of their workforce to such an extent that every employee must perform the work of two (or more) jobs. There is simply no allowance, therefore, for anyone to get the rest they need and deserve.

- Those in the second group, in contrast, are also being harmed, but not by their employers. Ironically, they are abusing themselves. They are undermining their own physical and mental health, their relationships with their families and friends, and the health of their careers. They are inflicting this damage because they have misinterpreted the controlling dynamic of the American Dream. They think their hard work, rather than their best work is the key to success.

Americans now spend more hours on-the-job than do English, French or German workers and even the famously devoted salarymen of Japan. We may be the richest nation on earth, but we have precious little time to enjoy our standard of living.

For example, according to the U. S. Bureau of Labor Statistics, the average workweek in the U.S. now drags on for 49 hours, or 350 more hours per year than the average workweek in Europe. Worse, a 2003 survey by Expedia found that one-out-of-every-seven American workers (13 percent) actually took no vacation time that year because they were too busy working.

A poll by Spherion uncovered even more troubling results. It asked 600 people about their work and personal lives and found that a staggering 51 percent spent seven or more hours of personal time each week thinking about work. To put it another way, even when Americans aren't laboring away in the workplace, they are still consumed by it.

When asked what impact this behavior has had on their lives:

- 32 percent said it adversely affected their family and relationships;

- 27 percent said it undermined their health and fitness;

  and

- 20 percent said it detracted from their sex lives and hobbies.

In other words, almost 80 percent of U.S. workers recognize the harmful impact of working too long and too hard. They know that such a pace eventually wears them down and undermines their performance on-the-job. And yet, they keep it up. For them, overdoing work has become an insidious addiction. There is even an organization that provides support and assistance for those who are struggling with this affliction. It's called Workaholics Anonymous (www.workaholics-anonymous.org).

The employment-related consequences of workaholism are bad enough, but there is another side effect of this condition that is not as obvious, but is just as damaging. Ironically, focusing too much of your time and effort on your job can cause irreparable harm to your career. It can blind you to what's best for you.

Such all-consuming behavior interferes with your ability to invest the personal attention and skill required to manage your workplace experience successfully. When you devote so much of your waking day to the accomplishment of your job, you deny yourself time for the accomplishment of your career. You set aside the Career Fitness Work-in and put off the actions you must take to pursue happiness in your work.

Moreover, the notion that you have no choice but to work at an unhealthy pace is just not true. As discussed in Chapter Five, what employers now need to compete successfully in the global economy is talent—the capacity for excellence—delivered on-the-job. While hard work is also necessary, that effort must now be integrated with a commitment to superior performance. And more and more, employers understand that superior performance can only be sustained with workers who are well rested and physically and mentally alert.

Most, however, will not initiate that restorative interval on your behalf. You have to claim it for yourself. Further, only you have the self-awareness to know when you need rest and recuperation and for how long. So, it's actually best that you set the pace for your career—one you judge to be sustainable and healthy.

Simple as it may sound and as obvious as it may seem, you must set boundaries on your work. Such limitations only have an impact, however, if you exercise self-control and self-discipline. Those words define responsibilities. They obligate you:

- to prioritize the goals you establish for personal growth in your field in order to manage employers' expectations of your work on-the-job;

  and

- to protect the time you allocate for rest and recuperation outside the workplace in order to perform at your peak in the workplace.

To put it another way, you must husband your energy and enthusiasm so they are always available to stimulate your best performance and thus maximize your contribution on-the-job. You have a lifetime to be successful at work, so you should pace your career so that it respects and supports your life.

Prioritize The Goals You Establish For Personal Growth

Establishing healthy expectations for your work on-the-job is an exercise in multitasking and reprioritization. You must now see your work as both a contribution to your employer's success and a step forward in your own pursuit of Happiness. Those tasks are equally important and, therefore, equally as deserving of your best effort.

To attain that balance, however, you will likely have to assign more priority to your self-task. Historically, many of us have viewed our work as a single activity focused exclusively on our employer's wellbeing. That outcome remains as important as it ever was, but now we must also give the same measure of attention to our own wellbeing. One is as vital as the other.

How do you install such a balance?

You must ensure that you select an employer whose culture fits your values and personality and whose mission is aligned with and advances your career. Unfortunately, achieving this match at any particular point in your career isn't easy. It won't happen by simply taking the first job offer you get or by relying solely on what you read at an employer's Web-site. To find the best match for you, you have to do your homework; you must research each prospective employer so you discover its true nature up front, before you make a commitment, not later, after you've accepted an offer.

In the 20th Century, this research was typically limited to wading through books that were often out-of-date and annual reports and other organizational material that employers published about themselves. Today, you have many more sources to tap, which collectively provide you with a more current and comprehensive view of alternative opportunities.

These sources include:

- Search engines on the Internet (e.g., Google, Yahoo!, Bing) that enable you to find and reach the latest articles and news reports published about specific organizations;

- Online databases (e.g., Hoovers Online (www.hoovers.com), the EDGAR database of the U.S. Securities and Exchange Commission (www.sec.gov)) that give you access to detailed financial, management and operational information for both public and private companies;

- Insights from employees—using the techniques described in Exercise II, you can network online and off to connect with the organization's current employees. These interactions will often give you a sense of their morale and esprit de corps as well as a more contemporaneous perspective on what it's like to work for one employer versus another.

- OPR—Other People's Research or information collected by other organizations that is available to you for free online. These include:

  o GlassDoor.com, which describes itself as "… a free jobs and career community that offers the world an inside look at jobs and companies. What sets us apart is our 'employee generated content'—anonymous salaries, company reviews, interview questions, and more—all posted by employees, job seekers, and sometimes the companies themselves."

  o CareerBliss.com, which describes itself as "… a leading job information-hub constantly improving our free valuable resources, like our happiness assessment developed by experts, database of millions of salaries, and hundreds of thousands of company reviews to guide you in your path of workplace happiness. The best part is that our info comes from feedback from real employees. We're the number one place to find out what job seekers and professionals are saying about their companies and jobs."

Collectively, the information you acquire will help you identify and select employers where the work you do for the organization is also worthwhile and beneficial to you. Such employers provide an environment in which you make a meaningful and measurable contribution to them by working at the three objectives you established for yourself: the Achievement, Advancement and Development goals in your Career Fitness Plan.

Though those two endeavors are very different, they have the same power source. They are accomplished by your drive to be your personal best. It alone makes two #1 priorities worthwhile and feasible. In effect, you are pacing your career to express and experience your Natural.

Centering your career on the realization of your own talent, however, does not mean you ignore the health of your employer. There are times when you can and should set aside your own interests for those of the organization. These situations involve:

- Surges in your employer's production or service delivery obligations;

- A special project that is critical to the organization's accomplishment of its mission;

  or

- Crises related to customer dissatisfaction or sudden changes in the marketplace or supply chain.

These occurrences are non-routine and short-lived. They do not dictate that you take on onerous workloads permanently or put your own career on hold indefinitely. They require, instead, that you pick up the pace for a reasonable period of time in order to protect or promote your employer. Said another way, giving your career the attention it deserves doesn't mean you shouldn't also be a good team player when the situation warrants.

No less important, giving your personal goals more priority in the workweek also creates a significant advantage for your employers. As an expert in your field, you are reinforcing the value of your skills and knowledge, and as an expert who shares that value through high performance on-the-job, you are delivering a real and substantial return on your employer's paycheck.

Pacing yourself with a focus on your Natural, therefore, establishes a new balance of benefit in the workplace. It nurtures the health and vigor of your career so you can nurture the health and vigor of your employers. That symbiotic relationship promotes mutual respect, mutual commitment, and mutual success. And, those three elements are the foundation for success in the 21st Century world of work.

Protect the Time You Allocate For Rest and Recuperation

Your work experience must, itself, be well designed and executed if it is to produce genuine and enduring happiness. An optimum experience on-the-job doesn't wear you out, it revives you; it doesn't deplete your focus and creativity, it reinforces them; it doesn't sap your commitment to being the best you can be, it positions you for peak performance.

Work, however, even in the best of circumstances, is strenuous; it is mental and/or physical effort. For that reason, your work experience must also include periods of non-work and recuperation. Think of these intervals as the days of rest a baseball pitcher needs between starts or the time golf and tennis champions give themselves to reinvigorate their talent between tournaments. No matter how good you are—indeed, to be the best you can be—you must pace your work so that your body and mind can refresh.

Workaholics deny themselves the time for such regeneration. That's self-abuse. Surveys have also found that some employers devise schedules, create expectations and set priorities that deny workers the opportunity for relaxation and recuperation. That's employee abuse

These distorted experiences are like heart disease. They block your access to the revitalizing rest that enhances your performance and sustains your career. And, unfortunately, both kinds of blockages are now on the rise in the American workplace.

For most of us, the workday is now filled with outsized demands that keep us on-the-job more hours of our day and more days of our week than ever before. According to a 2006 survey, fewer than 10 percent of U.S. office workers now take a full hour for a meal at midday. They do so despite the fact that three-quarters of the surveyed workers also said their productivity goes up when they take a break at lunchtime. Nevertheless, they avoid the healthy behavior because they believe it is the only way they can get their work done.

This relentless pushing on-the-job makes it all the more important to take the appropriate time away from work to recuperate. If there's no rest in the workplace, we must, at least, use our periods of earned vacations and holidays to get the regenerative time we need away from it. Unfortunately, however, that too doesn't happen.

Today, one-third of American workers don't use all of the vacation days they are allowed. And, when they do take vacation, four-in-ten of them take only a week off. In fact, just 16 percent of us now take a two-week vacation. Why? Once again, surveys indicate that many people feel they have too much work to do or that they will be seen as less committed, less supportive or less loyal by their employers.

Worse, even when we're on vacation, we're never actually cut off from the office. Over 90 percent of the respondents to a 2006 survey said they were either "very likely" or "somewhat likely" to check their e-mail while on vacation. Sit on the beach anywhere in North America, and you'll see men and women busily scrolling through the messages on their BlackBerries or iPhones. While some fear they will lose control if they're not in touch and others are convinced that the office can't function without them, a growing number of us simply don't know how to relax or feel guilty if we do.

For them, Wharton, the business school at the University of Pennsylvania, has an answer. The advertisements for its executive education programs are a huge white space with a single question: *Because what's vacation time for anyway?* The implication is clear. A vacation is wasteful if it's not focused on work. Absolutely, education is important, but so too is the rest humans need to absorb that education and use it effectively on-the-job.

The antidote to this unhealthy behavior is pacing. You must take control of the rate at which you work both day-in, day-out and over the course of the year. Pacing, in effect, is a commitment to self-moderation and self-regulation. It involves both managing the expectations of your employers and resetting the personal clock by which you manage yourself. The former is possible if you are at the top of your game—ironically, you are best able to secure time away from work when you have achieved a level of performance that makes your work indispensable to your employer—while the latter can only be realized by learning the art of restfulness.

Career Fitness gives you the power to assert your right to rest and recuperation. If you have developed your Natural to the point that it is invaluable to your employers, they will understand what it would do to them if they lost it. They will, therefore, respect your effort to keep it at its prime. They will accept that peak performance exacts a toll and recognize the importance of regular periods of appropriate regeneration—of unforgotten and uninterrupted vacations and holidays.

Then, you must actually use that time for your benefit. You must practice the art of restfulness. Restfulness is a state that can only be reached by ceasing work. As simple as that sounds, it is an elusive goal.

True cessation only occurs when the stoppage is complete and durable. It must take you physically, mentally and emotionally out of the workplace and away from your work. In other words, you must cease not only the activity of work but the long tail of internal demands it places on you. You haven't turned off your work if you go home and worry about it there or if you go on vacation and tether yourself to it with your cell phone or personal digital assistant.

Ceasing work means you consciously use a space you claim in your daily life, in your monthly schedule and in your planning for the year, to put aside your commitment to the development of your Natural. You create an inner environment that is as undirected but also as unconstrained and frictionless as outer space. In other words, you give yourself permission to halt your quest to be your personal best.

Experiencing the benefits of the space you have claimed for yourself when you stop work does not mean you cease being active. The Career Fitness Work-in is a course of action for strengthening the satisfaction and rewards of your time on-the-job. When you take a break from work, you reallocate that time to an increasingly unfamiliar activity in the American culture: personal leisure.

When you are at leisure, you are acting in a way that provides rest and recuperation. For that to happen, you must carefully plan and prepare for your leisure time. A carelessly designed vacation can be just as stressful (or more) as a bad day at the office. Similarly, a holiday won't help to regenerate you if you spend every waking moment doing things that tire you out and wear you down.

We are all different, however, so the most beneficial leisure for one person may not be appropriate for someone else. To experience the rest and recuperation you seek, therefore, you must identify the right leisure activity for you and devote your non-work time to that activity.

Pacing yourself imposes discipline on your career. It helps you to organize your time so that you are able to do your best work on-the-job, while still enjoying the life you have outside the workplace. It ensures that your efforts to build Career Fitness proceed in a fashion that is not too fast, but not too slow either, and never too much. As with your physical health, overexertion, no less than laziness, can diminish the power and promise of your career. The right pace enables you to avoid the danger of both and, as a result, invigorates your work and your life.

Exercise Strides for Pacing Yourself

Stride 1: Review your performance on-the-job to ensure you are multitasking in your work (assigning equal priority to both your employer's and your own wellbeing) and that its governing dynamic is the expression and experience of your Natural.

Repetitions: Perform this assessment 2 times per year, during every other personal performance review.

Using the realization of your Natural to pace your career will:

- Guide you to work for those organizations that are most likely to support the health of your career;

- Enable you to deliver a meaningful contribution to your employer through sustained superior performance on-the-job;

  and

- Position you to make the continuous personal progress that is essential to a successful and satisfying career in the long as well as the short term.

Where will you perform this stride in your work?

The pursuit of Happiness may be an inalienable right, but it is also hard work. It can only be accomplished through on-the-job experiences that develop and express your Natural. It is a daily commitment to performing at your peak that pushes you to your limits. You can't achieve that objective, therefore, unless you husband your strength. You can't continuously do your best work unless you know which leisure activities will refresh and regenerate you. You must acquire this self-knowledge so you can put it to work for you.

Repetitions: Devote 10 minutes at the beginning of every work day to acquiring and then affirming this personal insight. Instead of looking forward to a holiday or vacation as simply a halt to your work, anticipate these times for the rest and recuperation they will bring you.

Learning what you must do to rest and recuperate will:

• Assign your leisure time the importance it deserves in your career;

• Remind you to infuse your holidays and vacations with an activity that actually relaxes and regenerates you;

and

• Honor rest and recuperation for the role they play in helping you to lead a healthy career.

Where will you perform this stride in your work?

Stride 3: Review your Career Fitness Plan to ensure that the goals you are setting will stretch you to new accomplishments without harming you through overwork or overreaching.

The purpose of your Achievement, Advancement and Development goals is not to exhaust you from the effort, but rather to ensure that your effort elicits your best work at any particular moment in time. They must enable you to step up to the challenge of improving yourself, but not force you to trample on the rest of your life. Your plan, therefore, must include the periodic rest and recuperation that are the underpinnings of sustained peak performance.

Repetitions: Evaluate the pace you've set for the accomplishment of your goals every quarter, during your personal performance review.

Setting work limits and adhering to them will:

- Afford you the necessary time away from the workplace to replenish your electrolytes of energy and enthusiasm for the career goals you've set;

- Enable you to sustain a high level of performance during non-routine situations (i.e., the critical but short-lived requirements that occasionally arise in the workplace) as well as normal work operations;

    and

- Give you the time and space to appreciate the whole of who you are and hope to become.

Where will you perform this stride in your work?

Stride 4: Get what you need and deserve out of the time you have set aside for leisure activity.

The quality of your leisure time—the rest and recuperation it actually provides—depends upon your ability to plan and prepare appropriately for it. Therefore, you must monitor what you do on holidays and vacations to ensure you have selected activities that will reduce your stress and increase your motivation on-the-job.

Repetitions: Conduct this evaluation every quarter, during your personal performance review.

Critiquing the allotment and caliber of time you set aside for rest and recuperation will:

- Remind you of the importance of pacing as you build a healthy career;

- Ensure that you actually derive the benefits that come from rest and recuperation;

  and

- Prepare you to pursue happiness at work with the very best of your ability and from the first to the final day of your career.

Where will you perform this stride in your work?

Other Strides

The preceding exercise strides are the minimum essential for you to enhance your standard of life by stretching yoexercise strides are the minimum essential for you to pace your career so that you can achieve and sustain the fulfillment you deserve at work. If you are interested and able, you can supplement them with the following additional activities:

- Join a discussion group online or a club in your community whose members share your interest in a particular hobby or pastime.

- Turn off the television or computer and go to bed earlier each night so that you get as much rest as possible on a regular basis.

- Leave the office each day with enough time to get home and have dinner with your family.

What additional acitivies will you add to your Career Fitness strides?

My Exercise Record

Use the following worksheet to:

- Plan the time you are going to devote to each stride in the exercise and to set up a schedule for that activity in the upcoming months.

- Record your plan for and actual repetitions of each stride. Make sure your entries are accurate and up-to-date.

- Monitor your commitment to the work-in and to this exercise, in particular. Make corrective adjustments, as necessary.

The record is organized as an annual progression of monthly activity. Not every stride in every exercise is performed on a monthly basis, but the planning for and monitoring of your performance is. That continuous preparation and review optimizes the impact of your activity and ensures that you derive the maximum benefit from your effort.

Plan / Actual	Step 1	Step 2	Step 3	Step 4
Month				
Month				
Month				
Month				
Month				
Month				
Month				
Month				
Month				
Month				
Month				
Month				

VII. Stretch Your Soul

Exercise Strategy

Work that serves your own well-being and happiness is the external dimension of a successful career; work that serves the well-being and happiness of others is its internal dimension— its soul. Both kinds of work are essential to a healthy and rewarding career. Together, they compose a complete person in the world of work, a person capable of genuine success in their pursuit of Happiness.

As the previous five exercises indicate, Career Fitness involves the things you do to better yourself—the work you perform to expand the depth and richness of your personal best. The work-in identifies the activities in which you must engage to:

- build up your capacity in your own special talent—your Natural;

- express that unique capability in your work at every point in your career;

    and

- enjoy and be rewarded by that expression through your employment.

While the exercises do potentially contribute to the well-being of others—your spouse, life partner and children, if you have them—and to the success of others—your employers, coworkers and professional peers—their central focus and their ultimate goal are to maximize the benefits you derive. As it has been described to this point, Career Fitness is a strategy for taking charge of your career and ensuring that it serves you and your interests.

A healthy career, however, is not exclusively self-directed or self-absorbed. It has an individual focus and a collective purpose, as well. In other words, you can be your personal best only when you attend to both your own well-being and to the well-being of others, including those you may not know or even have met. Career Fitness, therefore, also involves the actions you take to assist others and improve the world around you. Think of it as work for your spirit.

This second dimension of Career Fitness is fundamentally an exercise in affirmative humanity. It acknowledges and addresses the opportunity and obligation each and all of us have to celebrate and respect the human species and the planet which supports it. Our collective purpose is not, however, an activity that exists in concept or theory. It is work, but work we do for those with whom we share:

- a social connection—our friends and neighbors;

- a civic connection—our fellow citizens of the United States of America;

- a global connection—our fellow members of the world community;

    and

- a custodial connection—our universal role as stewards of our home, the planet on which we live.

Soul work applies your Natural to the spiritual bonds that tie together all of humankind, whatever our individual age, gender, religious, ethnic, socio-economic, or other differences. Despite our increasingly fragmented and self-conscious world, it focuses on and strives to improve what connects us as people. It applies the best you can be to what others hope to be, need to be, deserve to be. In the process, it strengthens your compassion, reinforces your inherent goodness, and expands the purpose and impact of your life's work. When you work for yourself, you are developing your standard of living; when you work for others, you are developing your standard of life.

This collective purpose instills and nurtures a broader perspective in your career, a critical sense of communal responsibility. Your jobs and successes do not occur in a vacuum. They are intrinsically linked to the people and planet around you. They depend upon and, in turn, contribute to their well-being—as well as yours—in the present and the future.

A healthy career recognizes and honors that dual relationship; it serves the greater good as well as the personal good. It recognizes and respects our individual duty to serve us all. As a consequence, your dedication to both spheres of work is the penultimate expression of the champion inside you.

Soul work, however, involves far more than the occasional monetary contributions we make to charitable organizations or our participation in the annual company blood drive. These are helpful actions, to be sure, but they are not an expression of your personal best. Just as you can only achieve that supreme state in the physical world through the work you do on-the-job, the only way you can stretch your soul is through the work you do for the betterment of humankind. In essence, you must set aside some of the time and talent you could have applied to your own well-being and apply them, instead, to the well-being of others. You must be employed in their service. That is yet another and essential component of true work-life balance in the 21st Century.

In practical terms, this broader perspective means that you stretch your soul by recognizing and accepting a larger role for your Natural. You acknowledge certain social, civic, global and environmental responsibilities and attend to them through your work. You establish a goal—you define a career victory—that is larger than personal gain and strive to achieve that goal with all of the vigor and determination that you commit to serving yourself. You may still donate money or give blood, but you also contribute your special talent to those who need it, but cannot pay you for it. You labor not for what you can get, but for what you can give.

Ironically, that contribution leaves you richly compensated. By its very nature, soul work delivers an extraordinary personal paycheck. Not in cash certainly. And, not in the accoutrements of modern American culture. Instead, what you earn from your work for the collective good adds to the quality of your life. It accrues in your spirit. It is a direct deposit to the satisfaction and happiness you earn from having done some of your best work on behalf of others.

How Do You Perform Soul Work?

What does soul work look like? And, how do you perform it?

Soul work can involve your taking either or both of two paths. The first path directs your career into the not-for-profit sector, nongovernmental organizations (NGOs) or other institutions where the explicit mission is to serve the needs of others and/or the environment. In other words, soul work is your life's work. You choose to serve others as an occupation, as the work you do with your Natural in each and every job you take. The way you earn your living is the way you stretch your soul.

The second path to soul work is no less meaningful or fulfilling. Indeed, it requires as much commitment to sharing your Natural as the first. While it does not focus your career on serving others, it obliges you to take another job to do so. In addition to the two jobs you already have—the first involving the self-management of your career and the second pertaining to the work for which you are employed—you also volunteer for a third—a role where you can use your Natural to work for others and/or for the planet on which they and you live.

There are, of course, many different ways to embark on this third path. It is just as important, therefore, to pick the right job when you are working for others as it is to do so when you are working for yourself. Laboring for the good of others is not penance or punishment. It is not an exercise in denying yourself satisfaction or fulfillment. Quite the contrary, stretching your soul increases your capacity to be the best you can be. It extends the development and expression of your Natural. As a result, your third job enlarges the goodness within you. It leads you to yet another career victory.

That outcome can only be achieved, however, if you are in the right roles for you. Just as you will work in a range of positions during that part of your career which focuses on your own success, you are also likely to be employed in more than one role during the time you invest in working for others. The priorities and needs of the organizations where you will do your soul work will change from time-to-time, and your own abilities, outlook and opportunities will change, as well. These natural shifts may—indeed likely will—cause you to move from one kind of soul work to another as your career unfolds.

How do you select the best third job for you at any given point in your career? Evaluate your options using two criteria:

(1) Does the role engage you with its purpose, goal or mission? Is it an activity that seems particularly important and worthwhile to you?

(2) Does the role enable you to serve others to the best of your ability? Can you use your Natural to work for others in a meaningful and worthwhile way?

For example, you might participate in:

- a mentoring program that provides support and role models for at-risk youth in your area;

- a citizen's beautification program that maintains the shrubs and flowers in your community's park;

- a joint program between your employer and local schools that provides additional resources and educational support for students;

- a highway adoption program that improves the cleanliness and safety of local roads;

- a meal center and shelter that provides services and support for the homeless and others in need;

    or

- a construction and rehabilitation program that upgrades residences for the aged, infirm or disadvantaged.

Soul work is as varied as the human condition. Your selection of a particular activity or program, therefore, should be based on the opportunity it provides to apply your Natural effectively in the service of others. Your goal is to make a difference in their lives. To have a positive impact on one person or many, on the community you call home or on the only planet we all have.

Soul work is the legacy you create not to be remembered or celebrated, but to honor the humanity we all share. It is the antithesis of the self-congratulatory, name-the-building-after-me approach of so many of today's most "successful" people. For all of the benefit such financial commitments often provide, they are not work done for the good of others. They do not involve giving of one's special talent, but rather of one's wealth. They are a financial investment, not a spiritual investment. They are not, therefore, true soul work.

To stretch your soul, you must push yourself beyond what you do for yourself and do what you do, but for others. More than that, you must also reach for the best inside you and extend it to those around you. As you do in the organizations which employ you, you must agree to share your Natural with them. You must donate your talent and put it to work for them. In essence, you become their benefactor through the gift of your Natural.

Readying Yourself for Soul Work

Achieving an openness to the validity and centrality of soul work in your career requires that you pass through three stages of personal development.

The First Stage

The first stage is recognition. You must recognize the impact that you as a single person can have on the environment, on poverty, on homelessness, on the education of youth, on any of a myriad of situations that affect humankind's experience on planet Earth. These are clearly large and difficult challenges, and government programs—where an organization is responsible for the work involved—cannot completely solve them. Indeed, the only genuine solution—the one approach that produces the scale and durability necessary to achieve a lasting positive outcome—is the daily, sustained action that you and every other person can provide, if you chose to do so.

The Second Stage

The second stage is acceptance. You must accept personal responsibility for achieving a positive outcome for others either on-the-job or in some other workplace. Wherever it is done—in a human rights program building the moral and legal case for freeing political prisoners around the world, through your service on the Board of a not-for-profit promoting educational reform for high school students across the country, or in the time you volunteer at the local food bank—this work must become as central to your career as the work that you do for yourself. You must reach the point where you willingly accord it the same priority and level of commitment as your workplace deadlines. It must be a career victory that feels as important to you as your greatest accomplishment on-the-job or the growth you can achieve in your profession, craft or trade.

The Third Stage

The third stage is action. You must act on your recognition and acceptance. You must apply your Natural—your special talent—to a specific collective purpose, an organization or program where you can serve others. The goodness of your work is not measured by the time you put in, but by the caliber of the effort you make. A meaningful contribution to addressing whatever challenge you select doesn't demand all or even most of your time; it just requires some of your best time. It deserves your resolute determination to perform at your peak, to give your championship effort in support of its mission. That commitment is the career victory you achieve by expanding the limits of your optimal experience so that it encompasses not only what your work does for you, but what it does, as well, for the people and plant around you.

Getting Started on Soul Work

To execute this exercise, you must pass through all three stages. Not only is there no shortcut, but there is no way even to begin unless you first reject the egocentrism and self-absorption that dominate so much of modern business culture. You must excuse yourself from the sensatory, superficial crowd. You have to look within yourself and find the courage and conviction to pass through the first stage, the wisdom and maturity to pass through the second stage, and the resolve and magnanimity to pass through the third. That is why this exercise is fundamentally an act of affirmative humanity.

Moreover, the third stage—the initiation of action—is not the end of your passage, but it's perpetuation. It begins your work on behalf of others, but it also continues that work, as well. It is a stage and a state, a state of being in service to a purpose larger than yourself.

For example, if your Natural is:

- your ability to help people grow and develop their full potential, then you might volunteer to work as a counselor for a mentoring program that provides support and role models for at-risk youth in your area;

- your ability to create and sustain beautiful landscapes, then you might volunteer to work as a garden designer for a citizen's beautification program that maintains the shrubs and flowers in your community's park;

- your ability to perform complex mathematical operations and explain them to others, you might volunteer to work as a curriculum developer for a joint program between your employer and local schools that provides additional resources and educational support for students;

- your ability to communicate the importance of issues and ideas to the public, then you might volunteer to work as a public relations coordinator for a highway adoption program that improves the cleanliness and safety of local roads;

- your ability to provide friendly and helpful customer service, you might volunteer to work as a staff trainer at a meal center and shelter that provides services and support for the homeless and others in need;

    or

- your ability to organize and lead teams in executing complicated operations, you might volunteer to work as a project manager for a construction and rehabilitation program that upgrades residences for the aged, infirm or disadvantaged.

This commitment to action represents a very different approach to volunteering for or contributing to extant social service and civic organizations. In many cases, these groups have been habituated into viewing individual participation as either manual labor or a financial gift. As adding hands or dollars (or both) to the group's work.

Historically, they have not had the opportunity to draw on and, no less important, to apply the skills and knowledge—the special talent—of those who support them. As a consequence, some institutions may find it difficult to do so. At least initially, they may not know how to put you to work in your Natural in the accomplishment of their mission. Helping them to do so, then, may be your first assignment.

This preparatory instruction is as much a part of stretching your soul as the actual "job" you ultimately perform Indeed, it is an integral component of your role as a volunteer, for it opens such groups up to a deeper and richer form of talent than many have ever had access to before. It enables them to put your Natural and that of others into the service of their mission.

What does this instruction involve? What must you teach these organizations in order for them to tap your talent effectively?

First, you may have to help them visualize the "donation" of your Natural as a contribution in kind that has genuine value to them. They may not be familiar with your skill set or fully understand how it can be employed in the workplace. Second, you will likely have to show them the alternative ways they could realize that value through your employment in the organization. You may have to describe what you can do and where it can benefit them in the accomplishment of their mission.

For many in the business world, where the use of your skills is better understood, this preliminary activity may seem silly and a waste of time. In most cases, however, exactly the opposite is true. By definition, non-profit and voluntary organizations do not operate in the same way as the for-profit, commercial enterprises which likely employ you. This instruction, therefore, prepares them to realize the full potential of the best you have to offer. It sets the conditions of your soul work so that you use your special talent and do so in a way that actually benefits others.

Finally, this exercise explicitly acknowledges that working for the betterment of those around you and the planet on which we all coexist isn't something that you set aside until your "real" career is over. It is not the work you take up after you retire or after you've made your fortune (although it should certainly be done then, as well). Rather, stretching your soul is an activity that is central to the living of a healthy career. It cannot be postponed until your schedule or commitments make it more convenient. It must be integrated into your day, each and every day. Think of it as the vitamin you take to fortify your spirit on-the-job. It ensures you have the minimum essential elements to be the best you can be.

Exercise Strides for Stretching Your Soul

Stride 1: Join a local, national or international environmental or social service organization and participate in its activities.

While employer endorsed and/or supported programs are clearly convenient—they are often permitted to operate during lunch breaks and even during business hours—they may not be the best option for you. Your selection of a program, therefore, should primarily be based on your assessment of where you can have the greatest positive impact. Pick the program where you will be able to do the most good by volunteering your Natural.

Repetitions: Stretching your soul is not an exercise in meeting attendance, but rather a commitment to meeting the needs of others. To be performed effectively, therefore, it should involve work—the application of your Natural on behalf of the organization's mission, and that work should occur no less frequently than 1 time every 2 months.

This work on behalf of others will:

- Refresh your spirit and enrich the sense of well-being and happiness you derive from the application of your Natural;

- Counterbalance the personal focus and self-interest that, if overemphasized, can misshape your career;

  and

- Enable you to make a tangible contribution to the well-being and happiness of others and/or to the care of the planet on which we all live.

Where will you perform this stride in your work?

Make yourself as knowledgeable as possible about the soul work you have chosen to perform. Read about it, conduct research into it and talk to both those with whom you are working and those you are striving to serve.

Repetitions: Spend at least 1 hour per month performing this research and thinking about how to incorporate what you learn into your soul work.

Your research will:

• Give you the perspective and understanding you need to recognize the significance and value of your work on behalf of others;

• Enable you to pinpoint how best to apply your Natural so that you make the greatest contribution possible to the organization or program for which you are working;

and

• Help you better appreciate the power and the possibility of the extraordinary gift you have been given with your Natural.

Where will you perform this stride in your work?

Stride 3: Encourage others to do soul work.

Help your friends and coworkers recognize the integral and important role that spiritual wellness plays in building and enjoying a healthy career. Convey your message with gentle proselytizing, however, not with guilt or messianic zeal. Avoid strong-arm statements (e.g., "You really aren't doing your fair share.") and unflattering or unfair comparisons (e.g., "Everyone else is doing it, so why aren't you?").

Repetitions: Talk to someone about the importance of stretching their soul at least 2 times each quarter. If there's an opportunity to do so more frequently, certainly take advantage of it.

Your encouragement of friends and colleagues will:

- Help them better understand and, perhaps, even achieve the sense of purpose and satisfaction that can be derived from soul work;

- Multiply the good that is done in your local community and/or the world at large;

  and

- Give you a deeper connection to and appreciation for the work you do on behalf of others.

Where will you perform this stride in your work?

In most cases, it is not appropriate to describe your soul work on the public record of your career—your resume. Employers and recruiters may worry that your commitment to soul work will diminish your ability to perform on-the-job. Nevertheless, it's very important that you acknowledge and honor the commitment that you've made and the work that you've done on behalf of others.

Therefore, you should:

- Include your soul work in the personal and private record of your career, a document known as your Career Record (see Chapter Nine); and

- Remember and celebrate it by referring to that document regularly.

Repetitions: Give yourself this reward one time every quarter, during your personal performance review.

Rewarding yourself will:

- Ensure that you recognize and appreciate the career victories you achieve through your soul work;

- Reaffirm, in your own eyes, the value of the contributions you are making to the world around you;

    and

- Refresh your commitment to the spiritual dimension of your career.

Where will you perform this stride in your work?

Other Strides

The preceding exercise strides are the minimum essential for you to enhance your standard of life by stretching your soul. If you are interested and able, you can supplement them with the following additional activities:

- Conduct continuous research on your options for volunteering to ensure that you are always making the best use of your Natural in your soul work.

- Create a family foundation to address an unmet social, humanitarian or environmental need and find ways that each member of your family can donate their talent to it.

- Bring a colleague, a friend, and/or your children to work with you when you are performing this exercise so they can better understand the purpose and impact of soul work.

- Read a biography of someone who had a Natural similar to yours and put it to work in the service of others.

What additional acitivies will you add to your Career Fitness strides?

My Exercise Record

Use the following worksheet to:

- Plan the time you are going to devote to each stride in the exercise and to set up a schedule for that activity in the upcoming months.

- Record your plan for and actual repetitions of each stride. Make sure your entries are accurate and up-to-date.

- Monitor your commitment to the work-in and to this exercise, in particular. Make corrective adjustments, as necessary.

The record is organized as an annual progression of monthly activity. Not every stride in every exercise is performed on a monthly basis, but the planning for and monitoring of your performance is. That continuous preparation and review optimizes the impact of your activity and ensures that you derive the maximum benefit from your effort.

Plan / Actual	Step 1	Step 2	Step 3	Step 4
Month				
Month				
Month				
Month				
Month				
Month				
Month				
Month				
Month				
Month				
Month				
Month				

The Wisdom of the Work-in

The Career Fitness Work-in is a way for you to work personal growth and happiness into your career. It includes all of the activities necessary both:

- to practice the effective direction of your career so that it effectively supports your pursuit of Happiness;

  and

- to identify and be selected for employment opportunities that will enable you to do your best work.

The work-in produces beneficial and sustainable results because it is based on one of the most enduring principles of management: *what gets measured, gets done.*

Think of the work-in as a way for you to invest in yourself. It organizes and applies your best effort to your life's work and career on a continuous and regular basis. It gives you a plan with measurable steps that will protect you from the interruptions and demands that come your way every day. By performing the exercise strides according to the specified standards, you hold yourself accountable for the health of your career and you take the actions that will achieve it. You devote the same discipline and commitment to your occupational fitness as you devote (or should) to your physical fitness.

As with a physical workout, your Career Fitness Work-in will also ensure that you actually see results. These improvements, however, are not measured in promotions on an old-fashioned career ladder, but in the progress you make in realizing the special talent within you. Hence, the regimen. It moves you beyond career-self-management-by-chance—which is today's most prevalent form of work-related planning—to career-self-management-by-design. It enables you to establish the habit of committing clear, well reasoned personal direction and comprehensive, appropriate personal development to your experience in the workplace. The return on that effort is an ever expanding definition of your personal excellence.

Ultimately, the Career Fitness Work-in provides a structure that empowers you to reject and remove any and all constraints on who you are and what you can be at work. The expression of that self-optimized self, in turn, yields a career that rewards you with both self-respect and fulfillment. It transforms you into a champion. Naturally.

There are no artificial stimulants involved. There are no foreign compounds injected. It is all you and the all of you. That being—that ever more complete you—is the epitome of success; it is your pinnacle of achievement in the workplace. When you experience it, you reach the precious and penultimate objective of your career. You achieve Happiness.

Career Fitness Work-In Summary

Exercise I: Pump Up Your Cardiovascular System

Stride 1: Join your professional, technical or trade association and build your expertise by attending its events.

Repetitions: 1 session/2 months

Stride 2: Identify a social media community or employment Web-site that specializes in your field and offers an online platform (e.g., discussion forum, bulletin board or list server) for professional interaction and discussion. Join the peer-to-peer dialogue that occurs at such venues and draw on the knowledge that is shared.

Repetitions: Two 30-60 minute sessions/week

Stride 3: Using the medium with which you're most comfortable (i.e., print, online, audio), subscribe to and read one or more of the leading professional or trade publications in your field.

Repetitions: 2 hours/week

Stride 4: Using whatever medium is most effective for you (i.e., traditional classroom or online learning), take a class in your field that will optimize your performance on-the-job in the present and/or prepare you for moving to a more challenging and rewarding role in the future.

Repetitions: At least 1 course/2 years

Exercise II: Strengthen Your Circulatory System

Stride 1: While you are attending the local and/or national conferences, seminars and other events sponsored by your professional or trade association (see Exercise I), work on meeting and building a relationship with both people you know and those you don't.

Repetitions: Meet 2 new contacts and talk to 1 previous contact/meeting

Stride 2: Begin networking.

Repetitions: Interact with at least 1 person/session

Stride 3: Using whatever medium is most comfortable and effective for you (e.g., software, Rolodex or an old fashioned address book), set up an archive or database of professional contacts with whom you have established a relationship and keep it current.

Repetitions: Add 5 new contacts/quarter

Stride 4: Interact with the individuals in your archive/database on a regular basis. You can connect with them using Strides 1-2 or with a telephone call, an e-mail message or even a hand-written note delivered the old fashioned way by postal mail.

Repetitions: Network with at least 10% of your archive or database/month

Exercise III: Develop All of Your Muscle Groups

Stride 1: Enroll in a training or academic program that will build your functional capacity or performance expertise.

Repetitions: Take at least 1 but no more than 2 courses/2 year

Stride 2: Improve your peripheral vision by using your breaks at work as instructional opportunities.

Repetitions: Take 1 such walk/month

Stride 3: Join a local self-improvement group that will help you enhance your capabilities at work.

Repetitions: Invest 2 hours/month

Stride 4: Make yourself an apprentice. Seek out an expert and solicit their assistance in acquiring a specific functional or performance skill.

Repetitions: Interact with an expert at least 1 time/2 months

Exercise IV: Increase Your Flexibility and Range of Motion

Stride 1: Hold your finger up and see which way the wind is blowing in your organization.

Repetitions: Perform this assessment 1 time/quarter

Stride 2: Use the Internet to research what's being predicted for your career field, industry, employer, and location.

Repetitions: Devote 2 hours/month

Stride 3: Envision a successful change in your career.

Repetitions: Devote 4 hours/month

Stride 4: If you have a spouse or life partner, talk to them about the possibility and importance of transitions in your career. If you don't have a spouse or life partner, talk to members of your family.

Repetitions: Invest 4 hours/quarter

Exercise V: Work With Winners

Stride 1: Assess the caliber of those with whom you work.

Repetitions: Perform your assessment 1 time/quarter

Stride 2: Conduct a "winners watch"—an environmental scan of your career field and industry to identify the individuals and organizations that are either recognized as leaders today or viewed as the up-and-coming leaders of tomorrow.

Repetitions: Conduct your scan 1 time/6 months

Stride 3: Create a "career safety net" of potential employment opportunities and workplace contacts that could accelerate and multiply the success you achieve at work.

Repetitions: Devote at least 4 hours/2 months

Stride 4: Make sure you are working with the winners.

Repetitions: Review your work situation 1 time/6 months

Exercise VI: Pace Yourself

Stride 1: Review your performance on-the-job to ensure you are multitasking in your work (assigning equal priority to both your employer's and your own wellbeing) and that its governing dynamic is the expression and experience of your Natural.

Repetitions: Perform this assessment 2 times/year

Stride 2: Learn how to relax and rest.

Repetitions: Devote 10 minutes/work day

Stride 3: Review your Career Fitness Plan to ensure that the goals you are setting will stretch you to new accomplishments without harming you through overwork or overreaching.

Repetitions: Evaluate your pace 1 time/quarter

Stride 4: Get what you need and deserve out of the time you have set aside for leisure activity.

Repetitions: Check yourself 1 time/quarter

Exercise VII: Stretch Your Soul

Stride 1: Join a local, national or international environmental or social service organization and participate in its activities.

Repetitions: Work in the organization no less than 1 time/2 months

Stride 2: Expand the capacity of your spirit.

Repetitions: Invest 1 hour/month

Stride 3: Encourage others to do soul work.

Repetitions: Talk to others at least 2 times/quarter

Stride 4: Reward yourself.

Repetitions: Give yourself this reward 1 time/quarter

Chapter Nine

Step #5: Cool Down

Maintain a Career Record

How to Reward Yourself for Success

"It is time for us to stand and cheer the doer, the achiever, the one who recognizes the challenge and does something about it."

Vince Lombardi, Hall of Fame Football Coach

Most of us keep a record of vital health information—the medications that we take, the immunizations that we've had, and the results of our medical tests. Many of us also maintain a log of our income and day-to-day expenses, complete with an old shoe box full of receipts and stubs. Burdensome as all of this record keeping is, we stick to it because we recognize the importance of this information in our daily lives. It enables us to file health insurance claims, to register our kids for school, and to survive that mid-April deadline with the tax man.

Keeping a record of your Career Fitness is just as important because it memorializes your capabilities and achievements in the world of work. In fact, charting your progress in building Career Fitness actually gives you two important benefits.

- First, it enables <u>you</u> to recognize and take pride in your accomplishments in the workplace. It ensures you visualize the development of your Natural and the accumulation of your career victories.

- Second, this record of your Career Fitness permits you to document the status of your occupational credentials so that <u>others</u> (especially employers and recruiters) can see the continuing development of your capabilities and experience in the workplace.

The traditional name for this record, of course, is a resume, and that will continue to be the term of choice for recruiters and employers, even in the 21st Century. For you, on the other hand, this document is something else altogether; for you, it is a Career Record. It is a virtual trophy case for your career. A place to remember the challenges you accepted, the goals you achieved, and the happiness you attained in your work.

Equally as important, your Career Record is your antidote to silent supervisors. It is the way you compensate for inarticulate and uncaring managers. It's your alternative to bosses who never even acknowledge, let alone reward your contribution on-the-job.

Unlike a resume, however, your Career Record is a private document, something that you create with and for yourself. Think of it as a thunderous round of applause that only you can hear. It's a recitation of the efforts you've made and the results you've achieved, all for an audience of one. Your Career Record is a way to congratulate yourself outside of the public eye. It is the scorecard about yourself that you keep for yourself.

This record, of course, can also help you get a new or better job. It enables you to respond quickly and effectively to the employment opportunities that come and go at warp speed in the 21st Century. It gives you a ready-made marketing support document that can help to establish you as a dream candidate—one who both accepts personal responsibility for the health of their career and works at meeting that responsibility every single day.

Employers desperately want to hire such individuals, and your Career Record ensures that they desperately want you. Its focused, detailed information highlights the full scope of your credentials, increases the perceived value of your potential contribution on-the-job (and thus the salary you are offered), and positions you as the rare talent you truly are.

For all of these reasons, your Career Record is a personal and powerful device for effective career self-management. It is, in every respect, a far more important "personnel record" than that which is maintained by your employer, for it alone provides the full account of your pursuit of Happiness.

Your Career Record will:

- give you a good sense of the direction and status of your career so that you can make informed judgments about the rewards you are actually accruing in your current job and may potentially accrue in other roles and with other organizations;

  and

- ensure that the full dimensions of your talent and capabilities, results and accomplishments are clearly detailed and understood, and whenever appropriate and useful to you, appreciated by recruiters and prospective employers.

This combination of personal and public communication regarding the state of your career health is not possible, however, with a static document or one that is hurriedly thrown together at the beginning of an unexpected job search. Quite the contrary. It is achieved only when your record is a dynamic and complete representation of your personal best. In other words, your Career Record serves you most effectively when you treat it as a living document—when it is a creation that is always expanding and improving … just like you.

Keep Track of Your Victories

Your Career Record is both a place to document the totality of your career capabilities and achievements and a baseline you can use to scope the ongoing maturation of those capabilities and achievements as your career unfolds. It is as unique to you as your medical record, your driving record or your credit score. It establishes who you are in the world of work.

Unlike your health, driving and credit records, however, you control your Career Record; you maintain it. Not your doctor, not the government, not some credit bureau, and not your employer. It's a "personal record", not a personnel record, so it's more like a journal of your individual experiences and growth than a report card on your performance compiled by someone else.

At the same time, however, your Career Record is a private place where you can and should be honest and candid with yourself. You can use this document to clap yourself on the back when you deserve it, and give yourself a motivational kick in the pants when you've let yourself down. Whatever the case, the key point is that you should treat your Career Record as a reliable, practical resource in your management of your career.

You should refer to it regularly, pay attention to the insights it provides, and use that knowledge to reinforce (and, if necessary, redirect) the development of your occupational fitness. If you do that, your Career Record will be a winning record, as well.

> **Your Career Record serves you most effectively when you treat it as a living document—when it is a creation that is always expanding and improving ... just like you.**

While your Career Record must be a stand-alone document when it is reconfigured for external use as a resume, it should be supplemented by several other documents when you use it in private. These documents are:

- your Intention Commitment;

- your Achievement, Advancement and Development goals;

  and

- a summary of what you learned about yourself in each of your personal performance reviews.

Collectively, these documents, plus your work history, provide all of the information you need to take the five most important actions in successful career self-management. These actions are the fundamental building blocks of a healthy and rewarding career. They give you the strength, endurance and self-confidence to excel at your work and advance your career. They also give you the self-knowledge, commitment and capability to find and go to work for those employers that will aid and abet your success.

ACTION 1: Keep your career focused on your Natural—on that which you do best and most enjoy doing;

ACTION 2: Set career goals which develop your Natural, and hence hold meaning and challenge for you;

ACTION 3: Ensure that you make steady progress toward those goals in each of your work assignments and jobs;

ACTION 4: Recognize and enjoy the career victories you achieve through your work performance;

and

ACTION 5: Update your Intention Commitment, your Achievement, Advancement and Development goals and your Career Record, as appropriate, to reflect your progress toward being the best you can be as a person of talent.

Everything you need in order to be able to execute these actions is contained in your work history (described later in this chapter) and the documents you have produced in this workbook. The table below indicates which of the documents is involved in performing each action.

Action	Intention Commitment	Goals	Performance Review	Career Record
Action 1	•	•	•	
Action 2	•	•		
Action 3		•	•	
Action 4		•	•	•
Action 5	•	•	•	•

Clearly, your Intention Commitment, your Achievement, Advancement and Development goals, and your personal performance reviews are private documents meant for your use only. Your Career Record, however, is a personal document that forms the basis for a public one: your resume. It should be developed, therefore, with that dual purpose in mind. Think of it as a personal status report <u>and</u> as your foundation for a personalized sales "brochure." You use it to:

* measure and celebrate your own progress;

    and

* persuasively sell your capabilities to prospective employers.

How do you compose a Career Record that will detail the development of your Natural and the progress of your career so you can use that information effectively for career self-management? And, how do you draw on the same document to create a resume that will highlight your occupational strengths and accomplishments so they are noticed and appreciated by prospective employers? What must you do to develop a dual purpose document that serves you well in both instances?

The easiest way to begin is with the document you already know something about: your resume. Every person in the workforce quickly learns the rudiments of writing this public recitation of their skills and experience. For entry-level workers, a resume is the key to their first, full time employment experience. For mid-career workers and senior executives, a resume is the key to more interesting and rewarding employment opportunities. In both cases, it is the only way to translate one's hopes, dreams and goals into genuine advancement in the workplace.

Despite these advantages, however, the resume, at least as it is typically crafted, is widely regarded as imperfect. It cannot capture a person's drive, commitment or integrity. Employers and recruiters depend upon it, yet many dislike and disparage it. Why? Because it cannot reveal a person's values, principles or motivation. Even a well written resume will describe their actions and outcomes, but can only hint at their character.

Despite these flaws, your resume is the best tool available to:

- differentiate you from all of the other candidates who would also like to have the position you want;

  and

- demonstrate decisively that you are the single best prospect the organization can find for that position.

A resume that does any less, especially in today's notoriously fickle job market, is a waste of your time and effort or worse. A poorly written resume doesn't advance your career and may even set it back. A well written resume, on the other hand, can at least provide those two advantages and, as a result, help to position you for success in the workplace.

No less important, the work history included in such a resume has the power to sell you to you. It is not the whole of your Career Record, but the writing of a good resume interprets your progress in the world of work so that you appreciate what you've accomplished and "see" your career victories.

If the portrait it paints is both honest and positive, your resume will invigorate your pride and self-confidence by enabling you to reflect on your past successes and your current readiness for a specific new challenge. It will help to reinforce that self-respect by providing a gauge with which to measure the distance you've come in your quest to be the best you can be. And, it will provide a reliable indicator of your overall Career Fitness as well as the state of your Natural at any point in time.

You and Your Resume: A Winning Combination

The first step in developing your resume is to understand what you are trying to create. In other words, what is "a well written resume?" That should be your objective. Don't bother writing an adequate or even a good resume and certainly don't waste your time on a mediocre one.

If you want to land a great job—a position that will advance your career and promote your career security—you need a great resume. It doesn't have to be the equal of a Shakespearean sonnet or a page of Hemingway text, but it does need to be the single best statement about you that you've ever written. Why? Because you deserve it … and your happiness depends on it.

A well written resume is one that works for you in a number of different situations: in print, online and in the computerized databases that most companies are now using to manage the resumes they receive. It is a document that records your career victories—the goals you've achieved and the results you've delivered—and displays them in such a way that employers cannot misunderstand or overlook them.

Think of it as the key to an employer's front door. A well written resume will distinguish you from others in your field. It will pique the interest of employers and recruiters. It will create an image of you in their minds, and the image will be so compelling that it will convince them they have no other choice but to take some of their valuable time to contact and interview you.

A well written resume will get the door open—it will bring you into the zone of consideration—but that's all it can do. Once your resume has created that opportunity—once you're face-to-face in an interview with a recruiter or hiring manager—it's up to you to sell yourself as an employee. In other words, your resume positions you as a credible employment prospect. Then, you have to take over. You have to establish your right to remain there as an employee. That's how you grab hold of the next rung in your journey across the career jungle gym.

Using a resume successfully, therefore, is a lot like playing on a team. Each member of the team has an assigned role. If everyone executes their assignment effectively, the team will have a winning record. Similarly, if you write a resume that performs its role, and you, in turn, perform yours, then you'll have a winning combination, even in the challenging job market of the 21st Century.

The first step in forming that team, of course, is the development of a great resume. It requires a thorough understanding of:

- your Natural (as expressed by your Intention Commitment);

- the state of your career health (as expressed by your Achievement, Advancement and Development goals and the results of your personal performance reviews to date);

- the job market;

 and

- the human resource and recruiting community that will be the initial "customer" for your resume.

The previous chapters of this book dealt with the first three of these topics. The next section of this chapter will describe the human resource and recruiting community and its requirements for your resume.

What HR and Recruiting Professionals Want

Human Resource and recruiting professionals are charged with the responsibility of finding and evaluating prospective candidates for the vacant positions in their employer's organization. They seldom do the actual hiring—in most cases, it is a direct supervisor who will make the final decision about which person is selected—but they are extremely influential. In essence, they are the gatekeepers of the hiring process.

They are the ones who first screen all of the candidates. They are the ones who decide which candidates are qualified for a position and which are not. They are also the ones who determine which applicants go on to an interview and which do not. And, they make those decisions, in large part, by reading your resume. If your resume doesn't effectively sell you to them, you'll never even get in the door, let alone to a face-to-face interview with the hiring manager.

Not surprisingly, the extraordinary changes occurring in the world of work at large have also had a significant impact on the human resource and recruiting communities. Two of these changes, in particular, will also influence the way you develop your resume.

One is the pace of work facing many recruiters today, while the other is the growing reliance of Human Resource Departments on computers and other technology to get work done. If you ignore these changes and write your resume for a Human Resource Department and recruiter community that existed in the 20th Century, you're setting yourself up for quick disappointment in the 21st Century. If you recognize and accommodate them, on the other hand, you'll give a powerful boost to your candidacy for the next important challenge in your career.

The First Change

As we all know from the endless litany of layoff announcements, reductions in force, downsizing actions and restructuring decisions, organizations are moving rapidly to very tight staffing strategies. They are relying on fewer people to do as much or more work as larger staffs accomplished in the past. This approach is typically adopted to make employers more productive and hence more competitive in the global marketplace. It also means that each of their employees has less and less time to devote to each of the tasks they are supposed to perform.

That's particularly true for the Human Resource Department and the corporate staffing function. Why? Because in most for-profit organizations, these activities are treated as overhead. Despite the fact that human resource professionals, in general, and recruiters, in particular, determine the quality of an organization's so-called "human capital," they are viewed by most corporate executives as an expense, not as a revenue generator or profit maker. And, when business is difficult, as it often is in the 21st Century, the first place organizations look to balance the budget are those areas that they believe cost them money.

As a consequence, there has been a significant and continuing reduction in the staffs of many corporate Human Resource Departments. Employers have fewer recruiters at work, and in many cases, those who are recruiting are "human resource generalists." They have with minimal experience in recruiting and a number of other functions for which they are accountable in the workplace (e.g., compensation and benefits, labor relations).

This situation creates reality number one of the new job market: the window of opportunity is narrow and the pace is very fast in the Human Resource Department of the 21st Century. Each HR professional or recruiter is working on filling a number of open positions—sometimes fifty or more—and all at the same time. Therefore, when you send your resume into an employer for one of those jobs, your credentials will likely be reviewed by someone who has very little time, a very large stack of resumes to evaluate, and only modest training in doing so.

Your challenge is made even greater by the Internet. When an opening is posted online—and most vacancies now are—there's a very high probability that the employer will receive hundreds and sometimes even thousands of resumes for that single position. How does this situation impact on you? It narrows even further the opportunity you have to be considered a qualified applicant.

Historically, a recruiter would spend about 45 seconds reviewing your credentials. In effect, your resume had almost a minute to prove to the recruiter that you had the right stuff. Today, however, you're lucky if it gets 10 seconds to strut your stuff. Now, your resume must establish you as a dream candidate in the space of a glance. If it fails to do so, you're out of luck. You lose … even if you are qualified for the job. Even if you are the perfect person for the job!

The Second Change

The second change in the 21st Century is the widespread reliance on computers to get work done in the corporate Human Resource Department (and a growing number of staffing firms, as well). While computers and other advanced technology have been a fact of life in virtually every other area of business activity, it wasn't until the late 1990's that they began to creep into the management of human resources and recruiting activities.

Today, computer-based applications and databases are used to:

- process and archive candidate resumes;

- schedule interviews and record their results;

- test candidate skills and assess their work habits and personality;

  and

- keep track of and communicate with applicants as they move through the recruiting process.

In effect, the computer has become the coworker of the modern recruiting professional.

This transformation creates reality number two in the new job market: no matter how you submit your resume (whether it's over the Internet, via the mail, by hand at a career fair, or by fax), in all large employers and a growing number of smaller ones, that document will now be stored in a computerized database. Therefore, even to see a resume let alone read it, a recruiter must first use the computer to find it in the database. And, computers have their own peculiar way of looking at resumes. They identify the documents by searching for specific terms, called "keywords," that are provided to the computer by the recruiter.

Keywords are the nouns and phrases that describe the qualifications deemed necessary to perform a job. When recruiters use certain keywords to indicate the qualifications they want to see on a resume, the computer can only identify exact matches. It cannot "read between the lines" and make judgments about people by inferring or extrapolating from other words with a similar meaning. As a result, if your resume doesn't have the precise keywords specified by the recruiter, the computer will decide that you don't meet the requirements for a position … even if you do. For a computer, either you say it the right way (i.e., with exactly the keywords the computer recognizes), or you haven't said it at all.

Hence, the secret to writing a great resume is to design it so that overworked humans <u>and</u> single-minded computers can recognize your employment credentials. To do that, highlight your credentials so they are easy to find and to understand quickly. Summarize your key qualifications at the top of your resume using the vocabulary of HR professionals and recruiters. Begin your resume by detailing your expertise with their keywords.

How do you learn that language? Look at the vocabulary they use in their recruitment ads (especially the terms used in the ad for any specific position in which you're interested). Also check the words and phrases they use on their corporate Web-site and in any employment-related literature they may offer.

You must, of course, actually possess the skills and knowledge you're describing, so be careful about what you say as well as how you say it. The key is to lead with terms that are both appropriate and accurate, understandable (by recruiters and their computers) and true. Do that, and you'll have a resume that will work for you, even as you reach for the most challenging and rewarding opportunities in your field.

The Composition of Your Resume

A resume has two key elements: its content and its format. A well written resume carefully addresses each element and integrates both into a single, focused message that clearly and persuasively conveys your career strengths and victories. Developing such a resume in the 21st Century requires that you follow a number of new guidelines.

Content

New Guideline #1: Make sure your resume describes the right person.

A well-written resume will be complete and comprehensive, but not wordy or long-winded. It will focus on the work you do best and most enjoy doing. It is a record of your career strengths and victories, not your life story.

In most cases, a resume should be no longer than two pages of text. (The only exception is the Curriculum Vitae which is used exclusively in the education/academic field.)

Its content should be organized into headlines and bullets so that the information can be quickly scanned and absorbed. Don't make recruiters work (or read on and on) to figure out your potential value to their organization. They won't. They're too busy and moving too quickly. So, give them the pertinent facts and present those facts as clearly, as convincingly, but as succinctly as you can.

> **The secret to writing a great resume is to design it so that overworked humans <u>and</u> single-minded computers can recognize your employment credentials.**

Moreover, the discipline of limiting the presentation of your employment credentials to a maximum of two pages will force you to decide what you want to reveal about your record to a particular employer for a particular position. In the old world of work, the criterion for selecting the content to be included on your resume was what you thought the employer wanted to see.

You would try to determine—"guess" is the more accurate term—what the organization was looking for and, to the extent you could, that's what you provided in the document. In fact, career counselors would even tell their clients to write multiple resumes. They were to write one resume for one type of job and a different resume for another type of job, and send out whichever was appropriate for one organization or another.

Why did this happen? For two reasons:

- First, most people had only a vague notion of their employment objective—they lacked the clarity of purpose provided by an Intention Commitment and by Achievement, Advancement and Development goals. This ambivalence led employers to describe openings from their perspective. They used words like "requirements" and "responsibilities" to detail what they wanted to accomplish with a job. Either a job seeker conformed to those specifications or they were considered unfit for employment.

and

- Second, people knew that, with more workers than jobs in the workplace, their careers were controlled and defined by market forces beyond their control. As a consequence, looking for employment wasn't the fulfillment of a dream—the pursuit of Happiness—but an exercise in economics—the promotion of a product. They had to sell themselves to a buyer that had a large number of alternatives from which to pick. Either a job seeker positioned themselves as an employer's very best deal or someone else would be selected.

The concept of Career Fitness, on the other hand, enables you to apply a different criterion when deciding what content to include in your resume. The goal of Career Fitness is for you to be your personal best. The work you want to do, therefore, is what you most enjoy doing and do best. Your capability to perform that work is what you should highlight on your resume.

The information on that document shouldn't describe some make-believe person you've created (or contorted yourself into being) for an employer. It should be a description of you. The real you. It should detail your quest to explore and develop your Natural and to be the champion living inside you.

That kind of resume is as different from traditional resumes as it is powerful. It has two advantages.

- It's honest. It's about who you truly are and want to be. That candor is the one sure way to know what will optimize your experience in the world of work. It is the only perspective that will enable you to see what's best for you in your career.

- It's useful. It provides a template with which to evaluate alternative employers. The self-definition you establish is the basis for determining how well an organization's job(s) and culture will fit you. It enables you to determine where you will feel comfortable and flourish in your work.

Format

New Guideline #2: Make your resume "scanner ready."

As previously noted, when an organization's Human Resource Department receives resumes over the Internet, they will probably be entered directly (i.e., electronically) into a computerized resume database. Print resumes received via the mail, at a career fair, or from an employee referral are also entered into the database, but they must be processed first for that to happen.

Typically, the processing is accomplished with an optical scanner. This technology captures each document as an electronic image which is then transferred into the database where it can be searched by the computer. Optical scanners, however, are only as accurate as their ability to distinguish words and letters from the paper on which they are printed. And, unfortunately, many of today's scanners have limited vision:

- They can't read colored inks well;

- They can't read printing on colored paper well, especially if there is little contrast between the ink color and the paper color;

- They can't read fancy or ornate fonts well (e.g., *Script*, ROSEWOOD, **STENCIL**);

and

- They also often misread fonts that have serifs—the horizontal lines beneath the vertical lines in fonts such as this one: Times New Roman.

If you want your resume to get the attention it deserves, therefore, make sure that it's printed in dark black ink on bright white paper. Plain white paper is a good guideline even if a company doesn't use a computer to manage its resumes. The reason is simple: when a recruiter selects your resume for further review, it will be circulated to the appropriate hiring manager and others in the organization. Copies of the resume will be made to facilitate this exchange, and the value of that more expensive colored paper and ink will be lost.

Finally, if you decide to mail your resume to an employer, do not use a standard, number 10 business envelope. The crease of the folds you must make to insert it into that size envelope will disrupt the clarity of the printed type and confuse the scanner. Instead, send your resume underlined in an 81/2" x 11" or larger envelope. It will cost you a little more, but it will also help ensure that your resume gets through the scanner without a problem.

New Guideline #3: Make your resume "recruiter friendly."

The way the information on your resume is organized should also change to reflect the new environment in today's Human Resource Departments. As always, your name (with a date beneath it if you are going to post your resume online), address and contact information should appear at the top of the first page of the document.

In the past, these details were followed by an Objective statement that presented your goals for your job search. You were often encouraged to modify or, in some cases, completely change this statement to tailor it (and you) to the specific requirements and responsibilities of the job for which you were applying.

Career Fitness eliminates the need for such artifice and, hence, the need for an Objective statement on your resume. Since you now have a thorough understanding of what you want from your work and from any job that you might take (because you've written down your Intention Commitment and set your Achievement, Advancement and Development goals), everything on your resume supports and expands on that objective. There's no need, therefore, to articulate it in a formal (and often unclear) statement at the top of your resume.

That location, however, is prime real estate on the document and should be put to the best possible use. With recruiters now spending even less time than in the past reviewing resumes, it's critical that you lead with your strengths.

Replace the Objective statement with a new section at the top of your resume called a "Record Summary." Its purpose is to summarize and highlight the skills, knowledge and abilities described in the rest of your resume. It ensures that, even if the recruiter reads nothing else, they will have an accurate and detailed picture of your capabilities and experience.

A Record Summary is a string of single words or short phrases that itemize your greatest strengths as a worker (the attributes that employers call your "qualifications"). This list should include any specific terms and jargon appropriate to your field of work and/or regularly used to describe the credentials you have earned. Each individual entry or the first word of each phrase is capitalized, and all terms are followed by a period. The list should not run any longer than twenty-to-thirty discrete items covering approximately three-to-five lines of text.

In selecting the entries for your Record Summary, concentrate on three aspects of your background:

- Your skills, abilities and competencies (e.g., Project management, New account development, Systems analysis, Retail sales, XML programming, BA in business administration, TQM);

- Your experience using these skills, abilities, and competencies (e.g., HRIS installation, Plastics industry, Commercial/retail banking systems, Store management, E-commerce applications, Process re-engineering);

  and

- Your accomplishments in using these skills, abilities and competencies on-the-job (e.g., Project completion on time and within budget, $30 million in annual sales, Cost reductions totaling 12%, Customer service award, Annual productivity gains of 5%).

In effect, your Record Summary is both an "inventory of assets" that you can bring to a prospective employer and an advertisement about the quality of those assets. The inventory of assets tells an employer what you can do, and the advertisement provides proof (in the form of experience and accomplishments) of how well you can do it.

Developing a Record Summary does two things for you:

- First, it forces you to sit down and identify a list of the precise skills, knowledge, abilities, experiences, accomplishments, degrees, certificates, licenses and other work credentials that you offer to a prospective employer. It also obliges you to rank order these attributes so that only the most important are highlighted for any particular point in your career. In other words, building (and, then, updating) a Record Summary is a disciplined way for you to assess the current dimensions of your Natural.

- Second, the Record Summary puts these credentials right up front where the busy human recruiter can't miss them. In most large and mid-sized employers, this positioning compensates for the cursory review individual resumes initially receive in staffing organizations. In smaller employers, this positioning compensates for the lack of recruiting experience among many of those who will be reviewing your resume (e.g., a store manager, the company owner).

Here's what a Record Summary might look like on a resume:

RECORD SUMMARY: Sales Manager. Key client identification and management. Sales force development and management. Closing. Year-over-year profit growth exceeding 10%. Customer relationship management. Upselling. Repeat sales. Teamwork. Mentoring. Medical device industry experience.

The Foundation of Your Resume: Your Career Record

In order to keep a full and complete record of your career victories and, as a result, to have the necessary information for the development of a winning resume, you must build and maintain an accurate and complete work history. You must collect all of the details related to the following:

- Your Occupational Experience

- Your Occupational Education

- Your Occupational Affiliations and Awards.

While a resume can be developed in several different formats (i.e., chronological, functional, hybrid), your Career Record should always be organized in three consecutive sections (as listed above) and the information within each section should always be presented in chronological order. This structure enables you to find information quickly when you are writing your resume and, equally as important, to see the progressive maturation and expression of your Natural in the workplace.

Do not, however, add non-work-related personal information to your Career Record. Such information includes your marital status, age, gender, religion, ethnicity, or leisure time activities. While these details could be helpful to you in your career from time-to-time, they can also undermine your advancement.

For example, details about your personal life could be advantageous to you in a job search. They can establish a connection with or help you better relate to a recruiter or hiring manager. If there is some aspect of your background that you share with that individual, they might be more inclined to support your candidacy for a particular position.

The only appropriate time to forge such connections, however, is during an interview. Building rapport is a two-way activity, so both parties—you and the recruiter—must be willing to participate. Including personal information on your resume precludes that mutual consent and may, as a consequence, appear to be overreaching or presumptuous.

No less important, adding non-work related personal details on your resume can actually undermine your candidacy for a job. In most cases, they are simply not relevant to the hiring decision a company will be making about you. That decision should only be based on your skills, knowledge and experience as those factors—not your gender or age or ethnicity—will determine your potential performance on-the-job.

When you include personal characteristics on your resume, therefore, you insert them into the criteria that may be used—consciously or unconsciously—by the recruiter and hiring manager when evaluating your qualifications. In effect, including this information opens you up to prejudiced or biased behavior. While such behavior is clearly against the law, it can and does occur, even in the most progressive of organizations. So, rather than tempt fate, leave personal information out of your Career Record and off your resume.

Your Occupational Experience

Use the Occupational Experience section of your Career Record to list your employers in reverse chronological order (i.e., the most recent goes first). As shown in the illustrative Career Record at the end of this chapter, include the name of each employer and the inclusive dates of your employment at that organization. Also list the title(s) of the position(s) you held, beginning with the most recent, and the dates you held each position.

Under each position, describe your experience. Be as complete as you can in detailing the tasks you performed and the expertise you used to accomplish them. Avoid vague and nonspecific "responsibility pronouncements" (i.e., I was responsible for this. I was responsible for that.) Instead, use factual statements that detail the actions you took and the decisions you made on-the-job and the skills, abilities, competencies, capabilities, and knowledge you used to do so. The goal is to record everything you did to develop and express your Natural.

This section of your Career Record has two purposes. First and foremost, it provides the bottom shelf in your own personal career trophy case. It enables you to see how, when and where you did your best work. Second, this information can, of course, also be used when you want (or need) to make a move in your career. Its completeness ensures that nothing important is omitted when you write your resume and that you aspire to an appropriate employment opportunity, one that will advance your career.

For example:

Employment Experience

Haynes Computer Center (04/2005-Present)

- Store Manager (01/06-Present)

  - Direct sales staff in suburban mall store, grossing over $2.5 million in sales annually.

  - Select, train and supervise a sales team of four full time and five part time reps.

  - Provide direction and training to ensure the team delivers exemplary customer service and consistently meets quarterly and annual sales goals.

  - Deal quickly and effectively with customer issues and complaints.

  - Oversee the introduction of new products, including the preparation of sales reps and the installation of signage and displays.

  - Counsel underperforming sales reps and provide support for their improvement.

  - Periodically conduct inspections to ensure the cleanliness of the store and the good repair of all demonstrators and other equipment.

  - Prepare and submit store financial and operations summaries to regional vice president.

  - Participate in annual store managers conference, providing feedback on policies and programs.

- Senior Sales Rep (04/2005-12/2005)

  - Sold all lines of home computers and peripherals in a high volume retail store located in a major suburban mall.

  - Acquired an in-depth knowledge of all regular as well as special and/or seasonal products.

  - Honed interpersonal skills and developed a facility for dealing with upset or difficult customers.

  - Helped train new sales reps and get them acclimated to the store.

  - Contributed to the agenda for the store manager's weekly sales meeting.

Microcenter (01/2000-04/2005)

- Sales Representative

  - Joined the two-person sales team in a retail store offering computer products.

  - Read product literature and sales support material to obtain a thorough understanding of each product's features and capabilities.

  - Demonstrated products and answered customer questions.

  - Opened and closed the store when the manager wasn't present.

Practice: Using your current or last job, describe your Employment Experience.

Beneath the statements describing the skills, knowledge and expertise you applied in each position, record all of your accomplishments—the Achievement and Advancement goals that you reached in the process. While the details of your work tell you what you did, your realized goals indicate how well you did it. They remind you of the progress you've made, the distance you've traveled, the mileposts you've passed in your career. They are your career victories—the top shelf in your career trophy case—and they deserve special recognition.

When listing these accomplishments, adhere to the following guidelines:

- *Be comprehensive in your recognition.* Don't ignore or leave out any of your accomplishments, regardless of how they may be perceived by others. This is your trophy case, not theirs.

- *Be complete with the facts.* Don't stint on the details when recording your accomplishments or when describing their impact in the workplace.

- *Be precise in your descriptions.* Don't exaggerate the outcome of your work or the results you were able to achieve. Whenever possible, cite your accomplishments in quantitative terms (e.g., increased sales 30%).

- *Be honest with yourself.* Don't claim victories you didn't actually achieve or successes you haven't yet accomplished.

For example:

Work-Related Accomplishments

Haynes Computer Center

- Store Manager

  - Cut customer return and refund rate by 8% in 2007.

  - Met corporate sales goal of a 15% increase in annual gross receipts in 2006.

  - Received company award for Manager of the Year in 2006.

- Senior Sales Rep

  - Top sales agent by volume July-December, 2005.

  - Selected for bonus sales program reserved for top 1% of reps in 2005.

  - Helped reduce attrition among sales reps by 25% in 2005.

Microcenter

- Sales Representative

  - Achieved progressively higher sales totals year after year.

  - Sales leader among all reps in the store in 2004.

  - Selected for special vendor training program in 2003.

  - Received a letter of appreciation from a store patron highlighting my product knowledge and courtesy in 2002.

Practice: List your Work-Related Accomplishments for the job you described in the previous practice.

Your Occupational Education

Use this section of your Career Record to list all of your academic degrees and the Development goals you have attained in your career, in reverse chronological order. Include those education and training programs in which you are currently participating, as well as all of those which you have completed. These entries are also career victories. They recognize your commitment to keeping yourself up-to-date in your field and thus the continuous expansion of the dimensions of your Natural.

For each entry:

- state the degree or certificate you earned (or will earn) or course or program that you completed (or will complete);

- the name of the institution you attended or the vendor that delivered the training program you took;

- the dates of your participation. If you haven't yet completed a program or course, list its start date and add the term "Ongoing";

- the grade and any academic recognition you received;

    and

- the contribution the resulting expansion of your expertise made to the realization of our Achievement and Advancement goals. In other words connect the accomplishment of your Development goals to your performance in the workplace. Show yourself how one led to the other, as that dynamic—which you set in motion—is the essence of your career victory.

While your initial academic degrees (e.g., Certificate, Associate, Bachelor, Masters or PhD) are obviously important, they represent the baseline of your career. They are listed last because they indicate where you started, not where you are (or should be) in your acquisition of knowledge in your field.

An Occupational Education Section might look like this:

Education & Training

- Better Sales Through Better Marketing

  American Marketing Association 2012/On-going

  Is giving me a more strategic understanding of the sales process.

- Introduction to Conversational Spanish

  Northern Virginia Community College, 2007-2008

  Enables me to relate better with sales reps and aid their efforts to improve.

- Basic Course in Store Management

  Haynes Corporate Training Center, 02/2006

  Prepared me for promotion to store manager, especially in the area of financial metrics and reports.

- Communicating Clearly in Business

  Business Institute of Northern Virginia, 01-04/2004

  Helped me improve my performance as a sales rep by strengthening my verbal communication skills.

- Principles of Effective Retail Sales

  Microsoft Partner Training Program, 06-08/2002

  Updated my product knowledge and refreshed my customer service skills.

- Bachelors in Business Administration

  Penn State University, 1996-2000

Practice: Describe your Education & Training, including the course(s) you're taking now.

Your Occupational Affiliations & Awards

Use the Occupational Affiliations & Awards section of your Career Record to list your career victories that are not tied to a specific job or employer. They include accomplishments that were achieved through work in your field, but which you conducted independently or in conjunction with such organizations as a government agency, an academic institution or a professional society or trade association.

These career victories might be:

- articles or books you've written;

- speeches, seminars or workshops you've presented;

- awards or citations you've earned;

- elected or appointed positions you've held;

  or

- any other form of work-related accolade.

Such recognition represents progress in the development and expression of your Natural and, ultimately, in your pursuit of Happiness.

List these accomplishments in reverse chronological order. For each, indicate what was involved (e.g., what you did or were recognized for), the organization that was responsible for the award or recognition (if there was one), and the date it occurred.

Also list your membership in any professional, trade or academic associations and societies. Although they are not career victories per se, membership in these organizations is often an important part of your career advancement and success.

For example:

Professional Recognition & Awards

- Elected Regional Vice President of SMEA, 01/2012

- Selected to present "Optimizing Retail Sales" at Tri-State Regional Conference of SMEA, 07/2007

- Program Co-Chair, Fairfax Chapter of SMEA, 2006

- Member, Sales & Marketing Executives Association (SMEA), 2005-Present

- Member, Penn State Alumni Association, 2005-Present

Practice: List the Occupational Affiliations & Awards you've acquired in the last two years.

Putting It All Together

The three preceding sections will help you develop a Career Record that acknowledges and reinforces the effort and determination you devoted to your Career Fitness regimen. The outline below puts all of the information together so that you can see what the finished document looks like.

Your Career Record

Your Career Documents

- Your Intention Commitment

- Your Achievement, Advancement, Development Goals

- Your Notes from each Personal Performance Review

Your Occupational Experience

The Name of Your Current or Most Recent Employer

- Your Dates of Employment

- Your Position Title(s) and dates the position(s) were held

- A detailed description of your work

    o The tasks you performed and the expertise you used

- A complete list of your Career Victories while working in each position for this employer

    o The Achievement and Advancement goals you met

The name of Your Next Most Recent Employer

- Your dates of Employment

- Your position Title(s) and dates the position(s) were held

- A detailed description of your work

    o The tasks you performed and the expertise you used

- A complete list of your Career Victories while working in each position for this employer

    o The Achievement and Advancement goals you met

Provide the same information for all of your other employers, continuing the list in reverse chronological order.

Your Occupational Education

Your Most Recent Educational or Training Experience

- The dates of the program/course you took or are taking

- The degree or certificate you earned (or expect to)

- The name of the institution you attended or the vendor that delivered the program/course

- The Career Victory you achieved by completing the program/course

    o The Development goal you met and its connection to your Achievement or Advancement goal

Provide the same information for all of your other educational programs and courses of instruction, listing them in reverse chronological order. The last entries should be your initial academic degrees, which are listed in the same format shown.

Your Occupational Affiliations & Awards

- Your Most Recent Recognition or Award

- The organization that was responsible

- The date it occurred

Provide the same information for all of your other occupational achievements and awards, listing them in reverse chronological order. Also list your membership in professional, trade and academic associations and societies.

Turning Your Career Record into a Resume

There's an old saying that every person has a book inside them, waiting to be written. And many of us, from time-to-time, feel the creative urge, the desire to tell that tale, to coax it out of us and get it down on paper. Then, all too often, we stop. Why? Because the plot line isn't clear, and the protagonist of our story remains indistinct and unknown to us.

It's a common mental block, but one you can break through by changing how you view your Career Record. That document is your career story, a tale that traces your journey toward accomplishment and fulfillment in your work. It describes the challenges that you've faced and surmounted and the opportunities that you've grasped and transformed into new adventures.

The hero of this account, of course, is a person with whom you are very familiar: you. You are the champion at the center of it all, and thanks to your efforts, none of it is fiction. It is all true.

When you see your Career Record as a book about you—an unending tale of exploits and achievements—it suddenly becomes less of a burden to write and keep up-to-date. It's part diary, part autobiography, and part personal best seller. It is a new genre; it is a "self-serial."

Your Career Record is a book about yourself that you develop in installments over time. A self-serial is the work we all want to create—for our own enjoyment and for the edification of others—namely all of those employers out there that will be desperate to hire us … if they know just how accomplished we are.

Give Employers the Abridged Edition

Employers, however, are picky readers. They only want to read the parts of your self-serial that interest them. That's why you have to give them the abridged edition—your resume. You have to trim the story to fit their needs. In other words, you have to tailor your resume for the job you want.

In the 20th Century, you could get away with a generalized resume. Recruiters understood that it was simply asking too much to have each applicant rewrite their resume to address the particular aspects of each opening for which they applied. Instead, they expected job seekers to write a cover letter that provided the tailored information they wanted (and needed).

A person's resume was focused, of course, on their particular strengths, but the priority of the factual presentation was based on a vague or non-specific employment objective. Without an Intention Commitment, most people simply didn't know and/or couldn't clearly articulate their special talent.

This imprecision in self-knowledge had two harmful effects: it obscured a person's unique talent so that it was not easily recognized by recruiters and, as noted earlier, it caused almost everyone to create a self-portrait that was an image of the candidate they thought employers wanted to see.

> **Your Career Record is a book about yourself that you develop in installments over time.**

Today, that kind of generic, "I am whatever you want me to be" response (with a bit of superficial emphasis in a cover letter) simply will not work. Recruiters know that resumes are written on word processors, so making changes to tailor them is simply not the burden it used to be. They expect you, therefore, to shape the content of your self-serial to highlight those experiences and achievements that have the greatest bearing on their particular opening. They don't want to read about you in general; they want to read about the you that matters most to them.

That's the secret to writing a great resume in the 21st Century. Employers want to meet the genuine champion within you and understand what aspects of that persona you will contribute to them. They want you to tell the specific part of your career story that will show them how they can put your special talent to work for their mission and the needs of their organization.

Unlike in the 20th Century, however, you are not tailoring yourself. You are not trying to contort yourself into what an employer needs. Instead, you are tailoring your record. You are picking and highlighting the most important aspects of who you truly are. You are drawing on reality, not creating a fiction.

A cover letter is still appropriate, but its purpose is no longer to point out what's relevant in a long recitation of out-of-focus facts in your resume. Rather, this communication—whether it's conveyed on paper or by e-mail—must articulate the unique, personal contribution you can make to an employer as evidenced by <u>every</u> fact presented in your abridged and focused self-serial. In the 21st

Century job market, your cover letter stakes your claim to being a specific organization's dream candidate; your resume provides the proof.

Give Yourself the Unabridged Edition

While employers want the abridged edition of your self-serial, you, of course, deserve the complete story. The short version may be all that matters to an organization, but you can learn from and appreciate the whole of your record. That document is an account of your personal growth in the world of work.

Your Career Record includes all of your career victories—every employer to which you contributed your talent, every job where you accomplished goals and achieved success, and every work experience in which you enhanced your ability to be the best you can be through the expression of your Natural. It is your career epic and you should tell it with all of the richness of context and detailed information you can recall.

Writing such a book and keeping it up-to-date clearly require an investment of time and effort. Given the already hectic and over-scheduled lives most of us have these days, it's reasonable to ask: what do you get for all of that work? Is the commitment worth it? Said another way: why bother?

There are several reasons for investing the time and effort necessary to create a fulsome Career Record:

- First, the more complete the list of your career victories—the challenges you've faced, the goals you've met, the accomplishments you've achieved and the rewards you've earned—the deeper the inventory of supporting facts you have on which to draw when tailoring your resume for a specific employment opportunity. That saves you time—enabling you to respond to an opening more quickly—and ensures that you don't inadvertently omit anything that might be important to the employer or recruiter.

- Second, keeping your Career Record up-to-date and complete enables you to recognize and celebrate your own successes—the career victories you've achieved. Regularly setting your career milestones down in writing is a way of giving yourself a well-deserved pat on the back. You pause in life's hectic bustle and remember what you did on-the-job that made you more capable in your field and more satisfied with your work.

  You do more than just recall those situations, however; you memorialize them in writing, and the resulting document gives them permanence and a prominent role in the mosaic of your life. When times are difficult, that record is there to remind you of what's positive in your career. And, when times are good, it's there to help you remember all of the preparation and development you completed to make your success possible.

- Finally, keeping a complete record of your career victories enables you to build your Career Fitness carefully, methodically, effectively. Each of your personal performance reviews should yield a new entry for:

  o   the expertise you've acquired and added to your resume's Record Summary—the progress you've made toward being the best you can be;

  o   the tasks you've performed and/or the accomplishments you've attained through your employment and recorded in Your Occupational Experience—the progress you've made toward your Achievement and Advancement goals;

  o   the knowledge you've gained through the training and educational programs you've completed (or are taking) and cited in your Your Occupational Education—the progress you've made toward your Development goals;

and

o   the professional contributions you've made and the work-related awards you've earned and detailed in Your Professional Affiliations & Awards—the progress you've made as a career athlete.

When your Career Record does that—when you can visualize your progress toward being the champion within you—you release a powerful jolt of satisfaction and fulfillment into your consciousness. You create the career equivalent of the endorphin high that athletes achieve in meeting physical tests. This self-acknowledgement of work well done is the highest reward—the most enduring form of compensation—you can earn in the workplace. You enable yourself to feel each and every climax in your personal pursuit of Happiness.

What Happens if There is No Happiness?

None of us are perfect, so there may and likely will be times when your personal performance review does not yield the positive self-assessment we would all like to have all of the time. At these junctures, a candid personal evaluation confirms what you're probably already feeling inside: the happiness is missing. What happens then? What should you do when you look at your career and don't see any victories, when you are unable to note any progress on your Career Record?

Such a performance review is a clear and telling signal to you that you're letting your Career Fitness flag. It is the undeniable evidence that you've stalled in the development of your Natural. It is proof that you are no longer moving forward in your quest to be the best you can be. More than all of that, however, an unsuccessful personal review is the warning sign only you can see and only you can do something about.

What actions should you take if you see such a sign? Go back to the Career Fitness Work-in and recommit yourself to practicing its exercises in your work every day. That may seem onerous and even frustrating in the beginning because you have to expel the toxins of lethargy and inattention. Once they're eliminated, however, once you've reconnected your career with the powerful positive influence of working at your Natural, you will feel reengaged and reenergized.

If, after doing that, however, you still feel uninspired or sluggish—if you seem unable to do your best work and earn the self-fulfillment it provides—then you should stop what you're doing and return to the Career Fitness De-Stress Test and the Warm-up step. You can't build effective career health without a solid foundation of preparation and planning so:

•   Retake the Career De-Stress Test and ensure that your career is aligned with your Natural— what you most enjoy doing and do best.

•   Then, reformulate your Achievement, Advancement and Development goals to ensure your work enables you to develop and express your Natural.

Get those two aspects of Career Fitness right and you're on your way to a healthy and rewarding exploration of the best you can be in the workplace.

Appendices

Additional Tools & Information

Appendix 1

Rookies & Comeback Pros
How to Enter & Reenter the World of Work

"We're supposed to be perfect our first day on the job and then show constant improvement."

Ed Vargo, Major league baseball umpire

"When you're playing against a stacked deck, compete even harder. Show the world how much you'll fight for the winners circle. If you do, someday the cellophane will crackle off a fresh pack, one that belongs to you, and the cards will be stacked in your favor."

Pat Riley, Former National Basketball Association coach

Everyone in the workplace begins as a rookie—an entry-level worker—embarking on their first full time employment. In today's world of work, almost all of us will also find ourselves making a comeback (or two or three) in the workplace, usually from a personal obligation or a setback of some kind. The way we handle those two situations, therefore, affects the health of our careers. How well we start and re-start our work for employers significantly influences both the paycheck and the satisfaction we bring home from work.

To be successful in these situations, you must have both an understanding of and a commitment to the philosophy of Career Fitness. But, even that is not sufficient to ensure success, because finding your first job and reentering the workforce after a prolonged absence represent special challenges. Although they happen to all of us, they are not the norm in the workplace.

An entry-level job search and a job search after a career break of a year or more imposes obstacles and demands that are unlike any others in the world of work. To respond effectively, therefore, you must also be able to tailor the way you use the Career Fitness regimen in each situation. You must know how to adapt your practices—but not their underlying principles—to the reality of each challenge.

How do you tailor the Career Fitness regimen as a rookie or as a comeback pro? By:

- **Implementing a 2-phase strategy**
  Most of us do very little if any preparation for our first job search or our return to the workforce. We just start off. We launch into these transitions from a dead stop. Upfront planning, however, is the first and vital phase of both situations. It provides a baseline of credibility and capability that you can then leverage in the second phase to achieve your goal. It gives you a foundation on which to build success.

- **Emphasizing certain exercises and de-emphasizing others**
  All of the exercises in the Career Fitness Work-in are critical elements in building career health so you should continue to practice all of them. For these two situations, however, you must tailor your routine so that you devote 75 percent of your time and effort to a select subset of the exercises and 25 percent of your time and effort to the rest. In other words, you should focus on those activities that will best give you the strength and endurance necessary to meet each challenge.

The exercises on which you should concentrate in each phase of your experience as a rookie or a comeback pro are described below. After you've passed through these phases, you should revert to the normal routine of the Career Fitness Work-in and practice it regularly as prescribed.

If You're a Rookie

If you will be searching for your first full time employment at some point in the next 2-3 years, organize your application of the Career Fitness regimen into the following phases of activity:

Phase 1: Preparation Prior to Your Job Search

Phase 1 begins 2 years prior to your first job search and ends the day before you begin it. During this period of time, you should emphasize the following exercises:

- *I. Pump up your cardiovascular system.* Acquire the education and skills that will put you at the leading edge of knowledge in your field. This expertise is the only effective counterbalance to your lack of work experience.

- *II. Strengthen your circulatory system.* Nurture your contacts in school, both among your peers and your instructors. Do the same outside of school, focusing on family friends and acquaintances and on contacts you can make in the workplace through an intern program or part-time work.

- *III. Develop all of your muscle groups.* Resist efforts to force you into a single, circumscribed field of study. Seek coursework and experiences that will enable you to reinforce your core area of expertise with additional and complementary capabilities.

- *VI. Stretch your soul.* Broaden your perspective and sense of purpose by "sampling" a range of activities that enable you to work for the betterment of others. Search for an endeavor where you can apply your Natural for the greater good of your community, society at large, or the planet on which we live.

Phase 2: Your Job Search

Phase 2 runs from the first day of your first job search until its conclusion on your first day of employed work. During this period of time, you should emphasize the following exercises:

- *IV. Increase your flexibility and range of motion.* Be willing to adjust your employment goals (e.g., the kind of job you are willing to take, the compensation level you will accept or even the location where you would agree to live) in order to work at your Natural in a position that enables you to grow and advance.

- *V. Work with winners.* Pick your first job carefully. While the allure of a large paycheck can be strong, it's ultimately more beneficial for you to select a position where you can learn from and advance with a successful employer, boss and/or coworkers.

- *VII. Pace yourself.* Start fast, but remember to care for yourself so that you can always perform at your peak. You have many years of potential happiness ahead of you, but only if your work is governed by your own expectations and those expectations are challenging, but reasonable and sustainable.

Rookies, no less than seasoned pros, must carefully manage the course and content of their careers. As much harm can be done by starting off incorrectly as by making a wrong turn at some point later in life. Similarly, as much benefit can be gained from starting strong as by making a deft move in the middle of your career. It's important, therefore, that you learn the principles of Career Fitness even before you enter the workplace, and that you begin practicing those principles—as appropriate for your situation and on your own and without the training wheels of parental assistance—from the very first moment you begin to explore it.

If You're Making A Comeback

Comebacks can include two kinds of situations:

- **Returning**
  Returning is the process of coming back into the workplace after a self-initiated absence from the workplace of a year or more. These prolonged gaps typically involve women (although a growing number of men are also now experiencing them) who put their careers on hold to care for young children, elderly parents or both. They can also be caused, although more rarely, by a decision to "take a break" from employment in order to explore a long-held interest, hobby or other fascination.

- **Repairing**
  Repairing is the process of coming back into the workforce after a career disruption that forces a person backward on the career jungle gym against their wishes and/or plans. These setbacks are typically caused by a serious disagreement with a boss or coworkers, a misjudgment or mistake on-the-job, or a personal situation that degrades work performance. They are also increasingly caused by the prolonged inability to find a suitable job following a layoff or other involuntary termination.

Returning Phase 1: Preparation Prior to Your Job Search

Phase 1 begins the first day of your absence from the workplace and ends the day before you begin a job search to reenter it. During this period of time, you should emphasize the following exercises:

- *I. Pump up your cardiovascular system.* Take advantage of online courses and professional publications to maintain your occupational knowledge while still meeting the responsibilities you have assumed outside the workplace or continuing the exploration of that outside interest.

- *II. Strengthen your circulatory system.* Use e-mail and discussion forums at career portals and professional society sites to stay in touch with colleagues and maintain your work-related relationships even as you focus on that endeavor which takes you outside the workplace.

- *VI. Stretch your soul.* Look for ways to apply your Natural within the context of your work caring for children and/or elderly parents or in situations where you can work for the good of others while you are pursuing your own non-employment-related activity.

- *VII. Pace yourself.* Working outside the workplace is often as demanding as working inside it, so set aside the time and space necessary to keep yourself physically and mentally healthy and to recharge your energy and commitment so that you can be the best you can be both at whatever task you have undertaken and your job search preparation.

Returning Phase 2: Your Job Search

Phase 2 runs from the first day of your active job search for a new job until its conclusion on your first day of employed work. During this period of time, you should emphasize the following exercises:

- *III. Develop all of your muscle groups.* Demonstrate the agility of your mind and the strength of your resolve to contribute significantly on-the-job by acquiring additional career-strengthening skills even as you are engaged in an active job search. Note these developments on your resume as "On-going."

- *IV. Increase your flexibility and range of motion.* Keep your expectations reasonable (but not punitively low) and be willing to move outside your comfort zone in order to reestablish yourself in the workplace and in your profession, craft or trade.

- *V. Work with winners.* Reenter the workplace with those organizations and coworkers that can help you regain and accelerate the momentum in your career, even if you have to move back a rung or two on the career jungle gym in order to do so.

Comeback pros returning from an absence caused by family or other commitments constitute one of the fastest growing segments of the workforce. Their dedication, while noble, leaves a gaping hole in their resume that employers are loath to accept, despite their platitudes about family values. The reality is as simple as it is problematic: if all other attributes are equal among a group of candidates (and often, even if they're not), recruiters and hiring managers will always select the candidate with an unbroken work history. The only exception to that rule is the select group of individuals who make it a priority to take care of themselves (and their careers) even as they attend to the other responsibilities they take on during their absence from the workplace. And, that's precisely what the Career Fitness regimen enables you to do.

Repairing Phase 1: Preparation Prior to Your Job Search

Phase 1 begins on the first day of the disruption in your career and ends the day before you start a job search to reenter the workplace. During this period of time, you should emphasize the following exercises:

- *II. Strengthen your circulatory system.* Refresh and extend your professional and social networks and, where appropriate, tell your side of the story behind your setback, being forthright and self-aware enough to acknowledge where you might have done better.

- *III. Develop all of your muscle groups.* Reinforce the potential value of your contribution in the workplace by adding capabilities that you never seemed to have the time or energy to acquire while working full time.

- *VI. Stretch your soul.* Avoid the trap of self-pity that can compound the negative effect of a setback by disciplining yourself to exercise your Natural in the service of others outside the workplace.

- *VII. Pace yourself.* Don't stop the preparations necessary for your comeback by sulking off to lick your wounds, but also be realistic enough to acknowledge that it may take some time to recover fully from the setback and husband your strength accordingly.

Repairing Phase 2: Your Job Search

Phase 2 runs from the first day of your active search for a new job until its conclusion on your first day of employed work. During this period of time, you should emphasize the following exercises:

- *I. Pump up your cardiovascular system.* Keep yourself at the cutting edge of developments in your field in order to counter any negative fallout from your setback and to strengthen your credibility in the workplace.

- *IV. Increase your flexibility and range of motion.* Setbacks interrupt the momentum in your career, and that pause may mean that you have to accept a job or employment situation that's less than ideal in order to regain your footing and start moving forward again.

- *V. Work with winners.* Setbacks do not make you a loser unless you allow them to, so learn from such situations and then use that knowledge to position yourself as a stronger candidate for organizational winners and a more seasoned and durable coworker for individual winners.

Almost all of us, at one time or another, become comeback pros who must repair a negative situation in our careers. We are human, and humans have disagreements and make mistakes. The key to sustaining the health of your career when these situations occur, therefore, is to know which actions will help you rebound quickly and completely. By appropriately modifying your use of the Career Fitness regimen, you can rebuild your reputation, regain your self-esteem and self-confidence, and restart your career as a pathway to rewarding work and workplace success.

Work Strong

Appendix 2

Which Employers Should You Work For?
How to Pick Your Own Dream Team

"I can tell you one thing. I've done this my way. I don't have anybody to blame for this win but me, and I love it."

John Daly, Professional golfer

"A team in an ordinary frame of mind will do ordinary things. In the proper emotional stage, a team will do extraordinary things. To reach this stage, a team must have a motive that has an extraordinary appeal to them."

Knute Rockne, Legendary football coach

Research indicates that the number one reason a person does not work out when hired by an employer is not that they can't do the work. It's that they don't fit in. Their personality, beliefs and goals do not mesh well with the organization's culture, values and mission. That disconnect leaves them feeling uncomfortably out-of-step. They are a misfit in the organization. They are working with the wrong team. In that environment, they cannot perform at their peak; they cannot succeed on-the-job; and ultimately, they cannot maintain the health of their career.

Career Fitness, therefore, involves practicing the habits of a healthy career while working for employers that are healthy for you. Only employers that fit you, that match your values and goals—not the other way around—can position you to hone your Natural and pursue happiness through its expression.

To identify such organizations, you must apply two different screens:

- The first screen detects organizations don't value or respect the talent of workers. These are harmful employers that must be avoided at all costs. They create a toxic environment that will weaken and eventually destroy the health of your career.

- The second screen pinpoints those employers with policies, practices and norms that support and reinforce your best work and your ability to advance your career. All employers have unique cultures, so you must determine which of the best employers is best for you.

These two screens are provided below. Use them to evaluate any organization that you are considering for employment. If you determine that an employer is not a good fit for you, avoid it, no matter how lucrative an offer it may make or how well regarded it may be in the media.

The goal of using these screens is not to find "the best employers to work for" but rather, to identify "the best employers for you to work for." The former is a public relations exercise; the latter is the key to Career Fitness.

Pick Out the Bad Apples

Answer the following questions, either through your own observations or by conducting research among an organization's employees as well as published news and trade articles.

1. Do supervisors and managers publicly or privately denigrate and ridicule employees when they decide to leave the organization for a better opportunity with another employer?

        Yes = 0 points   No = 1 point

2. Is the person in charge of the employer's Human Resource function a senior executive in the organization (i.e., of equal stature to the Chief Financial Officer) and does that person report directly to the Chief Executive Officer?

        Yes = 1 point   No = 0 points

3. Does the organization provide some form of transportation assistance (e.g., a gas allowance, bus or van shuttles, a public transportation subsidy) if large numbers of employees have to commute an hour or more to work (each way) in order to own a home?

        Yes = 1 point   No = 0 points

4. Does the employer increase the cash compensation package of its CEO (i.e., their salary and annual bonus) at a percentage rate that is greater than the average annual rate of increase in cash compensation it provides to its top performers among rank and file workers?

        Yes = 0 points   No = 1 point

5. Do employees feel that they are regularly and meaningfully recognized and rewarded for their contributions to the success of the organization?

        Yes = 1 point   No = 0 points

6. Do employees say that their supervisors routinely expect them to work on weekends and during holidays and vacations, regardless of what the organization's official policy might be regarding such requirements?

        Yes = 0 points   No = 1 point

7. Do employees feel as if the organization provides them with the tools, resources, direction and training necessary to excel at their jobs?

        Yes = 1 point   No = 0 points

8. Does the employer offer preventative health programs (e.g., fitness club subsidies, classes on healthy diets), and are employees encouraged (with time, financial incentives and supervisor support) to participate?

Yes = 1 point   No = 0 points

9. Does the employer provide adequate notification of layoffs (at a minimum, as required by the Worker Adjustment and Retraining Notification Act) and are affected employees treated with dignity and respect?

Yes = 1 point   No = 0 points

10. Do employees feel as if they know what is expected of them and why and are organizational decisions, policies and financial results communicated to them regularly and clearly?

Yes = 1 point   No = 0 points

Tally the points earned by each of the employers you are considering. Those that earn 6 points or less out of the 10 possible points fail. They are bad apples and working for them will damage your career.

Pick Out Your Dream Team

In order to identify the employers that fit you best, you must first know what you want and need from an employer in order to feel comfortable and supported. To put it another way, to determine which employers you prefer, you must be aware of your own work preferences.

Questions for You

To determine those preferences, think about the employment situations in your career to-date where you have done your best work and then answer the following questions:

1. Do you prefer to work in:

_____ a hierarchical organization, one that has a vertical structure with numerous levels of positions?

_____ a horizontal organization, one that has a flat structure with few levels of positions?

2. Do you prefer to work:

_____ in teams?

_____ alone?

3. Do you like a work environment that:

_____ changes constantly with new assignments and projects?

_____ has relatively few or only minor changes over time?

4. Do you like:

_____ a lot of supervision when performing your work?

_____ minimal supervision when performing your work?

5. Do you enjoy an organizational culture where you:

_____ are able and encouraged to contribute your opinions about your employer's policies and programs?

_____ aren't encouraged or asked to contribute your opinions about your employer's policies and programs?

6. Do you like an organization where you:

_____ are expected to channel your work-related communications through a defined chain of command?

_____ can communicate with whomever you please within the organization?

7. Are you most comfortable in an organization where you are expected to:

_____ come up with new ideas and improvements in the way work is accomplished?

_____ focus only on doing your job as defined by the organization?

8. Do you like an environment where you are encouraged to:

_____ fix problems and deal with unexpected situations when they occur?

_____ seek guidance from supervisors when problems or unexpected situations arise?

9. Are you most comfortable in an organization that:

_____ requires, at some point, that you move into management in order to advance?

_____ offers advancement opportunities separate from its management positions?

10. Do you prefer an environment that is:

_____ informal, with causal dress the norm in the workplace, open offices and few or no distinctions between leaders and workers?

_____ formal, with business dress the norm, traditional offices, and clear distinctions between leaders and workers?

There are no right or wrong answers to these questions. You are who you are. The key, therefore, is to find employers that will provide the environment and cultural norms that best fit you. To do that, use the same questions as modified below, to investigate those organizations that you are considering as potential employers.

Questions for a Potential Employer

To determine the cultural norms and environment your current or a prospective employer provides, ask yourself or their current and former employees the following questions:

1. Does the employer have:

_____ a hierarchical organization, one that has a vertical structure with numerous levels of positions?

_____ a horizontal organization, one that has a flat structure with few levels of positions?

2. Does the organization require that individuals work:

_____ in teams?

_____ alone?

3. Does the work employees do in the organization:

_____ change constantly with new assignments and projects?

_____ have relatively few or only minor changes over time?

4. Do the employer's managers generally provide:

_____ a lot of supervision for the workers they oversee?

_____ minimal supervision for the workers they oversee?

5. Is the culture of the employer one where you:

_____ are able and encouraged to contribute your opinions about the employer's policies and programs?

_____ aren't encouraged or asked to contribute your opinions about the employer's policies and programs?

6. Is the norm of the organization one where you:

_____ must channel your work-related communications through a defined chain of command?

_____ can communicate with whomever you please within the organization?

7. Does the organization want its workers to:

_____ come up with new ideas and improvements in the way work is accomplished?

_____ focus only on doing their job as defined by the organization?

8. Does the employer have an environment where you are encouraged to:

_____ fix problems and deal with unexpected situations when they occur?

_____ seek guidance from supervisors when problems or unexpected situations arise?

9. Is the employer's organization one that:

_____ requires, at some point, that you move into management in order to advance?

_____ offers advancement opportunities separate from its management positions?

10. Is the environment of the employer:

_____ informal, with causal dress the norm in the workplace, open offices and few or no distinctions between leaders and workers?

_____ formal, with business dress the norm, traditional offices, and clear distinctions between leaders and workers?

The optimum employers—the ones that will support and encourage your peak performance—are those that match all 10 of your preferences. In no case should you ever accept employment from an organization that matches fewer than seven of your preferences. In most cases, if they're good employers they won't intentionally undermine your work—they are, after all, the cultures that they are—but the mismatch will slowly, but inevitably degrade the quality and quantity of your work and, as a consequence, impair your career.

Appendix 3

A Summary of Sources

John Branch, "An Immigrant Tale: Hard Life, Hard Work, All in the Family," *The New York Times*, November 17, 2006, p. D1.

Louis Uchitelle, "Job Security, Too, May Have a Happy Medium," *The New York Times*, February 25, 2007.

"Can't Disconnect? You Are Not Alone," *HR Mag.*, February, 2007, p. 14.

Arthur D. Levinson, Ph.D., "Letter to Stockholders," *Genentech 2005 Annual Report: 30 Years of Transforming Science*, www.gene.com.

"2004 DataBank Annual," *Workforce Management*, December, 2004, p. 89.

Fay Hansen, "HR jobs remain secure," *Workforce Management*, March 12, 2007, p. 14.

"Lawsuits allege mommy bias," *Staffing Industry Report*, September 15, 2006, p. 3.

Eduardo Porter, "After Years of Growth, What About Workers' Share," *The New York Times*, October 15, 2006, p. BU-3.

Eric Dash, "Compensation Experts Offer Ways to Help Curb Executive Salaries," *The New York Times*, December 30, 2006, pp C1, C9.

Andrew Ross Sorkin and Eric Dash, "Private Firms Lure C.E.O.'s With Top Pay," *The New York Times*, pp A1, A16.

Jessica Marquez, "Big Bucks at Door for Depot HR Leader," *Workforce Management*, pp 1, 3.

Eduardo Porter, "More Than Ever, It Pays to Be the Top Executive," *The New York Times*, May 25, 2007, pp A1, C7.

Jeffrey Pfeffer, "Ending CEO Pay Envy," *Business 2.0*, June, 2006, p. 62.

Matthew Boyle, "Exposing CEO pay," *Fortune*, March 25, 2007, www.cnnmoney.com.

Jennifer Waters and Angela Moore, "Home Depot chairman, CEO Nardelli resigns," *MarketWatch*, March 25, 2007, www.marketwatch.com.

Gary Carini and Bill Townsend, "$152,000 for Your Thoughts," *Harvard Business Review*, April 2007, p. 23.

"The Fight Against Pain," *USA Today*, May 9, 2005, p. D1.

"Job Stress," American Institute of Stress, www.stress.org.

"Stress at Work," National Institute for Occupational Safety and Health, at American Institute of Stress, www.stress.org.

Gordon T. Anderson, "Want a big payday? Get Fired," CNN/Money, http://money.cnn.com.

Lowell E. Gallaway and Richard K. Vedder, "Jobs and Plant-Closing Legislation: What to Expect," *American Enterprise*, January 1, 1994.

John Hollon, "You've been deleted," *Workforce Management*, September 11, 2006, p. 42.

Paul Kaihla, Erick Schonfeld, and Paul Sloan, "Job Boom," *Business 2.0*, May, 2006, pp 89-100.

Bio-W. Alan McCollough, President and CEO, Circuit City Stores, Inc., TimesDispatch.com, *Richmond Times-Dispatch*, December 12, 2006.

Carl Frappaolo, "The Empowered Document," Delphi Consulting Group, http://members.aol.com/dickdavies/delphi.htm, January 27, 2005.

Damon Hack, "Sorenstam Cruises to Her 3rd Open, And Gets Back to the Top of the Hill," *The New York Times*, July 4, 2006, p. D1.

"Stat Shot: Employees inspired by their jobs?," *Workforce Management*, May, 2005, p. 24.

E.L. Kersten, "Why They Call It Work," *Harvard Business Review*, February, 2006, pp 65-67.

Betsy Querna, "Finding Happiness at Work," *U.S. News & World Report/Best Health*, www.usnews.com, January 2, 2007.

Craig Lambert, "The Science of Happiness," *Harvard Magazine*, January-February, 2007, pp 26-30, 94.

"Someone's Gotta Love It," *Time*, April 9, 2007.

William C. Rhoden, "Krzyzewski is Putting His Reputation on the Line," *The New York Times*, July 26, 2006, pp D1-2.

Damon Darlin, "Using Web to Get Boss to Pay More," *The New York Times*, March 3, 2007, pp C1, C6.

"Scarlet Knights Show Off Their Chops," *The New York Times*, November 11, 2006, pp D1, D5.

J. Casner-Lotto and L. Barrington, "Are They Really Ready to Work," Top 10 Knowledge and Skills Expected to Increase in Importance Over the Next Five Years, in *Workplace Visions*, Society for Human Resource Management, January, 2007.

"Report of The National Commission on Writing," The College Board, September, 2004.

Krista Kafer, "High School, College Graduates Lack Basic and Applied Skills, Employers Say," *School Reform News*, December, 2006.

"Bilingual You're Valuable," CareerBuilder.com, July 16, 2007.

"Temp-to-perm for high level positions," *Staffing Industry Report*, February 9, 2007, pp 1-2.

"Training Temps," *SIReview*, July/August, 2006, p. 26.

"Promotion a Major Life Stressor," *HR Mag.*, July, 2007, p. 12.

Society for Human Resource Management, "2006 Access to Human Capital and Employment Verification Survey."

Peter Weddle, "How Workaholism Can Hurt Your Career," www.weddles.com, November 1, 2003.

Stephen P. Clark, "Private portal to education," *The Advocate & Greenwich Times*, February 27, 2007, p. 17.

Kathy Gurchiek, "Lunch Hour? More Like a Half Hour," *HR Mag.*, August, 2006, p. 35.

"The secret economy," Ode, May, 2007.

Tim Gray, "Vacation Deprivation," *Sky*, August, 2006, pp 47-49.

Nancy R. Lockwood, "Leveraging Employee Engagement for Competitive Advantage: HR's Strategic Role," SHRM Research, Society for Human Resource Management, undated.

"Executive Compensation Rises 41.3%," *SIReview*, September, 2006, p. 10.

Paul B. Brown, "Brand-Name Stock Picks," *The New York Times*, August 26, 2006, p. C5.

Ed Frauenheim and Mark Schoeff Jr., "Stagnating U.S. Wages Seen as Threat to Business Growth," Workforce Management, September 11, 2006, pp 3-4.

Louis Uchitelle, "Two Tiers, Slipping Into One," *The New York Times*, February 26, 2006, Section 3, pp 1, 7.

"HR on the Night Shift: An Offshoot of Offshoring," *Veritude*, www.veritude.com, December 15, 2006.

Peter F. Drucker, "What Executives Should Remember," *Harvard Business Review*, February, 2006, p. 152.

Ed Frauenheim, "Employers may want to get off sidelines in dialogue on worker economic security," *Workforce Management*, July 31, 2006, pp 38-39.

Barry Schwartz, Hazel Rose Markus, and Alana Conner Snibbe, "Is Freedom Just Another Word for Many Things to Buy?," *The New York Times Magazine*, February 26, 2006, pp 14, 16.

Peter Weddle, *The Career Activist Republic*, Weddle's LLC, 2010.

Peter Weddle, *A Multitude of Hope: A Novel About Rediscovering the American Dream*, Epicenter Books, 2012.

Don't miss any of Peter Weddle's thought-provoking and inspiring books.

Work Strong